Sense of History

# Sense of History

*The Place of the Past in American Life*

David Glassberg

University of Massachusetts Press   *Amherst*

Printed in the United States of America
LC 00-052743
ISBN 1-55849-280-1 (library cloth); 281-X (paper)
Designed by Dennis Anderson
Set in Janson Text by Keystone Typesetting, Inc.
Printed and bound by Sheridan Books, Inc.

Library of Congress Cataloging-in-Publication Data

Glassberg, David.
   Sense of history : the place of the past in American life / David Glassberg.
     p. cm.
Includes bibliographical references and index.
ISBN 1-55849-280-1 (library cloth : alk. paper ) — ISBN 1-55849-281-X (pbk. : alk. paper)
1. United States—History—Philosophy. 2. United States—History, Local—Philosophy.
3. Public history—United States. 4. United States—Historiography.
5. Historiography—United States. 6. Memory—Social aspects—United States.
7. National characteristics, American. I. Title.
E175.9 .G58 2001
973'.01—dc21                                      00-052743

British Library Cataloguing in Publication data are available.

To Rachel and Daniel, with love

# CONTENTS

# ILLUSTRATIONS

# PREFACE

THE ESSAYS IN this book explore the various ways Americans have understood and used the past in the twentieth century. I drafted them over a span of a decade, and although portions of some have appeared as conference papers or articles, they have all been extensively revised to create a coherent whole.

What binds these essays together, ultimately, is the idea of place, and the values that Americans attach to the environments they associate with their past. If we are a nation of immigrants, rootless, always in flux, then this instability has made us value the special places in our history all the more, from villages in New England to Civil War battlefields in Virginia to Gold Rush towns in California, as anchors for our personal and family identities. When many of us cannot find meaning in the present places where we live and work, we look for it in the places we remember from our family past.

The essays in *Sense of History* also concern the place of professional history and historians in contemporary American culture. I begin by discussing the enormous distance that exists between historians and the public, and end with some ideas about how the profession might better assist our neighbors in making sense of their present world. Drawing on personal experience as well as archival research, the essays offer examples of how the worlds of academic and public history interrelate.

The book owes its very existence to the creative tension arising from that interaction, and to the generous assistance and good ideas of many individuals and institutions. First and foremost among them is J. Michael Moore, a talented oral historian and museum curator who as a graduate student at the University of Massachusetts in the early 1990s became my collaborator in investigating the history of the war memorial in Orange, Massachusetts, described in chapter 2. Mike was my co-author on an earlier version of the story, published in 1996 as "Patriotism in Orange: The Memory of World War I in a Massachusetts Town," and deserves much of the credit for the initial research and argument. Our research was assisted in many ways by Wendy Chmielewski of the Swarthmore College Peace Collection; Richard Chaisson, formerly of the *Worcester Telegram and Gazette;* and Janice Lanou of the Wheeler Memorial Library in Orange.

Several other former University of Massachusetts students played crucial roles in research projects that ultimately became chapters. Elise Davis pored over microfilms of San Francisco newspapers for chapter 3, on urban festivals. Kimberly Crawford helped me to read through, categorize, and quantify, the letters that Ken Burns received in response to his film series *The Civil War,* the basis of chapter 4. I want to take this opportunity to thank Burns for allowing us into his office/studio in the spring of 1991 to read his mail, and for graciously answering questions and sharing his reaction to our data. Sean Godley transcribed tapes of the public meetings discussed in chapter 6. I have also learned much from the many students in my graduate seminars in public history over the years with whom I have shared ideas and chapter drafts.

The Special Places project profiled in chapter 6 was truly a team effort. It relied greatly on Deborah Tarricano, Kathleen Nutter, Carolyn Spencer, and Rosa Johnston in Northfield; Daniel Horowitz, Arthur Keene, Ellen Pader, Christine Thompson, and Stan Sherer in Amherst and Northampton; John Pearsall, Lawrence Duquette, and Linda Fuller in Wilbraham; and Gregory Farmer, Robert McCarroll, David Gaby, and Marjorie Guest in Springfield. The project also relied on the intellectual and financial support of the Massachusetts Foundation for the Humanities. Its executive director, David Tebaldi, joined the group studying Wilbraham and McKnight, and its former program officer,

Dolores Root, laid the groundwork for the Northfield project and was essential to its subsequent development. The chapter owes much to the foundation's bold vision of public humanities programming as a form of collaborative scholarship.

A Fellowship for University Teachers from the National Endowment for the Humanities in 1993–94 enabled me to start writing and conduct new research in California. The University of California, Davis, provided a wonderful home away from home that year, with office space, library access, stimulating faculty seminars, and bus service to the Bancroft Library at the University of California, Berkeley, where much of the research for chapter 7 was done. Special thanks at the Bancroft go to Bonnie Hardwick, David Kessler, and Mary Morganti for arranging access to the Joseph Knowland Papers, which at the time (1994) were off site and unprocessed. My research in California was also made more fruitful by the efforts of Patricia Keats at the California Historical Society in San Francisco and an army of librarians at the California State Library in Sacramento, in particular Ellen Harding, who was instrumental in obtaining many of the illustrations. My colleagues in the History Department at the University of Massachusetts helped the book along by granting me leaves from teaching during the fall semesters of 1994 and 1997, and assisting with the cost of photo reproduction.

Over the many years of writing and revising, I could not imagine having more astute and supportive readers. After part of chapter 1 appeared in *The Public Historian* under the title "Public History and the Study of Memory," Otis Graham and Lindsey Reed obtained perceptive comments from Michael Kammen, Michael Frisch, Linda Shopes, Edward Linenthal, David Lowenthal, Jo Blatti, Barbara Franco, and Robert Archibald, which I incorporated into the book version. Chapter 2, on the memory of World War I, benefited greatly from the comments of Stuart McConnell, Kirk Savage, John Bodnar, Karal Ann Marling, Charles Rearick, Joanne Fraser, Thomas Laqueur, and David Hollinger; chapter 3, on civic celebrations, from the comments of Rearick, Fraser, Carlin Barton, John Alviti, and Lewis Erenberg; chapter 4, on *The Civil War*, from the comments of McConnell, Carolyn Anderson, David Blight, and Amy Kinsel; chapter 5, on sense of place, from the comments of Hollinger, Michele H. Bogart, David Tebaldi, Sally F. Griffith, Brian Horrigan, and Mary Hufford; chapter 6, on New England town character, from the comments of Tebaldi, Robert Weible,

Dolores Root, Richard Fox, and the members of the Boston University New England Studies seminar; chapter 7, on California historic sites, from the comments of Ann Fabian, Jennifer Watts, Elizabeth Haas, Susan Lee Johnson, Anthony Platt, and others at the "Visualizing California History" session at the Western Historical Association annual meeting in Sacramento in 1998. I especially appreciate the close reading that Kenneth Owens of California State University, Sacramento, gave to this chapter; he tried his best to ensure that I got the story of his adopted home turf right. Back east, chapter 7 also benefited from the comments of Martha Sandweiss, Joyce Berkman, Bruce Laurie, Mary Wilson, and others at the Five College History Seminar. At the very end, Roy Rosenzweig and Michael Frisch read the entire manuscript and made many helpful suggestions, particularly concerning how I might knit these diverse essays into a coherent book. My intellectual debt to John Higham, with whom I have shared ideas about the relationship of the historical profession and the public for more than twenty years, is evident literally from page one.

As the book entered production, Gavin Lewis did an extraordinary copyediting job, greatly improving clarity; Carol Betsch added her hand and kept everything moving smoothly in house. My children, Rachel and Daniel, also assisted with some last-minute fact checking.

Two other individuals merit special mention. One is the late Roland Marchand, among the most dedicated and generous scholars the historical profession has known. Roland not only read several chapter drafts but invited me to spend my NEH fellowship year in California, where he helped in many ways great and small. This would have been a different book without him. The other is Clark Dougan, my editor at the University of Massachusetts Press. From the start, Clark believed that my diverse essays on public history and memory could hang together as a book and, based on his own extensive experience in oral and public history, suggested ways to make it happen. Equally important was his encouragement, when I needed it most, to finish up.

Over and above Clark's guidance, there is something essentially right about the University of Massachusetts Press's being the publisher of this book. For even though much of the manuscript was first drafted on the West Coast, and the book addresses issues of concern throughout the United States, it remains in many ways an intellectual product of the place where I live, of the students, professional colleagues, and residents of the western Massachusetts towns with whom I have talked about history over the past decade. The book is now materially a product of that place as well.

THANKS TO the following for permission to reprint material:

University of California Press for portions of chapter 1 that originally appeared in "Public History and the Study of Memory," *The Public Historian* 18 (Spring 1996): 7–23.

Princeton University Press for portions of chapter 2 that originally appeared in "Patriotism in Orange: The Memory of World War I in a Massachusetts Town," in *Bonds of Affection: Americans Define Their Patriotism*, ed. John Bodnar (Princeton: Princeton University Press, 1996), pp. 160–90.

The editors of *Mid-America* for portions of chapter 3 that originally appeared in "Civic Celebrations and the Invention of the Urban Public," *Mid-America* 82 (Winter–Summer 2000): 147–72.

DAVID GLASSBERG

*Amherst, Massachusetts*

# 1

## Sense of History

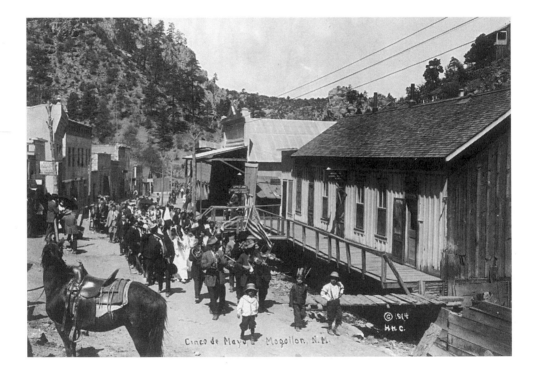

Cinco de Mayo. Mogollon, N.M.

W
HEN I RECALL my education as a historian, I think of
two tables. One was located where I went to graduate
school, at Johns Hopkins University, an ancient rectangu-
lar dark cherry that filled the seminar room on the second floor of Gil-
man Hall. Legend had it that the first generation of professional historians, Herbert Baxter Adams, Frederick Jackson Turner, and Woodrow
Wilson, had sat around the same table; we students, seeking to follow in
their footsteps, searched the underside for the places where they might
have carved their initials. Through fall and spring, seminar after seminar, I returned to the table, absorbed in what my professors and fellow
students called "History." If I had any doubt about what was and was not
History, I could ask my principal professor, who had studied with someone who had studied with Turner and written a book with that title
outlining the rise of the historical profession in America. But there were
no doubts expressed around the seminar table at Johns Hopkins in the
1970s, no wavering in the belief that history meant professional scholarship and an appointment at a research university. Around the table, we
learned that becoming a historian meant separating your personal uses
for the past from your professional career, putting aside the history of
the people and places you cared about, the history of your family or

3

hometown, and dedicating yourself instead to questions posed by the professional literature. Each of us sought to discover a gap in the literature, and the one thing about the past that we could know more about than anyone else, that would help us make an original contribution to knowledge. It was through the accumulation of these contributions, shared around the seminar table and published in scholarly journals and monographs from university presses, that History developed. The table was a monument to the common historical enterprise, its enduring presence a reminder of the continuity and solidity of the profession.[1]

Then the school year ended, and I departed for a seasonal ranger position at Mesa Verde National Park. On this "green table," stretching for miles above the semi-arid plain of southwestern Colorado, I experienced a much wider range of possibilities of what history could mean. Although this was an ancient landscape, with evidence of human occupation older than anything readily visible on the east coast, at the time the Park Service did not consider the lives of the puebloan peoples who had made their homes in the cliffs seven centuries ago part of the nation's history. The men, women, and children who had occupied the now picturesque ruins were "prehistoric"; Mesa Verde was a national park, not a national historic site. If I was looking for history, I could find it instead down below in the nearby towns, and it was comparatively short: dusty ranching, farming, and mining communities that seemed to have been built only yesterday. One was Moab, Utah, whose uranium boom of the 1950s and 1960s had just busted, and which was desperately courting new development to escape from passing into oblivion. Of course, the Hopi, Navajo, and Apache whom I met at the park had a very different relationship to that history of western discovery and settlement. In contrast to the history I studied at Hopkins, which had nothing to do with the natural surroundings of Baltimore and the Chesapeake Bay, understanding the natural setting at Mesa Verde was essential to the human story I told the public. My employers asked me to tell this story not only by talking about the ruins as I guided the visitors through, but also by demonstrating some of the activities that might have taken place there, such as grinding corn and making pottery; at my first pottery-making demonstration four Native American women tourists watched in amused silence. Most important, my concept of history expanded at Mesa Verde from listening, day after day, to the questions that the public asked as they tried to relate their own lives and histories to the people who had lived in the canyons centuries ago. The public asked questions about the past that did not correspond at all to what I was learning was history in graduate school.

The intellectual distance between the two tables in the 1970s seemed even greater than the 2,200 miles that separated them, yet both contributed to my development as a historian. Leaving graduate school in the fall of 1981 with a Ph.D. but no full-time academic position in sight, I moved back to Philadelphia, where I had grown up, and for the next four years continued to work intermittently for the National Park Service and area museums while teaching college part-time. My involuntary postgraduate education, shuttling back and forth between the worlds of academic and public history, not only led to my present position teaching public history at the University of Massachusetts, but also further provoked my curiosity about the place of the past in American life, and how popular ideas about history differed from those of the historical profession.

By the mid-1980s, when I arrived in Amherst, the enormous distance between professional historians and the larger culture had become a matter for public discussion, a discussion that is still raging today. Much of it has taken the form of a debate over the content of what Americans do or do not know about their past. Why, with the explosion of postsecondary education since World War II, do Americans seem to know so little about their history? Political conservatives, anxious to defend the patriotic verities of the Cold War era, blame the loss of "American memory" on professors too caught up in the identity politics of the 1960s and 1970s and the history of women and minorities to teach what American youth need to know to feel proud of their nation's past. But many on the political left also attack the college professors, for overspecialization and the failure to make their research intelligible to contemporary audiences or relevant to contemporary concerns. At the same time, other critics note that even if professional historians were to reach out beyond the walls of the academy to bring history to the masses, they face what the historian Michael Wallace has termed a "historicidal" American culture. The nation's rapid pace of technological innovation, insatiable hunger for novel forms of mass entertainment, and relentless transformation of the physical environment inevitably work against its citizens' sense of the past and foster a popular disregard for the traditions of yesteryear.[2]

I have little patience with these polemics attacking the public for their ignorance of history or the professors for being out of touch. From my perspective it seems that popular interest in the past has never been greater. Considering the frequency of commemorative ceremonies and historical festivals, the output of historical films and novels, the numbers of visitors to historic sites and museums, the intensity of campaigns to mark and preserve historic buildings, or the sales of software for probing family history and genealogy, it appears that if Americans do not have a strong sense of history, they certainly spend a lot of their leisure time looking for one, in historical pursuits of one kind or another.

Rather than trying to assess the degree of history-mindedness in America, we need to examine more closely its qualities. What are Americans looking for when they engage with the past? What do we mean when we talk about a "sense of history"? How is it nurtured and communicated? How does it change over time? How is it different from what the historical profession calls History? For years, we have traced the successive frameworks that historians have employed for interpreting the past and called it "historiography"—the catechism imparted around the seminar table at Hopkins and countless other graduate schools which is considered central to the training of future generations of professionals. It is now time to examine the place of the past in the wider culture.[3]

While professional historians talk about having an "interpretation of history," something that changes in the light of new evidence, others talk about having a "sense of history," a perspective on the past at the core of who they are and the people and places they care about. "Sense of history" reflects the intersection of the intimate and the historical— the way that past events of a personal and public nature are intertwined, so that public histories often forcefully, and surprisingly, hit home. It is the sensation I got in 1993 in Washington, D.C., on the fourth floor of the newly opened Holocaust Museum, when I saw a passport to Shanghai covered with swastikas mounted on the wall and realized that I had the same artifact in my attic, a legacy for my children from my father-in-law, who had escaped Germany for China in 1939. Or the sensation I get when I visit Atlanta, Georgia, where my late mother grew up, and hear her sisters tell stories about the time when all the Jews in town knew one another, or visit the cemetery where the gravestone of her immigrant father stands tightly clustered with those of his fellow *landslayt*, a shtetl of stones on an open, rolling hillside.

Although a sense of history is not based in physiology like a sense of smell or sight, reminders of a past event not personally experienced can evoke sensations deeply felt, such as feelings of loss, or reverie, or intense pride. Sense of history is akin to what environmental psychologists describe as sense of place—not quite territoriality, as among other animals, but a sense of locatedness and belonging. Sensing history, we explore fundamental questions concerning personal and group identity and our relationship to the environment. A sense of history locates us in space, with knowledge that helps us gain a sense of *where* we are, helping us to understand why our formerly thriving inner-city neighborhood is now a wilderness of vacant lots, or why a piece of erstwhile productive farmland nearby is now a shopping mall. A sense of history locates us in time, with knowledge that helps us gain a sense of *when* we are, filling in gaps in our personal recollection and family stories that allow us to understand our place in a succession of past and future generations. And a sense of history locates us in society, with knowledge that helps us gain a sense of *with whom we belong*, connecting our personal experiences and memories with those of a larger community, region, and nation.[4]

Where does a sense of history come from? At the most intimate of levels, we can talk about autobiographical memory and reminiscence, how individuals in reviewing their past experiences form a coherent personal identity and sense of self. We can also talk about communication about the past within families. But these intimate places for learning about the past inevitably interact with public ones, and it is those public histories that are the subject of this book. Such investigation includes the study of politics and collective identities—how some versions of history are institutionalized and disseminated by government as the public history through schools, museums, monuments, and civic celebrations, and how that public history intersects with other versions of the past communicated among family and friends. It includes the study of popular culture—those versions of the past created and disseminated not by government but through the marketplace in television, film, novels, and commercial tourist attractions, and how audiences understand what they see and hear. And it includes the study of environmental perception—the cognitive transformations that occur when a landscape is designated as "historic" either by government or by popular practice. A sense of history and sense of place are inextricably intertwined; we attach histories to places, and the environmental value we attach to a place comes largely through the historical associations we have with it.

In the following chapters I explore how a sense of history has been created, communicated, understood, and changed over time in twentieth-century America. They range across the many places where we encounter history in our lives—a war memorial in the town park, a parade of historical floats down Main Street, a television program about the Civil War, a neighborhood historic district—as well as about the contexts of family and community where we learn to interpret what these encounters with the past mean. Rather than weaving a single narrative, the chapters individually explore the images and uses of history in a particular time and place. They are arranged not by chronology or geography but rather as models of investigation, to exemplify the importance of politics, popular culture, and place in understanding the nature of Americans' connection with their past.

In studying the sense of history, I build not only on my firsthand experiences working with the public, but also on what others have written about popular images and uses of the past. For decades, scholars associated with American studies have investigated the role that historical myths and symbols play in forming distinctive national and regional identities. Literary critics and art historians have analyzed the often idiosyncratic historical imagery present in the works of artists and writers, while folklorists have investigated the historical tales of less prominent individuals. Political historians have explored the changing historical reputations of heroes such as Jefferson and Lincoln, the notion of history embedded in the ideology of political movements such as republicanism and populism, and how government officials have employed historical analogies in the making and selling of public policy.[5]

In recent years, this scholarship has appeared under the name of "memory." What distinguishes the new scholarship on memory from the old is not subject matter but approach. Where earlier studies primarily sought to characterize a single group or institution's beliefs about its past, the new studies primarily seek to understand the interrelationships between different versions of the past in the public arena. They investigate what the anthropologist Robert Redfield termed "the social organization of tradition": how various versions of the past are communicated in society through a multiplicity of institutions and media, including school, government ceremonies, popular amusements, art and literature, stories told by families and friends, and landscape features designated as historic by either government or popular practice. In a sense, the new memory scholarship expands the types of institutions and ideas that historians customarily examine in the traditional historiography course, situating professional historical scholarship as not the only thought about history but one of several versions of the past competing for public influence in a particular place and time.[6]

With this change in approach has come a shift in focus from studying the institutions that produce history—colleges and universities, government agencies, the mass media—to studying the minds of the individuals where all these versions of the past converge and are understood. Earlier approaches assumed that everyone who encountered a historical image understood it in more or less the same way—if George Bancroft's histories were popular in the mid-nineteenth century, it meant that they embodied the era's popular historical consciousness. New approaches, by contrast, emphasize the many different meanings we derive from the same historical representation. The meaning of a historical book, film, or display is not intrinsic, determined solely by the intention of its creator, but changes as we actively reinterpret what we see and hear by placing it in alternative contexts derived from our diverse social backgrounds. To paraphrase Carl Becker, every person is his or her own historian, creating idiosyncratic versions of the past that make sense based on personal situation and experiences. But then how can we make meaningful generalizations about a public history?[7]

Indeed, much of the new scholarship on memory examines communication about the past only on the most intimate of scales: autobiographical memory and reminiscence. Psychologists and oral historians explore how individuals in recalling the past form a coherent personal identity and sense of self. We tell stories about the past that place ourselves at the center of historical events, or reveal our "uchronic dreams" which combine recollections of events with our judgments concerning how history should have turned out. But our individual memories are not solely the product of idiosyncratic recollection; they are also established and confirmed through dialogue with others. An individual memory is the product of group communication, intimately linked to the "collective" memory of the community. The insight that memory is constructed out of social interaction, first advanced by the sociologist Maurice Halbwachs early in the twentieth century, links individuals and groups to the creation of a public history. Through conversations with others, we learn about a past before our own experience, share versions of that past with others, and seek to have our version of that past accepted in the larger society. This leads to a larger question, one that has been at the core of much of the recent scholarship on memory: with all the possible versions of the past that circulate in society, how do particular accounts of the past get established and disseminated as the public one? How do these public histories change over time?[8]

## Politics

One approach to these questions is to analyze how the prevailing images of the past in a society reflect its political culture. In recent years, debates about history have spilled into the national political arena. In September 1994, the United States Senate passed a resolution in response to the complaint of veterans' organizations that the exhibit being developed at the Smithsonian's National Air and Space Museum to commemorate the fiftieth anniversary of the end of World War II was going to question the necessity of the dropping of the atomic bomb. The Senate proclaimed that indeed the bomb was "momentous in helping to bring World War II to a merciful end." Bowing to pressure, the Smithsonian scaled back its plans and in 1995 displayed the fuselage of the *Enola Gay*, the plane that dropped the bomb, without reference to past or present controversies over its mission (figure 2). That same year, Congress went on record condemning the set of national history standards for public schools—a project developed at the University of California, Los Angeles, and funded by the National Endowment for the Humanities—that critics claimed contained more references to Sojourner Truth than to Thomas Edison. In this highly charged context, few can deny that the question of whose version of history gets institutionalized and disseminated as the public history is a political one. Public histories embody not only ideas about history, the relation of past, present, and future, but also ideas about the public itself, the relationship of diverse groups in political society. Contemporary debates have only increased the importance of understanding the political uses of public history, as reflected in the establishment of war memorials, civic celebrations, and public institutions such as museums, archives, and historic sites.[9]

For some scholars, public historical imagery supplies the myths and symbols that hold diverse groups in political society together. In the words of Benedict Anderson, a shared history—elements of a past remembered in common as well as elements forgotten in common—is the crucial element in the creation of an "imagined community" through which disparate individuals and groups envision themselves as members of a collective with a common present and future. From W. Lloyd Warner's analysis of commemorative rituals in "Yankee City" (Newburyport, Massachusetts) in the 1950s through Robert Bellah's characterization of a national civil religion in 1967, to recent analyses such as Pierre Nora's multivolume exploration of the "lieux de mémoire" in

Fig. 2. Hiroshima atomic bomb survivor Yasui Kouichi stands beside a photograph of the crew of the *Enola Gay*, the plane that dropped the bomb, at the National Air and Space Museum's exhibition in 1995 commemorating the fiftieth anniversary of the end of World War II. Photo by Ed Hedemann of the War Resisters League.

France and Michael Kammen's description of the "mystic chords of memory" in the United States, scholars have suggested that public historical representations have at least the potential to articulate an over-arching, broadly shared civic or national faith that can transcend particular ethnic and class loyalties.[10]

Other scholars depict the practices and representations of public history as instruments in the political struggle for power among various social groups. From the wide-ranging examinations of public ritual in the Eric Hobsbawm and Terence Ranger anthology *The Invention Of Tradition* (1983) through Michel Foucault's linkage of systems of knowledge and power in France, George Mosse's studies of the representation of the past in fascist Germany, and Raphael Samuel's investigations of the making of British national identity, this strand of analysis identifies public history with the master narratives that elite supporters of the nation-state impose from the top down to consolidate control over their citizenry. On one side, historical imagery disseminated by government and the mass media advance the imagined community of the nation; on the other, movement histories arise expressing authentic local and group memories and collective identities. The prevailing framework for analyzing the politics of public history versus popular memories sharply distinguishes between an official history that government agencies such as the military and the National Park Service employ to maintain the political status quo and a multiplicity of vernacular memories that ordinary citizens and social movements employ to sustain ties of family and local community.[11]

As the spirited contemporary battles over the nation's history show, a civil religion approach that emphasizes public history's role in holding political society together tends to overlook conflicts over the creation and dissemination of a public history. Many of these authors, nostalgic for a shared national culture—whether a conservative version that could reinforce the patriotic orthodoxy of the Cold War era or a liberal one that could promote understanding between particular racial, ethnic, class, and sexual identities and communities—see public histories as actually integrating society rather than as an effort by some to structure reality for others. But the prevailing conceptual framework pitting official history versus vernacular memories also oversimplifies the play of forces shaping public history. Concerned that depictions of the nation's "collective" beliefs and values might overwhelm the ability of minorities to express their unique historical visions, those who celebrate history at the grass roots tend to overlook the apparent spontaneity and depth of emotion associated with national histories—not only of the flag-waving kind on the political right but also of the progressive nationalist variety, such as that of the Congress of Industrial Organizations in the 1930s or Martin Luther King Jr. in the 1960s. Rather than being viewed primarily as a top-down phenomenon, communicated from an elite to the masses, the creation of national histories can also be understood as one that take place from the bottom up.[12]

As I show in chapters 2 and 3, on the memorialization of war and on urban civic celebrations, there are multiple official histories as well as multiple vernacular memories. Both chapters illustrate not only how public officials can appropriate and transform local memories into their official civic and national histories, but also how the official imagery they employ acquires diverse meanings from the local contexts in which it is displayed. The case studies demonstrate how public history simultaneously reproduces the unequal political relationships of a society, through the relative power of groups in society to have their version of history accepted as the public history. The chapters also show how public history serves as an instrument through which those relationships are transformed, through interaction at the local level with the other versions of the past that circulate among ethnic, fraternal, and labor organizations, as well as among family and friends.[13]

The new scholarship analyzing the politics of public history has important implications for how we think about historians' work. Inevitably, historians engaging in public projects enter a world of competing political forces. Since it is nearly impossible to reach a consensus on the public interpretation of a historical event that anyone still cares about, public historical representations such as a museum exhibit, war memorial, or commemorative ceremony are often kept deliberately ambiguous so as to satisfy competing factions. Such versions of the collective past are examples not of collective memory, but rather of what the literary critic James Young has termed "collected memory"—discrete and often conflicting memories brought together so as to converge in a common space, much like the Vietnam Veterans Memorial in Washington. The task of the historian in these situations may be more to create safe spaces for local dialogue about history and for the collection of memories, and to ensure that various voices are heard in those spaces, than to provide an original interpretation of the past or to translate the latest professional scholarship for a popular audience.[14]

## Popular Culture

The dialogical nature of public histories is especially evident when we examine historical imagery in commercial mass media and tourist attractions—representations shaped less by politics and the desire to communicate an official ideology or a sense of collective identity, than by the marketplace and the desire to appeal to large numbers of people in their leisure hours (figure 3). Popular appeal is the lifeblood of commercial historical ventures; with the decline of government and foundation funding for history, all but the most exclusive of historical institutions are increasing their marketing efforts to bring more visitors through their doors or reaching out to broaden the constituency for their work. In 1997, Colonial Williamsburg launched a $3 million–dollar advertising campaign packaging itself with other nearby tourist attractions such as Busch Garden and Water Country, USA. The Smithsonian's National Air and Space Museum drew enormous controversy with its *Enola Gay* exhibit in 1995, but also record-breaking crowds with its display of costumes and props from the movie *Star Wars* two years later. Similarly Mystic Seaport in Connecticut has displayed artifacts and videos from the Steven Spielberg film *Amistad*.[15]

As historical institutions in search of larger and larger audiences cater to popular expectations, will the conventions that shape other popular media play a greater role in shaping the form and content of the history they present? In the future, will every historical documentary or exhibit need to mimic the emotional drama of popular motion pictures based on past events, such as Steven Spielberg's *Saving Private Ryan*, Oliver Stone's *JFK*, and James Cameron's *Titanic*, to compete for a mass audience? Will historic sites and districts more and more resemble commercial theme parks, offering visitors experiences designed to re-create the sensation of living in the past—or will they even take the form of theme parks such as the one Disney Corporation proposed for Virginia in 1994? Plans for "Disney's America" included a whitewater raft ride through "Native America," a "Civil War village," and a re-created factory town with a high speed ride called the "Industrial Revolution." This particular project was rejected by local officials, primarily on traffic

Fig. 3. Turner Pictures feature film *Gettysburg* premiered in October 1993, starring Tom Berenger as James Longstreet and Martin Sheen as Robert E. Lee. Photo by Merrick Morton; © New Line Cinema Corporation.

and environmental grounds. However, it signals the larger role that multinational corporations may play in the future in presenting the history that the public sees and hears, carefully packaged to appeal to the largest possible audience around the globe.[16]

New scholarship on how we create meanings from popular culture can help us to understand the growing convergence of public and popular histories in the twentieth century. The historian George Lipsitz observes that we neither passively receive nor actively challenge the historical imagery we see and hear in popular television docudramas, music, film, novels, and tourist attractions; rather, we "negotiate" between the mass media versions of the past and the versions we have already encountered in our own particular subculture. To appeal to the widest possible audience, popular historical representations, like other pop culture forms, incorporate a wide variety of possible characters and themes with which we can identify our particular concerns. Embedded within even the most commercial and mass-produced representations of the American past, Lipsitz insists, are elements reflecting the historical experience of various subcultures; through close analysis, scholars can recover the hidden meanings and memories encoded in these narratives. Popular films and television programs do not impose a single view of history on the masses, but rather communicate a multiplicity of sub-merged alternative visions, each accessible to those with the particular social background to decipher them.[17]

The analysis of public history as popular culture, emphasizing the multiplicity of possible meanings for each historical image, suffers from the same limitation as the analysis of public history as political culture: neither approach tells us much about how actual people respond to the history they see and hear. Do we really view history primarily through the lens of our social characteristics such as gender, class, race, and ethnicity? Or is our education or political ideology a more powerful influence upon how we interpret what we see and hear? How competent are most of us to recover the hidden meanings in popular histories, or to construct an alternative interpretation of historical events by recon-figuring the information present and supplying what is left out? And what about the role of intermediaries in guiding reception? We not only see a film but read the review, with expert commentators helping us to classify it according to larger categories and interpretative conventions. Hearing a trusted personality such as David McCullough introduce a film on *The American Experience* as a "true story" will affect our under-standing of it at least as much as our particular social background. To discover the alternative ways in which various Americans might inter-pret the histories they see in the mass media, we first need to find out what other histories they might have encountered about the subject, and whether or not they considered the source of those histories to be reli-able. The Smithsonian Institution's reputation for accuracy leads most Americans to trust its representations of the past more than those of a commercial television network—though the controversy over the *Enola Gay* exhibit demonstrates how fragile that trust can be.[18]

Understanding the impact of popular historical imagery requires that we not only recover the range of possible meanings encoded within each image but also discover, through empirical research, what meanings actually surfaced in particular places and times. More than a decade ago, the literary critic Janice Radway surveyed a group of women readers in the Midwest about their reaction to different romance novels, and cre-ated, out of their likes and dislikes, a portrait of their thoughts concern-ing gender relations. Historians can conduct the same kind of field research, examining public historical representations not only as created by their authors but also as reshaped by the institutional bureaucracies that present them and reinterpreted by the various groups that see and hear them. If the meaning of a historical fact is not intrinsic but changes with context, then historians can investigate the successive contexts created by the authors, by the mass media, and by the public, tracing the path through each particular place where knowledge about the past is communicated. The aim of such research is not to discover how to make the histories we create more popular so as to attract a larger audience, but rather to understand better the preconceptions about history with which the public approaches our work.[19]

As an example of how we might analyze public history as popular culture, consider the experience of a family visiting a National Park Service site such as Mesa Verde. What at first glance seems a straightforward presentation of history and archeology, created by professionals working in a central Park Service office in Washington, Denver, or Harpers Ferry, turns out to be the product of a complex interaction between national and regional NPS offices, between park supervisory personnel and local interest groups (in the case of Mesa Verde, especially nearby Native nations), and finally, between the individual ranger and the visitor in the field.[20] Park staff have a great deal of autonomy in the selection of what information about the past to tell their visitors, and park visitors often continue to interpret and reinterpret that information within their families long after their visit ends. Each level of communication offers a new context that shapes the meanings of the history being presented. At the same time, as Interior Department budgets are stretched more thinly, the temptation to justify the level of a park's funding by the size of the audience that it serves generates pressure up and down the line to present its story in ways that will appeal to the greatest number of visitors. While the Park Service has yet to go the route of the cover of romance novels by placing a picture of an embracing couple in revealing period dress on an entrance sign, we might expect that over time the features of the Park Service's public programs will more and more resemble those of popular historical attractions.

Perhaps the most successful effort ever to combine the authority of public history with the appeal of popular culture is Ken Burns's documentary *The Civil War*. In chapter 4, I analyze the popular response to the film, based on the letters that Burns received at his home in New

Hampshire immediately after the series was first televised in fall 1990. The chapter characterizes not only how Burns constructed his compelling narrative of the conflict but also how the viewers who wrote to Burns about his film understood what they saw and heard. Many viewers compared the series to other television shows or films they had seen about the Civil War. Many more were moved to discuss how they had first learned about the war from their families or in school. And many thanked Burns for imaginatively transporting them back in time to places significant in both their families' and their nation's past.[21]

## Place

The histories we tell not only communicate our political ideologies and group identities, but also orient us in the environment. Public histories provide meaning to places. Whether in the form of televised images of a Civil War battlefield, or of the designation of a "pioneer saloon" as a historic site (figure 4), all such histories connect stories of past events to a particular physical setting. What cognitive changes occur when an environment is considered as "historical," either by government designation or popular practice, or when a civic organization such as a local chamber of commerce creates maps and historical atlases that recognize some historical places but not others? Scholarship on the politics of history helps us to understand how a particular version of the past becomes institutionalized in government museums and historic sites, and scholarship analyzing public history as popular culture helps us to understand how diverse audiences interpret the versions of the past they see in the mass media and at tourist attractions; likewise, scholarship examining how history shapes our perceptions of place can help us to understand the versions of the past underlying the historic preservation strategies that our communities employ to define and protect their special character.

Over the past decade, just as historians have studied the making of historical consciousness—how ideas about history are created, institutionalized, disseminated, understood, and change over time—other disciplines have investigated place consciousness, and the making of what scholars in environmental psychology, folklore, and cultural geography call "sense of place." Psychologists have explored how as children we bond emotionally with places as we develop, and how memories of these

Fig. 4. The Historic American Building Survey photographed this "pioneer saloon" in Columbia, Tuolumne County, California, in the 1930s. The sign on the side testifying to the building's historical significance was placed there in the 1920s as part of the development of a "Bret Harte Trail" for tourists. In 1945, the entire town of Columbia became a state historic park. Library of Congress, Prints and Photographs Division (HABS, Cal, 55-Colum, 7-2).

special childhood places remain a crucial anchor for our personal identity in adulthood. The social networks we participate in as adults can also further develop and reinforce our sense of place; the longer we live in a place, the more likely we are to associate local environmental features with memories of our significant life experiences involving family and friends. Psychologists have also explored the emotional consequences when the bonds between people and places are broken, such as the grieving for a lost home that occurs among the elderly or exiles forcibly deprived of their familiar environment and memory sites.[22]

Places loom large not only in our personal recollections but also in the collective memory of our communities. Through conversations among family and friends about past local characters, about the weather, about work, we transform ordinary environments into "storied places." Wallace Stegner notes, "No place is a place until the things that have happened in it are remembered in history, ballads, yarns, legends, or monuments."[23] Folklorists have observed the often conflicting meanings of the same environment communicated among different groups, and how the invention of a "collective" sense of place, like the invention of a public history, reflects the often unequal power relations between various local groups and interests. At the same time that psychologists and folklorists have investigated the subjective experience of place at the personal and communal level, geographers have analyzed the arrangement of space at the regional, national, and global level—how our environmental experiences are affected by larger social, economic, and political forces that determine the distribution of slums and suburbs in our locales, and which places we get to experience. The meanings established for a place, and the land use decisions that stem from those meanings, are shaped not only by the social, economic, and political relationships among the various residents of a town or neighborhood but also by local residents' relationships with the outside world.[24]

If individuals can experience a sense of place, they can also experience a sense of placelessness—the feeling of belonging in no particular place. Many critics have seen this as a particularly American problem. They charge that throughout its history the nation's high degree of geographical mobility—the pioneer leaving behind deserted villages and depleted soil in search of economic opportunity; the centralization of economic and political power under modern capitalism; the spread of a standardized, interchangeable, instant architecture; and new electronic forms of communication from the radio to the Internet—has made it difficult for Americans to identify with distinctive places and local histories. Towns such as Moab, Utah, so desperate for new development in the 1970s, experienced a tourist boom in the 1990s that transformed their main streets into strips of trendy shops and restaurants that are identical anywhere in the United States. While much of the critique that modern Americans lack a sense of place, like the complaint that they lack a sense of history, can be dismissed as merely intellectuals' nostalgia for past agricultural communities and ethnic neighborhoods, there remains, in the words of the folklorist Henry Glassie, a undeniable difference between a portable past made of paper and a stationary one made of dirt.[25] Surely population migration and dynamic changes in the physical landscape in the twentieth century, as working farms became residential suburbs, once-thriving city neighborhoods disappeared beneath superhighways, and rural villages remade themselves into tourist attractions, have affected the quality of Americans' relationship with their past and with their environment.[26]

Although I depict Americans' experiences of place and history in every chapter of this book, it is the particular focus of the later ones. Chapter 5 elaborates further on the importance of our understanding the processes through which, over time, Americans have made the environments where they lived part of their individual and communal identities.[27] Chapter 6, on New England town character, examines the relationship between land use practices and perceptions of local history in three present-day western Massachusetts communities. Through a series of public meetings to discuss the "special places" in their town or neighborhood, residents discovered the divergence between officially designated historic landmarks and community memory sites, and the different senses of history that underlay their different perceptions of the environment.[28] Chapter 7 traces the emergence of distinctive historical places in California between 1850 and 1940. It is a first attempt to put aside the assumption of American placelessness to examine the complex relationship between population migration, place attachment, and sense of history in the American past.

## New Histories, New Historians

Probing the connections between the histories Americans encounter and their political culture, popular culture, and sense of place will greatly enrich the historical profession as it enters the new century. The organization of tradition in society has a history; understanding this history, and the history-making practices we have inherited from the past, can help historians to understand the institutional contexts in which they operate as well as the presuppositions about history with which the public approaches their work. This understanding also offers a way for historians to ground their scholarly and professional identities in the larger culture, beyond the seminar tables of colleges and universities. In the future, as in the past, historians will work in a variety of professional settings; all can share the growing body of scholarship that investigates the place of the past in American life as a new foundation for professional training.

I began my career, like other professionally trained historians around the seminar table, equating the study of history with the world of colleges and universities. And like other scholars of my generation I discovered that this world alone could sustain me neither economically, nor ultimately, intellectually. Working in museums, historic sites, and community history projects, I encountered perspectives on the past that I never would have encountered solely in the world of professional academics. In presenting history to the public, I soon discovered that the public was presenting history back to me as well, and that it was impossible to uphold the separation between the history I practiced and the history I lived and understood. This book shares my insights from these interactions. I hope that my fellow professional historians gain insights into the place of their enterprise in the larger world, much as I hope that my other readers will gain insights into what professional historians do from the structure, documentation, and argument of each chapter. In the new century, as political and economic currents increasingly compel the historical profession to rethink its relationship with the rest of society, historical practice will be transformed, whether historians like it or not. What the historian Michael Frisch has called the "shared authority" of the public historical enterprise has profound implications for how all historians will do their work in the future, and the quality of the relationship that Americans will have with the past.[29]

# 2

# Remembering a War

T HROUGHOUT THE twentieth century, Americans have always had a war that they could remember. World War I veterans lived to see their children fight in World War II and Korea; World War II veterans watched their children struggle in Vietnam. The American landscape, relatively unscarred by battles of the twentieth century compared with those of Europe and Asia, nevertheless is dense with reminders of the nation's warriors and their wars. I take my daughter to Amherst's War Memorial Swimming Pool; watch baseball with my father in Philadelphia at Veterans Stadium; march with my son in the annual Memorial Day parade with the Boy Scouts. In almost any direction I drive in New England, retired artillery join statues of Civil War soldiers on town commons, along with statues of doughboys and monument stones carved with the names of war dead. The messages written across the land equating each generation's service in war and its service to country, its patriotism and its martial valor, are unmistakable.

Imagine my surprise, then, when I first saw the monument to the eleven men from Orange, Massachusetts, who died in World War I. The twelve-foot-high bronze depicts a seated, weary veteran recounting the horror of his war experience to a young boy. Rather than the usual military slogan, inscribed in the granite base are the words "It shall not be again."

How did this monument come to be built? What has it meant in the life of the community? What can it tell us about the politics of remembering war in the twentieth century, a politics evident in controversies such as that over the *Enola Gay* exhibit? Through the "biography" of this unusual monument, from its inception in the wake of the Armistice of 1918 to the present, we can trace the creation, institutionalization, dissemination, and transformation of a public memory of war. Along the way, we will consider the places in our communities set aside for remembering war, and the various ways that Americans have through those places identified their personal and family histories with those of their hometowns and their nation.[1]

The role of war in forging a link between person and nation has alternately fascinated and repelled generations of writers. In the decade after the First World War, social scientists sought to analyze the powerful emotional connections they had just witnessed between the government and the people. Focusing on the collective psychology of the home front at the height of the hostilities, the scholars equated feelings of national unity with an animal-like instinct to herd together when threatened. With the growth of fascism in the interwar years, the explanation that individuals identified with the nation to satisfy a deep psychological need to belong to a group grew more widespread.[2] Anthropologist W. Lloyd Warner, looking at Memorial Day ceremonies in Newburyport, Massachusetts, in the 1930s, concluded that "It is in time of war that the average American living in small cities and towns gets his deepest satisfactions as a member of his society." The public commemoration of war on holidays such as Memorial Day, Warner added, seeks to "recapture feelings of wellbeing when society was most integrated and feelings of unity most intense."[3]

More recently, scholars seeking to explain the connection between war and how citizens identify with the nation have relied less on questionable assumptions about the psychology of the home front during wartime than on the ways in which governments promote a collective memory of the nation's war experience long after the last shots have been fired. Public monuments and rituals that direct each citizen to remember a war in similar ways form a crucial element in the construction of an imagined community through which disparate groups envision themselves as part of a collective with a common past, present, and future. Historians of modern Europe in particular have explored how governments after World War I developed elaborate war memorials, holidays, and rituals to link service in war and service to country, and how the myth of the war experience and the cult of the fallen soldier became powerful symbols helping the modern nation-state to consolidate control over its citizenry.[4]

But the recent historical studies of how governments have created and disseminated a national memory of war leave unanswered questions that the initial generation of scholars raised about the apparent spontaneity and depth of personal emotion associated with war memorialization. If the myth of the war experience was a top-down phenomenon, communicated from the elite to the masses, why did the masses buy it? How did the government's war stories connect with the everyday worlds of family and local community that social historians insist are most important? The question is especially vexing for the United States, where the ability of the federal government to disseminate a national memory of war has been far more limited than in other nations. While the U.S. government during World War I created new national agencies for mobilizing public opinion and conserving scarce resources, mixed recruits from across the nation in the same military units, and even distributed the same graphic images of the war nationally via the Committee on Public Information, it did little to shape how the war was remembered in towns and cities across America. Once the mobilization ended and the troops came home, each town and city became an arena where different memories of war competed for public expression. The story of Orange, Massachusetts, and its monument prompts us to rethink our assumptions about the memory of war and national identity, and the ways in which a living memory of war passes into the history of a community.

ORANGE IS a small industrial town located on Millers River in north-central Massachusetts. Never an especially prosperous town, its population of approximately 5,500 hardly changed in the forty years from the turn of the century to World War II.[5] As in other American towns, at the declaration of war in April 1917 the men and women of Orange organized a host of local committees to support the war effort, the local manufacturers obtained government contracts to produce war materials, and the young men went off to fight.

Most of Orange's 264 soldiers served in units scattered throughout the army and navy. But a substantial number—more than one in five— fought in the Great War as members of their local state guard unit, Company E of the 104th Infantry Regiment, 26th (Yankee) Division. The unit shipped out to France in October 1917; it received the Croix de Guerre for its heroism while attached to the French army at the battle of Apremont in April 1918, and saw extensive action with the American Expeditionary Force in the summer and fall. Five men died— nearly half of the town's total of eleven war dead. Unlike most American soldiers in World War I, including other veterans from Orange, the men of Company E fought alongside men from their hometown and region; their distinctive war experience served as a source of identity and solidarity for them when they returned to Orange after the war, and the Company E experience came to stand for the experience of all of Orange's veterans.[6]

The men returned to Orange in April 1919 amid a public debate about the proper way to honor them and memorialize their deeds. Some in town proposed the erection of a stone shaft or triumphal arch, in keeping with the commemorative traditions of the late nineteenth century which suggested that symbolic memorial art could promote idealism and influence the behavior of present and future generations of viewers.[7] Indeed, Orange had erected an imposing obelisk in the town cemetery as its Civil War monument in 1870. Topped by a memorial urn, the thirty-foot-high shaft became the principal focus for the town's annual Memorial Day commemorations. A new World War monument, argued a letter to the local newspaper, would serve a similar didactic purpose, standing "for generations to come, an object lesson in patriotism and loyalty to country." Another writer extolled the particular value of the plaque that such a monument would hold, as a remembrance of the individual soldiers and a bridge between generations to keep the memory of their deeds alive. "The present and future generations to come will be proud to point to certain names and say, this is my son, this is my father; that's my grandfather's name. They served their country in the World War."[8]

But there were others in Orange openly disdainful of the prospect of the traditional monument. The local paper editorialized that a memorial obelisk or statue would be a "backward step." "No better dead memorial can be provided than a big marble shaft or statue toward which small boys in after years can shoot small stones and snowballs and aged people can sit complacently about and by squinting their eyes through strong lenses satisfy their curiosity in reading the names of those who responded to duty."[9] Echoing national trends, this group preferred a "living memorial," such as a community building, gymnasium, or park, that could honor the veterans' spirit of service while also providing something useful to the town.[10]

Debate was heated. It seemed that the town would vote for the completion of a new gymnasium, a project for which it had begun to raise funds before the war. But after four special town meetings, in May 1919 the town voted to create a new memorial park by clearing a rundown section of town between the railroad tracks and the Millers River.[11] Much of the support for the park came from local businesses wanting to create an attractive town common near the railroad station to greet visitors, a strategy popular with village improvement societies throughout New England; merchants also saw the plan as providing additional parking space for their stores.

Although space was reserved in the park for a World War monument, the decision for the park left many of the recently returned veterans feeling used and left out. One veteran stated: "The boys did not relish the idea of being used as a lever by the townspeople to obtain something they could get in no other way," adding that the new park "would serve more as a benefit to the townspeople than the servicemen."[12] The ex-soldiers' feeling of separation from the rest of the town was reinforced when the first anniversary of the Armistice came and went in November 1919 unobserved by the townspeople.

But by then, the veterans had their own organization to perpetuate the memory of the world war in town. With the help of $2,600 that the town had originally set aside—but never used—for a welcome home celebration, the veterans founded a local chapter of the American Legion in August 1919. On the evening of November 11, Legion members gathered in Memorial Hall, a space dedicated to the Civil War veterans of the Grand Army of the Republic, for an Armistice Day ball. Post membership soon grew to over one hundred, including leading citizens who gave the Legion prominence within the community.[13]

By May 1920, the Legionnaires had not only taken over the head-quarters of the Grand Army of the Republic as their post building but had also assumed direction of the town's annual Memorial Day celebration. They transformed the focus of the observance from the Civil War dead to those of the World War, while keeping intact old rituals such as veterans visiting schools and children decorating soldiers' graves. In 1922, the Legion made the commemoration of November 11 into a public event for the first time, organizing a short parade to the newly landscaped memorial park during the day and hosting an Armistice Day ball at night. While the Legion could not convince local businesses to close on the day, many observed three minutes of silence at 11 A.M.—a silence that was enforced in one local foundry in 1925 when two workers who did not stop work were forced to kiss the American flag. A third who refused to comply was dunked in water.[14] At the open house before the Legion Ball the following year, a speaker reminded his audience of the importance of observing the day: "Armistice Day is not a holiday, but let us not forget the great thrill of eight years ago when the Great War came to an end, let us not forget those 'buddies' who never came back. Ex-servicemen, mothers, fathers, friends, be with us on this night. We don't forget."[15]

The ex-soldiers' desire to remember and to be remembered kept the idea of a permanent memorial alive. When the state returned $3,100 in unspent veterans' bonus money to the town in 1926, the veterans insisted that it be earmarked for a memorial in the vacant park.[16] The town committee that had been appointed to recommend a design heard from ten different firms that manufactured war memorials. While the Orange memorial committee records are lost, we know the type of monument that several commercial firms had available. American Doughboy Statues of Spencer, Indiana, touted *The Spirit of the American Doughboy*, a realistic lifesize bronze with rifle in one hand, grenade in the other, stepping over barbed wire. The firm's promotional brochure reprinted an endorsement by the American Legion and a testimonial letter from Sergeant Alvin York.[17] But wanting "a memorial designed especially for Orange, rather than a stock model which may be seen anywhere," the committee rejected the commercially produced statues of the doughboy in action. Instead, it sought to commission an original bronze statue by John T. Hardy. The committee had seen Hardy's work in the nearby town of Templeton, where he had created a memorial doughboy in combat gear holding a rifle in one hand while bending over to place a wreath on the grave of a fallen comrade (figure 6).

When the Orange monument committee approached Hardy to create a similar mourning statue for Orange, however, the sculptor wanted more than double the money the veterans had available.[18] Frustrated, the veterans moved ahead with less expensive alternatives. In November 1929, amid strains of "America the Beautiful" and popular songs from 1917–19 played by the high school orchestra, the veterans unveiled a large wooden frame containing photographs of the eleven men from Orange who had died in the World War grouped around a silk-embroidered emblem of the coat of arms of the United States. Though the dedication ceremony was in the town hall, the photo memorial was soon removed to the Legion headquarters (figure 7).[19] In 1931, the Legion persuaded the town to memorialize its eleven war dead in public by placing bronze markers at eleven intersections around the town, "as near as possible to a spot which the man whose memory it perpetuates passed in his daily life."[20] Turning to Memorial Park, in August 1932 the Company E Veterans Association dedicated a boulder "to the buddies who never returned."[21] Former company members from throughout western Massachusetts attended the Saturday evening dedication ceremony, then stayed overnight for a clambake. Two months later, in October 1932, the newly organized Damon-Spooner Veterans of Foreign Wars Post added a French 88-millimeter World War cannon to the landscape of the park, with a plaque reading "In memory of our departed comrades."[22]

The veterans wanted the markers, boulder, and cannon as permanent reminders of their war experience. What did this experience mean to Orange's World War veterans? We don't know what motivated the men of Orange to go to war in 1917—what combination of sense of duty to nation and boredom with small town life. But we do know how their experience was retroactively explained in the decade following the war. Even before the World War had ended, the town had transformed the soldiers into model citizens and patriotic exemplars, sliding them into the social role that had been occupied by the thinning ranks of Civil War veterans.[23] By the early 1930s, townspeople were accustomed to viewing the soldiers' war experience as an abstraction with didactic value for local youth. Newspaper accounts of the veterans' commemorative ceremonies praised their spirit of self-sacrifice more than their actual accomplishments, which, in the context of a resurgent militarism in Germany and the failure of the League of Nations, were left ill-defined. Reporting on the dedication of the Company E memorial boulder in 1932, the local newspaper proclaimed simply that the large rock would "inspire future generations with a spirit of patriotism."[24] Orange's veterans did not shy away from the patriotic role they had been assigned or the national iconography that went with it—the photographic memorial hanging in the Legion Hall intertwined the pictures of the men with the American eagle, and veterans hoped to add a flagpole to Memorial

Fig. 6. Joseph T. Hardy's war memorial sculpture for Templeton, Massachusetts. Photo by J. Michael Moore.

Fig. 7. The photographic tribute to Orange's World War I dead still hangs in the American Legion hall. Photo by the author.

Park with a plaque to Gold Star mothers. But the focus of the veterans' efforts to mark the landscape, like their other public activities of the early 1930s—encouraging military training for youth, sponsoring a drum corps, organizing Memorial Day and Armistice Day ceremonies—was as much to reinforce the ex-soldiers' camaraderie with one another and special position in the community as to inspire national loyalty among their fellow citizens.

The increase in the Legion's public activities in the 1930s gains additional meaning when placed in the context of the Great Depression. The Company E clambake and boulder dedication of August 1932 took place six weeks after federal troops had routed the thousands of World War veterans who had gathered in Washington to request an advance on the cash value of the life insurance policies they had been given for their service. Not only did the ex-soldiers not get their bonus that year, but in March 1933 the Government Economy Act slashed veterans' benefits by 40 percent. As the Depression worsened, Legion membership offered veterans not only an important source of personal identity but also mutual economic support and a base from which to retain their claim on civil society.[25] Veterans of the early 1930s had reason to fear that their special position in town would be lost as the story of what they did in the war was forgotten, and their direct testimony was replaced with books and films about the war.[26]

Thus as Orange's veterans dedicated the boulder and cannon on the perimeter of Memorial Park in late 1932, they left room at the center for a more imposing monument—one that unmistakably would embody the veterans themselves and their central place in town life, as well as the centrality of their story over others about the war. A statue of a doughboy could speak to the town more eloquently than any boulder could. In 1933, as the Depression deflated prices and raised the value of the funds the town had set aside for a memorial in 1926, the ex-soldiers launched yet another effort to realize their long-sought goal of a doughboy statue for Memorial Park.

BY THE EARLY 1930S, however, the veterans were not the only group in town keeping alive the memory of the war. Reflecting national trends, there was a veritable eruption of internationalist and pacifist sentiment in the community, much of it directed toward using the memory of the World War to transform the traditional rituals that connected war and patriotism. This sentiment left a permanent mark on Orange, ensuring that while the town would stick to its commitment to erect a statue of a doughboy, the unique design ultimately created would not depict him in martial glory.

Orange's churches were among the earliest centers of pacifist sentiment. Arthur Blair, pastor of the Universalist Church from 1922 to 1931, regularly wove antiwar themes into his sermons.[27] On Memorial Day in 1923, Blair warned that "if civilization does not do away with war, war will destroy civilization." In 1924, on Armistice Day, Blair called for the town to "make war on war psychology," including the elimination of children's toy guns and soldiers. On Memorial Day in 1929 he called for the nation to honor its "peace heroes" such as Edison as well as its war heroes, and intoned "Let us not forget that the world is larger than our nation, as large and as important as we think our nation is, and we must have due regard for the rights of other and especially smaller nations."[28] Blair played an active role in the town's commemoration of the world war, speaking at the first Armistice Day ceremonies in Memorial Park in 1922, as well as at the dedication of the memorial street markers in 1931; he also chaired the war memorial committee in 1926 that had preferred Hardy's original statue of a mourning veteran to the commercially available ones depicting a doughboy going over the top.

Another center of antiwar sentiment was the high school, under the influence of civics and government teacher Henry Littlefield and Principal Dwight Davis. Littlefield, only twenty-four years old in 1929 and fresh out of New York University, encouraged his students to question the results of the Armistice, the system of war reparations, and the role of arms manufacturers.[29] Davis, in an article in the school paper (reprinted in the town paper), provoked the imagination of the students who would view the 1931 Memorial Day parade:

> As you watch the parade swing from the old town hall down East Main Street toward the cemetery, I hope that you will see more than the veterans, old and young, more than the members of the various organizations who will be marching there. I hope that you will see shell-torn, mud-spattered, bleeding humanity as it was on the fields of France. While the band is playing a stirring march, I hope that you will hear the cry of suffering humanity as God has heard it through all the wars of the ages. I hope that in some way you can sense the awful futility of war as a means of settling national disputes.[30]

Local efforts in 1931 to transform the traditional rituals that connected war and patriotism were bolstered by a statewide campaign of the Massachusetts chapter of the Women's International League for Peace and Freedom. Proclaiming that "the new patriotism is peace," Massachusetts WILPF mailed over a thousand kits to teachers, including holiday programs for schools developed by the National Council for Prevention of War. The kits included exercises not only for Memorial Day and Armistice Day, but also for July 4, Flag Day, and Washington's Birthday (a play depicting Washington negotiating peace treaties). Among the items in the Armistice Day kit for 1931 were plays about the Kellogg-Briand Pact and a list of suggested topics for student talks such as "War versus Prosperity: Munitions Makers and Disarmament."[31] In

September 1931, two WILPF members drove into Orange as part of a disarmament caravan. An offshoot of the national Peace Caravan that traveled from Hollywood to Washington between June and October 1931, this "baby caravan" circulated petitions throughout rural Massachusetts calling for the total disarmament of all nations. Those who took copies of the petition for circulation in Orange included ministers from the Congregational, Universalist, and Methodist churches, as well as representatives from the Orange Women's Club, the Millers River Grange and, interestingly, the Catholic Women's Club.[32]

In the spring of 1932, Wallace Fiske, age twenty-four, replaced Arthur Blair as pastor of the Universalist Church and as a member of the town monument committee. The new minister wasted no time in letting the veterans know how he felt about the war. On the Sunday before Memorial Day in 1933, Fiske began his sermon with a recollection of being in grammar school and seeing soldiers returning home from the World War "broken in body and mind and spirit." He went on to implore the veterans in his congregation to join him in teaching that war was horrible and futile: "You who tasted battle know that war is not music and flags and clean uniforms. It is filth and suffering and death. Let us join our energy then to tear away the mask and see war as it really is, a death dealing monster. [Let the memory of the war dead serve as an] 'inspiring influence' in a peacetime 'war on poverty . . . ignorance, superstition, vice, oppression, and exploitation."[33]

Fiske was severe in his condemnation of the Great War, claiming that deep down the veterans knew "that every nation lost the war," and that it had established none of the principles for which it was fought. As a member of the town monument committee, Fiske wanted the residents of Orange to face this fact squarely. But would the veterans support a monument to the futility of their effort? Could a monument honor the men while condemning the war?

Fiske sat down with the other two members of the committee, Herbert Macdonald, owner of a local jewelry store, and Cora Bangs, a prominent member of the local chapter of the Daughters of the American Revolution and former chair of the Women's Club, to review the proposed monument designs the American Legion had collected over the years. The Legion still had a monument committee of its own, consisting of Luther Horton and former post commanders Howard Warren and Arthur Lundgren. Fiske recalled circulating through town, asking various community leaders for their ideas.[34] Among the suggestions he received were "alternative" memorials such as a collection of books on peace for the public library and the endowment of a hospital bed. But Fiske, mindful of the need to win the approval of the veterans, sought a suitable monument for Memorial Park. As in 1926, the committee placed a high priority on originality; there could be no duplicate of a design used elsewhere. To avoid the problem they had encountered with Hardy, they let sculptors know in advance that they only had $4,300 to spend. The committee received numerous sketches, including a design by Paul Saint-Gaudens, nephew of Augustus Saint-Gaudens, consisting of a large stone tablet with a bronze relief of a draped figure holding a wreath above an honor roll, with a broken sword below (figure 8). The inscription read "Let the Word Be Peace." The back of the tablet displayed an American eagle over a dedication "To the Men of Orange Who Gave Their Lives for Their Country."[35] But this symbolic memorial, in the allegorical style of an earlier generation, was not the figurative statue that the veterans wanted.

Unhappy with the proposals it received, the committee began to develop a monument design of its own. Fiske sketched a soldier and boy—a scene perhaps recalled from his own youth—and refined it with the help of the other committee members and Joseph P. Pollia, a forty-year-old Boston-trained sculptor who had a number of pieces in the area by 1933.[36] Among these were Spanish-American War monuments in Stoneham and Greenfield, unveiled in 1928, and World War I statues in Barre and Franklin, unveiled in 1929. The Spanish-American War memorials, modeled on "Hiker" statues nationwide, showed a soldier with a rifle striding through a field. The Barre World War memorial depicted a doughboy thrusting forward his bayonet (figure 9). The Franklin doughboy stands in prayer, with his gun at rest. Pollia had a well-deserved reputation in western Massachusetts for the quality of his doughboy statues—but none of them hinted at the design he would execute in Orange.

The Orange World War I monument (figure 10) contains no helmets, no rifles, no bayonets. It depicts the soldier not on the battlefield, but back in his community. He is seated, wearing his service hat, boots, and leggings, leaving the impression that he has just arrived home. At his side stands a young boy, a book under one arm. One imagines the insistence of the boy on hearing "all about" the war, not even giving the

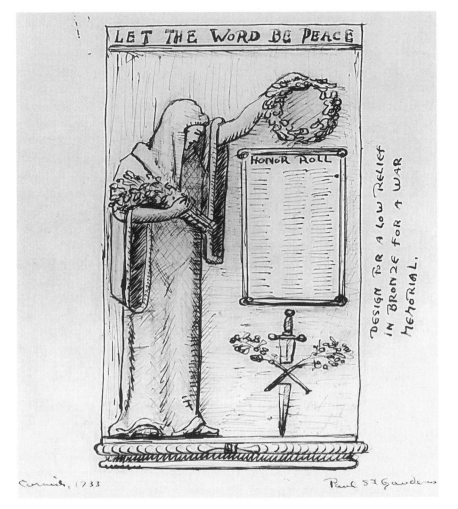

Fig. 8. Paul Saint-Gaudens submitted this sketch for the proposed new World War I memorial in Orange in 1933. Peace Monuments and Symbols Collection, Swarthmore College Peace Collection.

soldier time to get out of his uniform. Viewed from the front the soldier's expression appears stern, but from the viewpoint of the boy, to whom his gaze is turned, it appears compassionate and concerned. His right arm is extended in a gesture, the hand half-opened as he relates his story to the child. The bronze tablet on the front of the granite base suggests the soldier's words: "It Shall Not Be Again." A shrouded figure

Fig. 9. Joseph Pollia's sculpture for the World War I memorial in Barre, Massachusetts. Photo by J. Michael Moore.

Fig. 10. Pollia's sculpture for the World War I memorial in Orange, viewed from the side. Photo by the author.

reminiscent of Saint-Gaudens's design frames the tablet, crushing beneath its feet the weapons of modern war. Eleven stars, representing the eleven men from Orange who died in the war, float in the background. On the rear of the base is a plaque "Dedicated in Memory of Those of Orange Who Served Their Country during the World War, 1917–19."

The historian J. Michael Moore notes that while the monument suggests the ease of communicating the veteran's experience across generations, the boy's posture suggests that he is reacting angrily to what he is hearing. The boy tightly grips his textbook, pugnaciously thrusting out his fist; his initial reaction to the eyewitness account of the soldier is to hold on to the happier stories of martial valor and heroism with which he has grown up. The confrontation between the soldier, reluctant but nevertheless determined to tell the tale of what war is really life, and the boy, drawing back from the soldier while clinging tenaciously to his storybook version, gives the monument enormous power. At the same time that it conveys its message against war it dramatizes the need for the message—to educate the children.

The Orange monument is unique in its depiction of a returning soldier in the classic "educator" statue pose of an adult teaching a youth.[37] But it is akin to a number of other memorials erected in the United States and Europe in the 1920s and 1930s that emphasized the human cost of war. Americans and Europeans dedicated figurative statues of mourning comrades, such as John Hardy's doughboy at Templeton, Massachusetts (see figure 6), and Albert Toft's at Streatham in England; of mourning parents, such as the one Käthe Kollwitz sculpted in memory of her son in Belgium; even of mourning children, as in Saint Bertrand de Comminges, France, where a young boy stands by a shaft listing the names of the war dead (figure 11). These memorials emphasizing bereavement erected after World War I contrast sharply with the war memorials erected in the late nineteenth century that emphasized the national cause for which the soldiers fought.[38]

The monument committee left space on the sides of the base for an honor roll plaque listing every Orange resident who served in the World War. Names for an honor roll had been compiled immediately after the war, with a "final list" of names published for inspection in the local newspaper in May 1919. But when the Legion met to consider the plaque in 1934, shortly before the monument was finished, members voiced concern about some of the names that had been included. In a

debate that lasted until midnight, the Legion decided that the plaque
would retain the names of soldiers and Red Cross nurses but not the
names of those who served in the Salvation Army, YMCA, or merchant
marine, those who had been dishonorably discharged, and those from
surrounding towns who did not live in Orange. Despite the mention of
nurses, none of the 241 names printed in 1919 were women, suggesting
the larger absence of a women's role in war commemoration.[39]

Orange dedicated its new monument on Memorial Day 1934, inserting the unveiling into the annual holiday program, between the main
exercises in the town hall and the march to the Civil War monument in
the central cemetery. Arthur Lundgren, former American Legion post
commander and chair of the board of selectmen, accepted the statue on
behalf of the town and laid a wreath at the base of the monument. Fiske

Fig. 11. This World War I memorial in Saint Bertrand de Comminges, in the Basque
region of France, is similar to others in Europe and America in its emphasis on the local
community's losses rather than the nation's victories. Photo by Anne Rearick.

delivered the main address in Memorial Park, in which he explained that "the committee, in cooperation with the local post of the American Legion, specified that their memorial was to suitably memorialize the veterans of the world war without glorifying the idea of arms and equipment of war in the minds of the younger generation." Proudly putting Pollia's statue in the context of the times, he continued: "With representative clergymen of every denomination speaking against participation in armed conflict and refusing to consider any idea of aid or assistance in another war, with college students rioting against military instruction, with college professors teaching and preaching against excessive military preparation, the feeling is spreading among laymen that War Memorials which they propose to erect should reflect the new spirit."[40]

Why did the members of the American Legion—an organization whose national office earlier that month had decried the "subversive" activities of pacifist ministers—accept Pollia's monument?[41] How did Fiske—a newcomer to town and barely ten years old in 1918—gain the authority to design it? Clearly the distance between the antiwar ministers and the Legionnaires at the local level was not as great as historians might suppose. Former Legion commander Howard Warren belonged to Fiske's Universalist church, serving as its treasurer. Fiske, who invited a number of pacifist speakers to town in 1934 under the auspices of the Orange Community Forum, was also president of the Kiwanis Club that year.[42] Henry Littlefield, the high school teacher who the month before the monument dedication supervised a contest for the best essay on "The Part Played by Armaments Industries in Making Wars" (with a first prize of twenty-five dollars and a book autographed by Senator Gerald Nye), also organized the town's George Washington bicentennial celebration and historical pageant, dedicated to the Civil War veterans of the Grand Army of the Republic. It was the Daughters of the American Revolution that sponsored an essay contest in honor of the monument dedication with the title "How Can War Be Avoided and Peace Be Sustained?" Coming of age in the 1960s and 1970s, I was accustomed to seeing a great polarization between members of "left-wing" antiwar groups and "right-wing" patriotic and hereditary organizations, but clearly in Orange in the 1930s, they shared common ground.

It is also likely that Legion members were not the militarists one might expect from reading the literature produced by the national headquarters. In a national survey of Legion members later in the 1930s, 44 percent felt that World War I was a "mistake," even though 38 percent described their own time in the military as a "great experience."[43] Perhaps the Pollia statue spoke against war in ways that the veterans could not, given the expectations of civilian society concerning manliness and war.[44]

But the most likely reason that the members of the local American Legion chapter endorsed Fiske's design was that they saw Pollia's statue not as antiwar, but as a portrait of themselves in the community. These were, after all, the same men who promoted military training for local youth. Despite Fiske's desire to "unmask" the horror of war, the monument shows the soldier returning home intact; a handsome likeness occupying a central place in the park established fifteen years earlier in the veterans' honor. Although they might have been disappointed that Pollia's doughboy was not laying a wreath at the grave of a fallen comrade, like Joseph Hardy's doughboy statue in Templeton, it depicted him in another activity, educating youth, in which the ex-soldiers felt important.

That the veterans' endorsement of the monument's design did not extend to Fiske's interpretation of its meaning is suggested by the speaker they chose for the Memorial Day exercises at the town hall in 1934, General Frederick Pierce. The Spanish-American War veteran, who also had spoken at the ceremonies dedicating the cannon placed in Memorial Park by the VFW in 1932, made no reference at all to the town's newest war memorial. Instead, this soldier of an earlier generation offered a history lesson, reviewing the succession of lustrous military campaigns that had enabled the United States to realize its manifest destiny. "Let us not forget that through the soldiery of our Nation . . . the glorious insignia of our country, the stars and stripes of this republic, floats proudly in every clime on the face of the globe."[45] It may be too much to assume that the veterans in charge of the Memorial Day ceremonies asked Pierce to speak specifically in reaction to the pacifism of the clergy. But the contrast between his speech and Fiske's memorial dedication, both of them part of the same Memorial Day observance, is striking.

The dedication of the monument in 1934 must be seen as part of a continuum of activities through which Orange and its ex-soldiers recalled the World War. The month before the dedication, the Legion put

on the play *Buddies* at Town Hall, and read installments of the diary
of an Apremont veteran published in the local newspaper. The local
veterans' commemoration of Apremont culminated the following year
when the entire 104th Division held its reunion in Orange. A poem
published on that occasion, titled "Your Pal at Apremont," concluded
that although the ex-soldiers might come to know famous men, mil-
lionaires, and movie stars, "the friends worthwhile and true, are the
happy smiling few, who shared with you the Hell at Apremont."[46] If the
veterans' commemorative activities sought to put words in the mouth of
the monumental soldier in Memorial Park, it was likely to be tales of his
buddies at Apremont—a hell—not pacifist abstractions about war.

THE COMPROMISES and ambiguities of that Memorial Day in 1934,
cast in bronze, remained with the monument long after the popular
pacifist sentiment of the early 1930s subsided. Very soon after the dedication, local newspapers boasted that Pollia's memorial had put the
town on the map. In the mid-1930s, brief profiles of the Orange monument appeared in the *Boston Herald*, the *Christian Science Monitor*, the
*New York Times*, the *WPA Guide to Massachusetts*, and, of course, journals
of national peace organizations. It made the cover of the *Church School
Journal* for November 1936. These articles described Pollia's statue as a
peace monument, emphasizing its antiwar message, and quoted praise
from prominent pacifist clergy John Haynes Holmes and Harry Emerson Fosdick, as well as Eleanor Roosevelt and former navy secretary
Josephus Daniels.[47] That these nationally known figures liked the monument is not surprising; what's significant is that their comments were
reprinted in the same local paper that elsewhere attacked the New Deal
as socialist and pacifist church groups as "tearing down" America.[48]
Orange was still the same town that in November 1936 voted three to
one for Alf Landon, and heard Baptist minister Stephen Talbot's Armistice Day address attacking the "peace propagandists of communism."[49]
But for better or worse, Orange had become "internationally known"
through its monument. And the local paper reprinting comments from
afar reinforced the monument's inscribed meaning as a "peace statue" as
well as established a new meaning for it as a local tourist attraction—
an attraction the local chamber of commerce tried to capitalize on in
1945 in its bid to get the United Nations to locate its headquarters in
Orange.[50] Meanwhile, Pollia also capitalized on the fame his monument

Fig. 12. This editorial cartoon appeared in the Orange *Enterprise and Journal* on November 11, 1937.

brought, securing commissions for statues of Philip Sheridan, Stonewall Jackson, and Babe Ruth.

By the late 1930s, as war broke out in Asia and Europe, the residents of Orange found other meanings in their statue, and in its slogan "It Shall Not Be Again." A local newspaper cartoonist in 1937 sketched a picture of the statue with the slogan, and added a "We Wonder?" (figure 12). Speaking on November 11, 1938, the first year that Armistice Day was a federal holiday, Methodist minister Ernest Lyman Mills lamented the nation's lack of military preparedness in 1917 and declared, "We must not be caught napping again." Taking an isolationist tack, the following year the editor of the Orange paper explained the appropriateness of the ceremonies in front of the statue whose message warned that "this country should refrain from solving Europe's troubles." Then in 1940, with France on the verge of surrender to Nazi Germany, a Memorial Day editorial pointedly stated that "it shall be again if it is necessary to preserve our independence, our liberty, and our democracy."[51]

During World War II, the contemporary meanings of the monument all but displaced its references to World War I veterans. The local paper reported that state senator Ralph Mahar, speaking on Armistice Day 1941, "pointed to the irony of the inscription on the peace monument." "It need not have been again," he said,"if American politicians had won the peace as their armed forces won the war." There were no Armistice Day celebrations in 1942, 1943, or 1944, except for brief ceremonies at Memorial Park at the World War II honor roll, newly erected near the World War I statue. By the time that Orange's soldiers returned home from World War II, more than doubling the size of the Legion post in 1946, memories of more recent battles than Apremont loomed larger in the consciousness of the Legion and its veterans.

Orange's World War II veterans expressed no interest in commemorating their deeds with a memorial statue. Nor did they consider adding the names of the town's twenty-two World War II dead to the World War I monument, as several other towns did after the war. In fact, as if to separate their experience from those of earlier wars, the veterans moved the World War II honor roll away from Memorial Park to a site in front of the town library. Mirroring national trends, there was no effort to commemorate VE Day or VJ Day in town. When 35 veterans met in August 1946 to discuss a World War II memorial, they unanimously opted for a "living memorial" in the form of a new field house near the athletic field, an idea endorsed the following year in a public meeting of 125 veterans (out of an estimated 600 World War II veterans in town). Significantly, there was no evidence of the participation of ministers or women in the World War II memorial committee.[52]

In the decade after World War II, Pollia's statue in Memorial Park lost its particular association with World War I veterans. The commemorative ceremonies around it every November 11 mentioned service in all wars, a phenomenon paralleled at the national level in 1954 when Congress changed the name of Armistice Day to Veterans Day. In postwar decades, the statue continued to prompt homilies on war and peace. A speaker in 1948 placed the customary wreath on the "peace monument" (as the local paper described it), which he saw as underscoring the "importance of keeping America militarily strong in order to prevent World War III." A speaker on Veterans Day in 1956 pointed to the statue as a symbol of humankind's desire for peace, though he did not allude to either the Great War, contemporary events, or even World War II.[53] But as Veterans Day ceremonies diminished in size through the 1950s, and the passing seasons turned the memorial's bronze to a weathered green, it seemed to fade into its park surroundings, with little of the political meanings that it had been given in the 1930s.

That would change in the following decade, during the Vietnam War. In 1965, veterans' organizations sought to bolster the patriotic associations of Memorial Park by renaming it Veterans Memorial Park and enlisting the Boy Scouts in a townwide campaign for a flagpole, which was dedicated Memorial Day, 1966.[54] At the same time, local peace activists rediscovered the statue. In 1971, the Athol-Orange Peace Action Committee tried to enter into the patriotic rituals of the town by joining the Memorial Day ceremonies. Denied a place in the procession (on the grounds that it would be "inappropriate on Memorial Day and not in the best interests of the town of Orange" and might cause "a serious public safety hazard"), the seventy-five protesters held their vigil at Pollia's World War I monument in Memorial Park, standing in silence before the statue that itself commemorates the act of communication about war across generations (figure 13).[55]

Since the 1970s, the monument has remained "a favorite of pacifist groups."[56] In 1984, the Rural Peace Coalition persuaded the Junior Women's Club to commemorate the fiftieth anniversary of the statue by sponsoring an essay contest for high school students on "How to Obtain Peace in 1984." The winning entries were published in the local paper. Seven years later, peace groups gathered again at the Pollia statue to protest the Gulf War.[57] As these actions reinforced the monument's meaning as a peace statue, the same veterans' organizations that dedicated the statue in 1934 seemed to grow more distant from it. On Memorial Day 1991, the procession to the Civil War monument in the town cemetery paused for ceremonies before the honor roll erected for veterans of World War II, Korea, and Vietnam in front of the town library, but twice passed by the World War I statue in Memorial Park without stopping.[58] Although Legion members continued to hold Veterans Day ceremonies in Memorial Park in which children played a prominent role, in effect reenacting the scene cast in bronze in the statue, it was the women of the Universalist Church, not the veterans' organizations, who assumed the primary role in caring for the monument against deterioration from vandalism and weather.

While the memorialization of World War I in Orange, the source of the town's fame in the 1930s, had all but disappeared from the public life of the town, elements of it remained within the Legion Hall. The memorial pictures of the eleven soldiers who died in that war hang on the wall of the new hall, along with numerous World War I–era photographs of the buddies in camp, the Last Man's Club, and the charter membership roll—all relics significant to the members' identity as Legion members. Among those relics was the honor roll from World War I; it was never attached to the statue, and in 1993, Michael Moore and I found it in the hall's attic.[59] Interestingly, in 1993 the walls of the Legion Hall contained practically nothing from World War II or later wars.

Fig. 13. Local residents beside the Orange war memorial on Memorial Day in 1971 protesting the United States military intervention in Vietnam. Photo by Richard Chaisson; Richard Chaisson collection.

Fig. 14. This editorial cartoon appeared in the Orange *Enterprise and Journal* on June 3, 1937.

It ✦ Shall Not Be Again

The political themes that surface during times when issues of war and peace are foremost on the minds of Orange residents constitute one set of meanings for the statue in Memorial Park. But there is another set of meanings to the statue that emerge not through the organized activities of various political groups but through day-to-day interaction with the townspeople. Three years after the dedication in 1934, the local newspaper ran a picture of Pollia's statue depicting the veteran handing the youth a tax bill, complete with the caption "It Shall Not Be Again" (figure 14). In 1956 the slogan accompanied a photograph of the monument in the snow, as a caption wondering if this was the last of the season.[60] Over time, the soldier and boy in the statue have come to symbolize not only national issues of war and peace but also the townspeople themselves.

Unlike figures on war memorials that depict death and sacrifice on the battlefield, the Orange doughboy is down to earth; you can talk to this doughboy and he talks back. The returning soldier talking to the young boy is talking to all children; by embracing the civilian child he is embracing the town. And over the years the town has embraced him back. During the Gulf War in 1991, the soldier was given a yellow ribbon and an American flag, as if in an effort to complete Pollia's statue by adding what was missing in the 1930s. The monument serves as an icon through which local residents can express their concern about family members in the service and hope for their safe return, as well as a prompt which leads residents to recall their own military service. Fifty years after the monument dedication of 1934, Kenneth Richards remembered identifying with the boy in the statue: "Expecting a heroically postured soldier depicted in the heat of battle, my childish concepts were disappointed when the statue was unveiled." But then his reminiscence linked the statue with his own military experience—"Years later when I returned from World War II, I saw that memorial in a different light"—and he identified with the seated soldier telling the child about war's inhumanities. Richards's reminiscence reminds us of what we do not know about the memory of war in Orange—what real veterans tell their children and grandchildren in private about their war experiences.[61]

We also have the story of Robert P. Collen, whose uncle Oscar was one of the eleven men from Orange who died in World War I. Robert Collen recalled growing up in the 1930s in a family of "America Firsters" bitterly opposed to American intervention in World War II (until Pearl Harbor). He also recalled that local high school students who wanted to join the military during World War II were required to page through a book of explicit photographs of World War I casualties before being allowed to enlist. Collen did not fight in World War II but did serve in Korea. He mentioned that he is still interested in the history of World War I—more so than in that of later conflicts—and has taught his children and grandchildren songs popular during the war.[62]

The statue may have come to represent not only the promise of the safe return of local residents in the service but also the continuity of the town itself. In a town with declining industry after World War II (Orange is now the sixth-poorest in the state in per capita income), the statue of the man and boy, sometimes explained as a "father and son," may stand for generational continuity—the iconographic message of father and son symbolizing the endurance of the town.[63] Unlike World War I memorials in Europe that depicted mourning widows and children and the disruption of families, Pollia's monument appears as a

family scene, much like the images of parents and children common in
Depression-era photography. The boy's clenched fist—common in Depression iconography as a symbol of determination to survive—may be
especially important to local residents in the context of the industrial
flight from Orange since the 1970s.[64] This is one son who is not leaving
town. In 1984, the town's veterans may have been associating the economic well-being of the town with defense of Memorial Park by leading
the fight against a proposal to erect a monument to the New Home
Sewing Machine Company in the park. While the New Home had been
among the most important businesses in town history, it had left Orange
long before and had been taken over by a Japanese firm.[65] Over the years
the seated veteran has come to embody loyal service not only to the
nation but also to the town, and local residents' commitment to the
maintenance of the town's way of life for their children.

Certainly many local residents now view the monument as integral
to the town's identity. In 1995, with the assistance of my collaborator
Michael Moore, a Save Our Statue Committee was formed to raise
money to restore the statue's weathered bronze. To publicize its efforts,
the committee sponsored an essay contest, reminiscent of the one the
Daughters of the American Revolution sponsored in 1934 when the
monument was first built. Robert Collen served as one of the judges and
read a poem he had written about the statue at the awards ceremony, at
which Moore also spoke. The committee's restoration efforts culminated on Memorial Day 1998, at an elaborate ceremony rededicating
the newly refurbished statue. Wallace Fiske, now eighty-eight years old,
returned to Orange to address the crowd in a voice that had lost none of
its power over the intervening six decades (figure 15). To help pay for
the restoration, the statue is now surrounded by a new walkway of
bricks, each inscribed with the name of a person the donor wanted to
remember. My cousin Trudy, who lives in a town adjacent to Orange,
purchased one in memory of my mother. What had been a rundown
section of town in the 1910s had by the 1990s become a sacred space in
which most local residents had some memorial presence.[66]

THE STORY of the World War I memorial in Orange prompts us to
consider the many different ways in which wars have been remembered
and forgotten in twentieth-century America. The particular form of the
Orange monument and its identity as a "peace statue" was the result of

an unusual intersection of events and feelings in the early 1930s. Had
the statue been built just a few years earlier or later it likely would have
looked quite different. The monument offers a permanent record of the
feeling in the 1930s that a town could honor its warriors but not their
war; of the efforts nationwide in the period to replace the powerful
commemorative rituals linking military and national glory that had
arisen in the decades after the Civil War and consolidated in the 1890s,
with ones that would promote a nonmilitaristic love of country.[67]

Orange's ministers and teachers saw the seated veteran educating the

Fig. 15. Reverend
Wallace Fiske speaking
at the ceremony
rededicating the newly
restored Orange war
memorial on May 25,
1998. Photo by the
author.

child about the horrors of war as a patriotic act, just as much as his fighting in battle. This memory of war that combined pacifism and patriotism was all but extinguished after World War II—as evidenced in town officials' response to antiwar activities during the Vietnam era as unpatriotic. As Armistice Day gave way to Veterans Day, so went the memory that Congress had originally set aside the holiday in 1938 as "a day to be dedicated to the cause of world peace."[68] Headlines such as the one in the Orange newspaper on that day—"Armistice Day Will Be Observed/Orange Post American Legion Announces Program/Exercises at Peace Monument at 10:45 A.M.," now look strange to us. The Orange monument was one of a number of activities in the 1930s that sought to expand the boundaries of patriotic belief and behavior only to see those boundaries constrict in the aftermath of World War II, when Cold War orthodoxy and the popularity of the Allied cause made public rituals that questioned national purpose in war unacceptable.

The memorialization of World War I in Orange also suggests much about the nature of "collective memory." Joseph Pollia's monument was not an expression of the town's collective memory of World War I but rather of what the literary critic James Young has termed a "collected memory"—a process by which discrete memories converge in a common memorial space and are assigned a common meaning.[69] Through the 1920s and 1930s, local veterans—especially the minority of the town's veterans who had fought together in Company E—were given a privileged position in narrating their version of the war and assigning a meaning to Memorial Park, but they did not have a monopoly on the memory of the war. What made Orange unusual was that its veterans were not the only ones who seized the right to inscribe their version of history on the local landscape: young men such as Henry Littlefield and Wallace Fiske also had a large say in the design of how the war would be remembered. So did the women of the town, though their role in the conflict was not memorialized—no women appeared on the final version of the honor roll. The ministers and veterans had different ideas about the meaning of the monument; the design embodied a compromise but not a common vision. Pollia's statue became a special place in the town, one where veterans and other residents could project their meanings and memories—much as a later generation would do with the Vietnam Veterans Memorial in Washington. War memorials tend to be ambiguous so as to satisfy competing groups. As multivocal embodiments of compromise, the monuments invite different groups to read their own meanings into what they see.

Although the Orange monument reflected the collection of memories within the town, it did surprisingly little to consolidate local residents' relationship to the nation-state. Scholars have insisted that war memorials are designated common spaces for shared memories, sites that create the illusion that the residents of a town, region, or nation have a common past, present, and future; and that creating a "common" memory of war is important for the formation of a national identity, of creating an overarching framework into which particular and diverse local interests can be inserted.[70] Yet the U.S. government in the interwar years had a limited role in directing this practice, especially when compared to other nations. Other than establishing battlefield cemeteries overseas and the Tomb of the Unknown Soldier in Arlington, it did not build war memorials of its own, or subsidize local memorials, or supply lists of names to be enshrined on local honor rolls, as in France; nor did it officially attempt to guide memorial design, as in Great Britain. The federal government in 1934 was unable even to answer Orange veterans' request for a list of local residents who had served in the World War, to check against the honor roll they had compiled. With a comparatively weak federal presence, no single World War I experience emerged as the official one, and the symbolism employed in local war memorials such as Orange's varied greatly with local conditions. Unlike monuments erected in the aftermath of the Civil War, when towns erected near-identical common soldiers' memorials that demonstrated their identification with the nation, Orange's war memorial was the product of a quest for local distinctiveness, a claim that only grew with time. To a far greater degree than in other countries, memorialization of World War I in the United States was shaped by local political cultures rather than the dictates of the nation-state—though recent research has shown local and regional variation in war memorial practices in European countries as well.[71]

Over time, the memorial's importance in the life of the community as a symbol of local distinctiveness surpassed its importance as a reminder of the Great War. In an often-quoted passage, Robert Musil observed that monuments repel viewers because the causes they commemorate inevitably become less important with the passage of time.[72] In Orange over the past seven decades new meanings have become attached to the memorial, making it more pliant than the original bronze. The monument's meaning was not fixed in time; it changed through the townspeople's continuing interaction with it, and its relationship with the public may have even grown more close as new, personal memories attached to it. By the 1990s, these memories of the monument had displaced the memory of the war it commemorated. No one in Orange remembers World War I—the town's last veteran of that war died in 1991—or how the monument was built—yet the citizens of Orange are eager to hear the story of the creation of the monument, and to raise money to preserve and protect it. The fact that no other town has such a monument now seems its most important attribute.[73] Still, as the symbolic battle over Memorial Park during the Vietnam era shows, while the original antiwar message has not always loomed large in Orange in the half-century since the monument's dedication, neither has it entirely disappeared.

Local residents' attachment to their monument also suggests the importance of figurative war memorials in the twentieth century. Professional artists concerned with how Americans would memorialize World War I had nothing but harsh words for the Civil War soldier monuments, and heaped contempt on the commercial doughboy statues that proliferated in the America of the 1920s. This critical contempt for figurative memorials continued after the Second World War—the Iwo Jima monument in Arlington is one of only a handful of such memorials commemorating World War II. It erupted again with the placement of the Frederick Hart statue by the Vietnam Veterans Memorial in Washington in 1984, and with the unveiling of the new statue of women veterans by Glenna Goodacre in November 1993. Contemporary art critics condemn the Hart and Goodacre statues as degrading the original intent of Maya Lin's wall of names.[74] But by insisting on aesthetic purity, these critics miss an important aspect of war memorials. Lin's long black wall, built in 1982, was paid for by contributions from Vietnam veterans and serves as a powerful memorial to those who died there, but it has no representation of the veterans themselves—those who fought and survived. Like the World War I veterans in Orange, many Vietnam veterans rejected the idea that an abstract memorial, such as a boulder or granite slab, could stand alone; their powerful drive for a figurative memorial suggests that they wanted a realistic figure to testify to the reality of their experience, to narrate the particular circumstances of their service and embody the centrality of their story over that of others about the war. The surprising number of Vietnam veterans memorials across the United States that incorporate figurative statues, and the figurative Korean War memorial unveiled in Washington in 1995, reflect the continuing importance of a documentary style rather than abstraction in war memorials. This might be especially true for memorials associated with wars such as World War I, Korea, and Vietnam, whose veterans feared neglect and little consensus existed in society concerning the results of their efforts.[75] Perhaps it is not coincidental that a campaign for a massive new World War II memorial on the Mall in Washington was launched in the aftermath of the controversy over the proposed exhibit of the *Enola Gay* at the Smithsonian, an exhibit that would have questioned America's motives for dropping the atomic bomb at the close of World War II and that evoked a fear among veterans that the current generation of "revisionist" historians would not get their story straight.[76]

This fear on the part of World War II veterans, as their own conflict fades from living memory into history, returns us to our initial question about how the memory of a war is institutionalized and communicated across generations. The monument in Orange, dedicated in 1934 to the promise that veterans could share what they learned about the horrors of war, has forever been mocked by silences between generations. Veterans assume that unless you were there you cannot possibly understand their experience; that their war memories are essentially a private possession to be communicated only with other veterans in dark Legion hall bars. In public ceremonies, we hear only the patriotic slogans that the veterans are expected to say and that the next generation can never quite understand.

Constructed largely as an expression of the camaraderie of the doughboys of Company E and the fear that their deeds would be forgotten in the Depression, and modified by the desire of local pacifists to teach a lesson about war, the Orange World War I monument remains a vivid presence on the landscape. It recalls not the militant 100 percent Americanism and patriotic slogans traditionally associated with veterans' groups and war memorials, but rather a kind of patriotism from the ground up, one that uses the symbolism of stars, flags, and the memory of the war dead to address local concerns and diverse but powerful emotions close to home. The statue of the returning soldier and the young boy reminds local residents that wars have been fought not only for the progress of the nation, but also for the preservation of the town's way of life for its children. Remembering a war as a defense of buddies, family, and hometown, rather than as an extension of America's ideological and economic interests, would prove an important theme in the years after World War II and throughout the remainder of the century.[77]

# 3

# Celebrating the City

The idea in back of the parade is not only
to give the holiday meaning, but to reveal
the city to itself.
—E. B. Mero, 1914

Modern images of crowds have consequences
for modern ideas of community.
—Richard Sennett, 1976

The people owned the streets.
—San Francisco *Chronicle*, 1909

Fig. 16. Souvenir program for
San Francisco's Portolá Festival of 1909.
San Francisco History Center,
San Francisco Public Library.

IN THE PRECEDING chapter, we saw how the residents of one New England municipality set aside a place in their town to remember a national event, and how this place soon became an important symbol of local community identity. Indeed, many of the public historical places we create—war memorials, history museums, roadside markers or plaques on buildings—make claims to local distinctiveness as well as tell stories about the past. This is especially true for perhaps the most popular, yet ephemeral, way of representing local history in public, the local civic celebration or historical reenactment. The public commemoration of events from local history projects a distinctive collective identity for people of different classes, ethnic backgrounds, and lengths of residence who happen to live in the same locale.

Such commemorative rituals—often celebrating the origins of a community—have always been part of the American scene. As early as the eighteenth century, Plymouth, Massachusetts, held commemorative ceremonies on the anniversary of the Pilgrim landing. Throughout the nineteenth century, as the nation moved west, among the first activities of newly organized historical societies was to hold a fete to mark the anniversary of the arrival of the first "white" settler. Elaborate small town parades with floats depicting scenes of pioneer life lie at the center of our portrait of America at the turn of the twentieth century, idealized in Disneyland's "Main Street USA" and theatrical productions such as *The Music Man*. Such nostalgic images of small town America on parade serve as a counterpoint to the urban, industrial America that existed at the time, and that mostly shaped how Americans have lived their lives ever since.

Yet when we cut through the haze of our twenty-first-century nostalgia for small town America, we see that cities, too, staged elaborate civic celebrations at the turn of the century, in which history played an important part. Such commemorative celebrations invited diverse local populations to identify the history of their particular group or neighborhood with a distinctive overarching urban identity. Why did efforts to invest the city with a unique aura through celebrations of its history become more prominent at the turn of the twentieth century than ever before? In what sense, if any, did these civic celebrations "reveal the city to itself?" What made some historical representations of "the city" more compelling to the urban public than others? And how have these turn-of-the-century representations of the urban past continued to influence American urban politics and culture as we begin a new century? These questions are worth addressing both on a general level, and in terms of a specific example: San Francisco's Portolá Festival of 1909. The Portolá Festival demonstrates how urban businesses in collaboration with city governments at the turn of the century transformed city streets that were ordinarily arenas for social conflict into elaborate stage sets for dazzling spectacle.

CIVIC CELEBRATIONS first and foremost are forms of communication, arenas for the expression of ideas and emotions. They do not necessarily function to integrate society and resolve social tensions. Nor do they necessarily project some kind of collective mentality. To the extent that civic celebrations represent a collective history, they are representations of and for the collective but not necessarily by the collective. Such representations primarily serve as tools that some groups use to structure a common reality for others. True, the open character of urban civic celebrations, incorporating various elements in order to appeal people of diverse social and cultural backgrounds, limits the extent of this structuring: urban residents can interpret what they see and hear according to their particular background and experiences; historical images can evoke meanings other than those intended by their creators. Nevertheless, as various groups in the city view the "collective" imagery, read explanations of the imagery in their newspapers, and are unable to articulate alternative explanations, civic celebrations express a "common" ideology, a framework for understanding the workings of urban social and political life at a level once removed from the immediate surroundings of neighborhood, workplace, or ethnic group. Another way to think about the place of historical imagery in urban civic celebrations is in terms of the struggle of various groups to define the center of urban politics and public life. In a society where invoking the name of the public legitimizes a variety of actions, each group seeks to have its particular interests, embedded in its definition of the city's history, accepted as the public interest.[1]

There is a long tradition of civic celebrations in American cities. Among the earliest forms of commemoration were holiday customs transplanted from overseas, which referred to their participants' pasts in Europe or Africa. Despite Puritan antipathy to the festival calendar of early modern England, celebrations of Christmas, May Day, and Pope's Day crossed the Atlantic to Boston, while in Philadelphia, Quaker influence did not prevent German immigrants from "belsnickeling" in fantastic costume on Christmas and participating in New Years shooters brigades, or the Welsh from Christmas mumming door to door. Slaves in New England celebrated Election Day, and in New York and New Jersey, they celebrated "Pinkster," with elaborate dances and rituals clearly of African origin. A new wave of Irish and German immigrants in the mid–nineteenth century expanded the urban holiday calendar. By the 1850s, tens of thousands marched in St. Patrick's Day parades in New York, Boston, and Philadelphia, while Germans in Milwaukee and elsewhere celebrated the birthdays of national heroes such as Schiller and held annual pre-Lenten Carnivals. While such ethnic holiday rituals employed historical imagery to build group consciousness, they also had clear contemporary political overtones; when Philadelphia's Irish demonstrated the strength of their numbers on St. Patrick's Day, or the city's African Americans marched annually after 1808 to commemorate the anniversary of the end of the slave trade, or beginning in 1834, the anniversary of the abolition of slavery in the West Indies, they endured the blows of the city's overwhelmingly native-born white Protestant population.[2]

Another form of urban celebration incorporating historical imagery, also with roots overseas, was more directly political: the street procession as protest march. During the American Revolution, angry processions in Boston and Philadelphia participated in rituals against the British such as raising the Liberty Pole, as well as confronted merchants who raised the price of bread. In the antebellum city, street processions with ideologically charged historical references routinely accompanied campaigns for political office, for labor unions (such as the spectacular strike parade that accompanied the General Trade Union's movement for a ten-hour day in 1835) and for causes such as temperance, nativism, and abolitionism. Like the celebrations of ethnic identity on holidays, these partisan political demonstrations, whether in "rough" or "respectable" form, often prompted conflict and violence between the participants and their opponents.[3]

Members of the local elite sought to submerge these militant displays of ethnic and political identity, arising more or less spontaneously from the city's streets, within a third type of celebration, associated with American national history. On July Fourth or Washington's birthday, or at a reception for a visiting dignitary such as Lafayette, civic leaders invited various local groups who seldom socialized with one another to march together in lengthy, elaborately planned processions celebrating the development of the new nation. The Grand Federal Procession in Philadelphia celebrating the ratification of the Constitution in 1788 took the form of a guild procession from medieval Europe, incorporating various trades demonstrating their vocations on parade floats. While employee and employer marched together, displaying their common interest in the new federal government's encouragement of domestic manufactures, lines of status remained clear as master craftsmen marched in the front, their journeymen and apprentices at the rear. In contrast to ethnic and political demonstrations, these patriotic processions organized by the local elite purportedly represented the city as a whole and displayed the cohesive social hierarchy of all local groups. Evidence suggests, however, that over time, even as the frequency of such patriotic demonstrations increased, the sense of hierarchy that the celebrations were meant to reinforce was breaking down. By midcentury, employees began to march apart from their employers in a host of new voluntary associations, including trade unions and fire companies. State and national holidays such as Muster Day were occasions not only for the local elite, organized into militia companies, to parade at the head of urban society in a conspicuous display of wealth, but also for the working classes to impersonate their social betters in burlesque processions featuring blackface and women's dress. Clearly, events designated for the display of national patriotic sentiment wound up also as occasions for the further expression of local ethnic and class rivalries.[4]

Celebrations in the nineteenth-century city, then, reinforced existing ethnic and class identities while offering newly established voluntary organizations opportunities to display their ideas and numerical strength before the public. Since no place was reserved in the procession line-up for the unorganized, the occasion of a civic celebration even prompted new organizations to come into existence. By obliging members of groups to march together so as to express their distinctive identity to others, the discipline of the parade also enabled group leaders to consolidate their power and authority. The civic celebrations may also have reinforced differences in public status between men and women. Historians have assumed that the streets of the antebellum city were closed to women, except as allegorical figures adorning parade floats, but enough exceptions have been found recently in the historical record to suggest that this assumption needs reexamination.[5]

In general, two aspects of civic celebrations in American cities at midcentury stand out. One is that despite the claims of celebration organizers, various urban groups rarely showed up to commemorate the same historical event at the same place and time. Even on the most widely celebrated holiday, July Fourth, the elite downtown enjoyed programs of orations and demonstrations of militia companies, while working-class and immigrant groups cavorted in their own outlying neighborhoods. Moreover, it appears that in several cities by midcentury, the elite groups had stopped bothering to attend July Fourth ceremonies at all.[6]

Also striking is how these celebrations, while replete with symbolic imagery representing the history of various ethnic groups or the American nation, lacked any symbolic representations of "the city." To the extent that these celebrations in any sense stood for the city as a whole, it was in the eyes of artists and writers, who by and large viewed the degree of discipline and order in the procession as a barometer of urban social order. John Lewis Krimmel's painting of the guild-style procession of Philadelphia's victuallers in 1821 (figure 17) idealized the extent of social harmony in the city, since employees had already begun to march

Fig. 17. "White's Great Cattle Show and Grand Procession of the Victuallers of Philadelphia, March 15, 1821," by John Lewis Krimmel. Atwater Kent Museum, Philadelphia.

apart from their employers, and contemporary newspaper accounts described the behavior of holiday crowds as rowdy and dangerous. At the same time, accounts such as one describing July Fourth as a "lawless saturnalia"[7] may have overemphasized the extent of social disorder on holidays, as part of their authors' general lament that American cities, teeming with immigrants and the poor, afforded no possibilities for civilized urban life in comparison with the picturesque and festive cities of Europe.

By the end of the century, both of these aspects of civic celebrations had changed. Celebration organizers made a greater effort to incorporate diverse urban groups and their customs into a single citywide celebration, and they displayed more symbolic representations of "the city" and of events from local history in their holiday programs.

The giant, citywide celebration with the history of the city, rather than the nation, as a focus resulted from the convergence of several factors. Downtown businessmen and merchants wanted larger civic celebrations to attract tourists from outlying areas; politicians wanted larger civic celebrations as venues for distributing patronage and amusing the million, associating themselves with a burgeoning commercial popular culture; and elite and middle-class reform groups wanted larger civic celebrations as a new medium to communicate their ideas to the masses. In response to this pressure to expand the scope of civic celebrations, city governments moved from sponsoring a single day's program to an entire week of activities in an effort to provide something for everyone. But along with this expansion came more central control, and the effort to provide a common focus for these diverse new holiday activities. In a sense, civic celebrations evolved like other urban institutions at the turn of the twentieth century; parallel with municipal consolidation and the annexation of suburbs was the creation of new symbols for a unified city: official flags, banners, seals, and histories. And along with these icons came new public rituals of common citizenship, designed to promote loyalty to the city as a whole. Like the municipal symphony orchestra, art museum, library, or city-beautiful plaza, the large civic celebration—or even better a world's fair—announced the city's status to the outside world while offering a focus for civic identity within. While the downtown plaza represented a distinctive civic space, the civic celebration represented distinctive civic time. Various groups in the city valued the giant civic celebration both as a tool to obtain other ends—more business, wider recognition for their organization or political agenda—and as an end in itself, to foster the idea that despite urban residents' diverse social and cultural backgrounds, they all lived in the same place.[8]

But unlike other symbolic representations of the civic ideal that emerged in American cities at the turn of the century, such as public libraries, museums, statues, or murals, civic celebrations could not be created solely by private donation and subscription. If the purpose of the celebration was to embody a unified city, then it required a large and enthusiastic turnout for its success. Yet the prospect of bringing large numbers of urban residents together at the same place and time was fraught with danger. Enthusiastic expressions of public sentiment could also degenerate into rioting. If downtown businesses, politicians, and reform groups would use urban residents like "pigment" to paint a unified portrait of the city, there was also the danger that the wrong pigments would appear, or worse, that chaos would reign.[9]

The danger of urban mobs had been obvious since before the French Revolution. The pervasive labor conflicts of the Gilded Age, especially the great upheaval of 1877, proved especially unsettling to self-appointed guardians of the existing social order. Added to this were the concerns about the anonymity of urban life expressed by a new generation of sociologists such as Edward A. Ross, who viewed the "mob mind" and human suggestibility in crowds as evidence of the loss of individual conscience in urban-industrial America.[10]

Yet the opportunity to create these giant events to announce a city's economic vitality to the outside and to reach a large culturally diverse audience within (especially a largely non–English-speaking audience in an age before motion pictures) proved irresistible. One promoter of citywide "Safe and Sane" July Fourth celebrations described the civic celebration as a "psychologically opportune" moment, in which the "glow of enthusiasm and the ardor of excitement fuse the day's experience and instruction into the mental make-up of the participants." Human suggestibility in the crowd was a source of danger—but also of opportunity. Offsetting the dangers of the mob mind was the prospect of the beautiful crowd acting as one.[11]

The particular dilemma of those planning civic celebrations—like those planning political campaigns at this time—was eliciting mass participation to give the illusion of an outpouring of public sentiment while maintaining control of the prevailing imagery and institutions. The solution was not only to invent a new visual vocabulary enshrining "the city" through architecture, murals, and banners, but also to refashion images of the urban crowd. Like July Fourth celebrations in the antebellum years that, in a sense, invented American nationhood through representations of national history, the new celebrations sought to invent urban citizenship through emotionally compelling representations of the city's history. The new municipal extravaganzas of the twentieth century did not replace the traditional forms of public display through which urban residents expressed their loyalty to ethnic group, neighborhood, and nation in the nineteenth-century city—in fact ethnic holidays such as St. Patrick's Day and new political demonstrations such as Labor Day continued to proliferate, along with displays of American nationalism such as the elaborate receptions many cities gave returning Spanish-American war veterans in 1898. Rather, the new civic celebrations superimposed upon the customary occasions and imagery another level of allegiance.[12]

Among the new public rituals through which business and government leaders sought to forge a new civic identity were municipal historical pageants, a team deliberately selected by its promoters for its association with Europe in the early modern era—another period when the

Fig. 18. The "Consolidation of the City" float from Philadelphia's Founders Week celebration of 1908. This photo by William H. Rau originally appeared in King's Booklets, *Philadelphia Historical Pageant, 1908*. Free Library of Philadelphia.

city was purportedly the focus of popular loyalty and the elite the focus of popular deference.[13] In Philadelphia in 1908, as part of the weeklong celebration of the 225th anniversary of the city's founding, the local historian Ellis Paxson Oberholtzer presented a succession of floats depicting a "common" history beginning with founder William Penn and culminating in a final float entitled the "City Beautiful" (that originally was to display a plaster model of the proposed Benjamin Franklin Parkway and art museum). The procession included an image of a Quaker woman unifying the twenty-eight formerly independent districts of Philadelphia (figure 18). Oberholtzer invited spectators to visualize the city's diverse population as a cohesive social hierarchy arranged by heredity, carefully selecting each participating group. He invited descendants of early settlers and prominent families to impersonate their ancestors while rebuffing organizations composed of later arrivals such as Irish, Italians, and Poles.[14]

Less common in cities was the historical pageant in dramatic form. In

Fig. 19. Poster for the Pageant and Masque of St. Louis, 1914. The artist, Joseph C. Leyendecker, was best known as a creator of advertisements for Arrow Shirts. A. W. Proetz Collection, Western Historical Manuscript Collection, Thomas Jefferson Library, University of Missouri–St. Louis.

St. Louis in 1914, downtown businessmen staged a drama of municipal development before nearly one hundred thousand spectators, reworking local history since the ancient Mound Builders into an allegory of the triumph of "social civilization" over "chaos," culminating in St. Louis, in his knightly armor, leading the townspeople in the crusade for several municipal reforms (figure 19). The thousands of actors on stage represented the heterogeneous urban population united as a mighty chorus acclaiming the enlightened leadership of St. Louis, much as those behind the pageant were in the midst of a campaign for a new city charter that would strengthen the power of the mayor. While the organizers of the St. Louis pageant made a greater effort than those in Philadelphia to elicit the participation of recent immigrants, they still slighted African Americans and organized labor. Significantly, organized labor opposed the political goals of the pageant organizers such as the charter change, while the omission of African Americans in 1914 reflected their exclusion from other aspects of the city's public life, a separation made formal by the passage of a segregated housing ordinance two years later.[15]

When all is said and done, the elaborately orchestrated pageants were of limited impact in refashioning a popular image of the city and its history. Oberholtzer claimed that there was much appreciation of his Philadelphia pageant from all classes of people, but his Anglocentric and hierarchical vision simply did not play in the heterogeneous city. Similarly, although the St. Louis pageant organizers claimed that spectators fell "under the spell of a unifying idealism" that lifted the campaign for the new city charter over the top, newspaper evidence suggests that the audience did not take the production so seriously, and the atmosphere in the crowd was more like that of a popular sporting event than of serious dramatic ritual. Sustained not only by the boosterism of downtown businesses but also by a strong reform and didactic impulse, the urban historical pageant by and large died after World War I with the end of that crusading impulse.[16]

By contrast, the urban carnival, another form of civic celebration incorporating local historical imagery at the turn of the century, proved much longer-lived. Carnival in America had roots in popular burlesque traditions such as the mock militia, "anticks," and "horribles" processions in which the working classes parodied their social betters. By the late nineteenth century, however, new versions of these popular events wound up in the hands of the elite themselves, and ultimately, under the sponsorship of city government. The best-known example of an urban carnival, of course, is New Orleans's Mardi Gras. In the decades after the Civil War, Mardi Gras transformed from a participatory ritual among local residents into a spectacle for tourists, as New Orleans merchants craftily invited northern businessmen to the pre-Lenten carnival to promote investment in their city. But other American cities—Baltimore, Louisville, Cincinnati, St. Louis, Omaha, Los Angeles—also staged annual carnivals to attract tourists at the turn of the century. The Philadelphia municipal government enticed the rowdy but colorful New Year's Mummers parade to move from the back streets of the city's working-class neighborhoods, where it had been confined for most of the nineteenth century, into a major thoroughfare downtown with the promise of prize money for participants. New York City produced a carnival procession in 1909 as part of its commemoration of the three hundredth anniversary of the "discovery" of the Hudson River and the centennial of Fulton's steamboat—hiring Mardi Gras artists from New Orleans to create the fantastic historical floats. Increasingly the product of entertainment professionals who employed the same imagery in their productions for the commercial stage, urban carnivals earned the enmity of those who saw civic celebrations as a way to propagandize for reform. Oberholtzer refused to allow mummers or troupes of professional entertainers to join his Founders Week procession in Philadelphia. Similarly, planners of the St. Louis pageant rejected a suggestion that it be combined with the annual Veiled Prophets carnival (as the Missouri centennial celebration of 1909 had been). Yet ultimately, it was the elements of a shared popular culture borrowed from commercial entrepreneurs, not the images of a shared past presented by a conservative elite or the images of a shared future presented by progressive reformers, that were most effective in giving civic celebrations the power to promote the idea of an urban public united as one.[17]

SAN FRANCISCO's Portolá Festival of 1909, ostensibly honoring the city's founder Gaspar de Portolá, exemplifies how the citywide carnival and accompanying historical imagery could be employed for political ends. Like the originators of the celebrations in Philadelphia and St. Louis, those behind the Portolá Festival wanted to publicize their campaign for a host of municipal improvements, including a new downtown plaza, auditorium, and city hall. They also wanted to bring money to town, encouraging outside investment by demonstrating the economic dynamism of the city that had been devastated by the earthquake three years earlier. And they hoped to regain political power from the labor movement that had been running the city. Former mayor James D. Phelan's vision of the "New San Francisco," spelled out in a wide-ranging address in 1896 that made reference to Athens, Rome, Paris, and the "burgher spirit" that had animated the builders of medieval towns and cities, had been abruptly halted by organized labor's reaction against his use of police to protect strikebreakers during a bitter teamsters' strike in 1901. Since then, and with the election of a Union Labor Party mayor, San Francisco's business leaders had felt on the defensive, trying to regain control of the city where, as Ray Stannard Baker reported to the nation in *McClure's Magazine*, "unionism holds undisputed sway." They scheduled their giant commemoration of the city's history for October 1909, two weeks before the mayoral election; interspersed in committee correspondence were references to the importance of averting the "calamity" of the Union Labor Party candidate Patrick McCarthy's election.[18]

Those planning the Portolá Festival were a tightly knit group acting in the name of the public. The Downtown Merchants Association, the principal organization behind the affair, simultaneously wanted to get credit for the celebration in the form of acknowledgment of its leadership, yet also to project the impression of the city's acting spontaneously. Executive committee member Edgar Peixotta recalled, "The idea of the fiesta from the first was to make it impersonal and never to let the world know who was the originator of the idea—to let the results be judged by itself, and not by the personalities which produced it." The festival had the backing of neighborhood associations and Phelan. It set up headquarters in the Phelan building, where the former mayor gave the committee rent-free accommodation for ten months.[19]

The weeklong celebration included a military procession featuring sailors from various nations, an evening costume ball, and a civic and industrial procession, but what distinguished the Portolá Festival was the executive committee's willingness to use carnival imagery to get its message across. A Saturday evening parade included twenty-one electrified floats, built by theatrical professionals and ridden by female department store clerks and men from local colleges, depicting successive scenes of local history from the Indians and missionaries through the forty-niners and the completion of the transcontinental railroad. Behind the floats walked a ragtag collection of comic bands and clowns, in some cases parodying the dignified figures who marched ahead of them. A squad riding miniature horses mocked the Spanish founder Portolá and his entourage at the front of the parade. At the conclusion of the parade route, seven of the electrified floats became bandstands for public dancing in the streets.[20]

On the surface, the historical focus of the city celebration, the aristocratic Don Gaspar de Portolá, the "discoverer" of San Francisco Bay, combined the image of an urban founding father like Philadelphia's William Penn, and that of an idealistic knight like St. Louis. The merchants went to great lengths to bring in Nicholas Covarrubias, a seventy-year-old descendant of a prominent Spanish family of California, to impersonate Portolá (figure 20). The irony of associating the city with the Spanish—conquered not only in the 1840s, but again in the 1890s—was not lost on local newspapers; one noted that the public display of the red and yellow banners of Spain would have caused a riot only ten years before. In fact, marching directly behind Portolá in the civic parade was a brigade of Spanish-American War veterans carrying an enormous American flag. But in keeping with the carnival theme, festival organizers compared Gaspar de Portolá not with a founding father but rather with King Rex of Mardi Gras. The chair of the executive committee, Philip Clay, explained, "This new Gaspar is to be the rollicking, carefree, laugh-loving soldier of fortune, not the stern ascetic pioneer." Portolá's "proclamation" to the city ordered play and revelry, not solemn reverence for the past; organizers praised Portolá less for his contribution to the future development of the city than for his "lusty blood." Similarly, while newspapers made much of the distinguished ancestry of the young festival "queen," Virgilia Bogue, they also identified her as the author of a steamy novel, *The Strength to Yield*.[21]

Both Portolá and his queen were eclipsed by another historical image in the festival—that of the Spanish dancer. The dark, overtly sexual figure, cigarette in hand, who graced the organizers' official stationery (figure 21) was no Quaker or shining knight.[22] The same businessmen who attacked candidate McCarthy in their newspaper editorials and campaign literature by associating him with the prostitution of the "Barbary Coast," the city's red light district, appropriated the same provocative imagery to represent their fun city, and by extension, win the allegiance of its working-class residents. The imagery on the official souvenir program (see figure 16) also was suggestive of ethnic mixing and, metaphorically, sexual promiscuity—from the dark Mexican woman on the cover (clearly not of "pure" Spanish blood) to the revelry in the background. The theme of ethnic mixing carried through to the civic and industrial parade. Although members of the largest contingent, the Native Sons and Daughters of the Golden West, were primarily of English, German, and Irish ancestry, also prominently on display were organizations of Chinese and Japanese residents. This was apparently the first time that the Chinese marched in a civic celebration in San Francisco outside of Chinatown; they also appeared in the Saturday evening carnival procession (figure 22).[23]

Organized labor of any kind was conspicuous by its absence. The Chinese dragon and Japanese cherry blossom floats were not only evidence of San Francisco's cosmopolitanism but also a direct affront to the

Fig. 20. Nicholas Covarrubias as Gaspar de Portolá, 1909. San Francisco History Center, San Francisco Public Library.

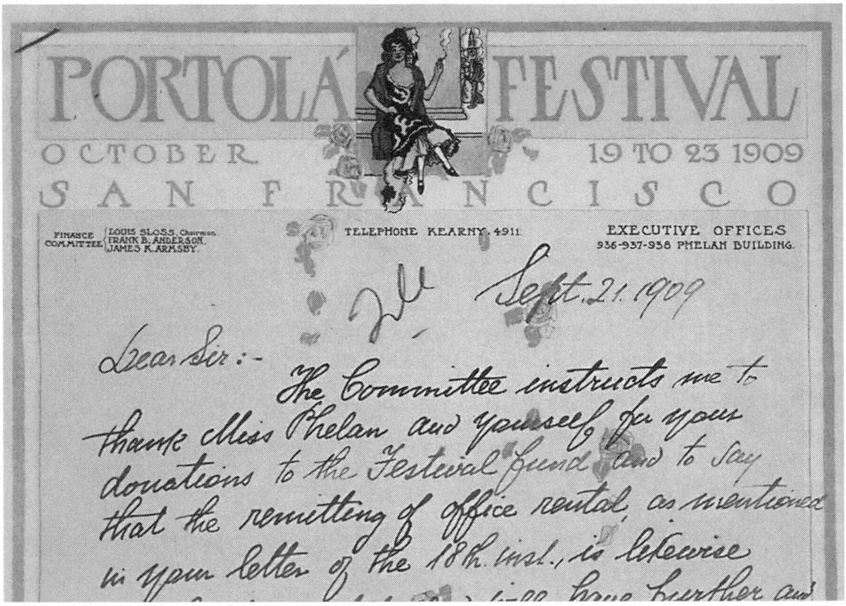
PORTOLÁ FESTIVAL
OCTOBER 19 TO 23 1909
SAN FRANCISCO

FINANCE COMMITTEE: LOUIS SLOSS, Chairman. FRANK B. ANDERSON. JAMES K. ARMSBY.
TELEPHONE KEARNY 4911
EXECUTIVE OFFICES 936-937-938 PHELAN BUILDING.

Sept. 21. 1909

Dear Sir:-

The Committee instructs me to thank Miss Phelan and yourself for your donations to the Festival fund and to say that the remitting of office rental, as mentioned in your letter of the 18th inst., is likewise

Fig. 21. This thank-you note from Charles Gayles of the Portolá Festival Finance Committee to former San Francisco mayor James D. Phelan featured a Spanish dancer smoking a cigarette on its letterhead. James D. Phelan Papers (C-B 800, box 97, folder 5), The Bancroft Library, University of California, Berkeley.

city's labor unions, which had been campaigning to expand the laws excluding Chinese immigrants to exclude Japanese immigrants as well. While the festival committee circulated a fund-raising pamphlet declaring that "all the commercial, fraternal, civic, and labor societies of the city" were behind the celebration, organized labor kept its distance from the event. Labor unions did not march in the downtown procession, and labor newspapers all but ignored the festival—one editorializing that the festival was an example of "Bread and the Circus. Thus was the Roman populace amused by the holders of Special Privilege, and thus do the Republican-corporation managers seek to divert the attention of the people of San Francisco from the real issues of an important municipal election." But the San Francisco Labor Council, seeking to take advantage of the extra visitors drawn to San Francisco during Portolá Week, sponsored its own weeklong "Labor Carnival" in a park near downtown to raise funds to build a new union hall, designating one day "Portolá Day."[24]

The festival, especially the evening carnival procession, projected a particular historical image of San Francisco and the urban public that claimed to embrace all while deliberately excluding a significant segment of the local population. But even more important than the festival imagery itself was how local newspapers explained the celebration and gave it meaning. Newspapers were the primary chroniclers of these ephemeral events, consolidating experience into memory. They were also downtown businesses themselves, with owners who shared the festival organizers' interest in promoting a particular view of the city.

Newspapers pointed to the affair as evidence of the city's "pull to-

Fig. 22. Residents of San Francisco's Chinatown carry a dragon float through downtown in 1909 as part of the city's Portolá Festival. San Francisco History Center, San Francisco Public Library.

gether spirit," an example of "what may be accomplished when the community is undivided." Yet news of October's Portolá Festival was interlaced with that of the enormously divisive mayoral election scheduled for November. During Portolá Week, editorials in the *Chronicle* blasted Union Labor Party candidate Patrick McCarthy as dangerous, warning that his election would signal to the rest of the nation that "San Francisco had deliberately returned to government by the criminal classes," and that "public welfare demands that we carry the Portolá spirit into the coming election." Newspapers helped the Portolá Committee to foster the impression that the festival was created by public-spirited citizens for the good of the city, and that those opposed to their plans—or their candidates—were disloyal.[25]

Newspapers also pointed to the festival as evidence of the city's ethnic unity—especially the warm welcome accorded the Chinese and Japanese participants along the parade route, "even the little brown men from the *Idzumo*," the Japanese ship. One had to look hard to discover that the crowd had set the Chinese float afire on Saturday night—with the Chinese in it. Neither the city's Mexican nor its African American residents were invited to march in the civic and industrial procession.[26] But that did not stop the boxing champion Jack Johnson, in town after successfully defending his crown against Stanley Ketchel in nearby Colma, from speeding down Market Street ahead of the procession in his car (likely accompanied by the two white prostitutes with whom he shared his quarters at the Seal Rock Hotel). Police promptly forced him off the road.[27]

Newspapers explained the significance of the Portolá Festival in terms not only of its contribution to local class and ethnic harmony but also of profits. They downplayed the fact that the festival lost money, emphasizing instead the increased business downtown during festival week and the good impression that the festival made on visitors who would make San Francisco a mecca for conventions. "Henceforth," proclaimed the *Call*, "the city should be one of convention and carnival." Soon after the festival, the city's papers began promoting the Panama Pacific Exposition planned for 1915.[28]

While newspapers reported on the social and economic benefits of urban togetherness as exemplified by the various ethnic and fraternal organizations participating in parades, their instant histories of the festival devoted even more attention to crowd behavior. Newspapers pointed to the crowd, not the formal processions, as the most important symbol of "San Francisco unity." Newspaper accounts of the Portolá Festival depicted the urban public not as a cohesive hierarchy based on heredity as in Philadelphia, or as under the spell of a unifying idealism as in St. Louis, but rather as a frolicking, undifferentiated mob. "The people owned the streets," proclaimed the *Chronicle*, quickly adding that this was not the same kind of purposeful mob as that of the French Revolution, which went "snarling on its way from Paris to Versailles to cry to Louis for bread."[29] Rather it was a good-natured gathering of all social classes, in which the "men who sit in the councils of great corporations mingled in the bonhomie of the night with their laborers. Women who shine in the circles of the socially elect laughed and jested with the girls from the factories and the shops."[30] Headlines proclaimed the "people's unabated joyousness," as the city's residents, under the "carnival spirit" and a "reign of mirth," put aside everyday social distinctions.[31] The most common metaphors that newspapers employed to describe the crowd were liquid. The crowds "surged like a swollen stream" and flowed like "mountain torrents"; a "storm of pleasure . . . drenched everyone" as the city was "inebriated with ecstasy."[32] Of course, as with the Festival Committee's fantastic historical iconography of the Spanish dancer and the lusty Don, newspaper writers also tried to titillate readers with thinly veiled sexual imagery. Like the dancer waiting to consummate her passion, one reporter noted, "the city throbs in expectation of tonight's crashing finale"; and after the Saturday evening event: "The glory of Portolá Week in culminating waves, has grown and spread until it wove the heart of every man and woman into unity, and as the merrymaking broke forth into joy that knew no restraint, there seemed to be a rhythmic unity to all the motion as if the heart of San Francisco was bare before the world and beating with the love of all humanity."[33]

On the same page as this description of municipal orgasm was a more prosaic description of the police fighting the crowds, as children screamed and women defended themselves with hat pins. Other articles describe the police using horses to drive back the crowds.[34] Which account is to be believed? Discounting the newspaper hyperbole, crowds really may have behaved in an ecstatic manner with wild abandon; the event could plausibly have triggered a psychic release after the stress of the 1906 earthquake, similar to the street celebrations at the end of

World War II. It is also possible that crowds interpreted some elements of the carnival procession on Saturday night as a genuine lampoon of the social order, like the burlesque militia processions in antebellum Philadelphia or the carnival imagery of the Abbeys of Misrule in early modern France. The clowns riding miniature horses at the rear of the procession in a parody of the Portolá Dragoons, the young businessmen who rode at the front, seemed a jibe at the businessmen who staged the event.[35] It is difficult to ascertain what actually happened, or what it meant to participants at the time—but we do have the newspaper explanations of how and why it happened. The newspaper accounts helped to shape participants' memories of what they experienced, as well as provided the principal impressions of the event for those not in attendance. In a city with a reputation for class and ethnic conflict, newspaper descriptions of local residents pulling together in the Portolá Festival had important political and economic uses. Pointing to the celebration as evidence of San Francisco's innately fun-loving historical character, the festival organizers touted their city as an ideal place for businessmen and professionals to hold conventions.

Of course, the festival imagery of a city in the grip of ecstasy, suggestive of sexual release and of class and ethnic mixing, went only so far. It is true that working-class female department store clerks rode with elite male college students on the same parade floats, and that the dark-hued Spanish dancer flirted with the aristocratic Don in newspaper cartoons and official publications, but Jack Johnson and his white girlfriends were still forced off the road. The same newspaper descriptions of the crowd's wild abandon also mentioned its instinctive "regard for order and decorum." The city's residents lost control, but not entirely; their dancing was "free almost to the point of madness, but far from the point of obscenity." Local residents demonstrated a playful camaraderie yet instinctive sense of boundaries; compared to the residents of eastern cities, one paper noted, when San Franciscans celebrate they are "never in need of the upraised club of the police." Newspapers attributed San Franciscans' exemplary festival behavior to their history: their "tincture" of Spanish blood being balanced by a spirit of "American" self-restraint, much as in the procession of historical floats seductive images of "Spanish languor"—the early Californios lazily smoking cigarettes, were balanced by scenes showing the accomplishments of the energetic forty-niners who built the city. The population's unique historical character included both a "natural carnival spirit" and the will to get things done.[36]

Although this particular representation of the population of San Francisco united by a common history, ancestry, and love of a good time met with little political success in the short run—two weeks after the Portolá Festival Union Labor Party candidate Patrick McCarthy was elected mayor—it may have helped James Rolph Jr., head of the Merchants Association in 1909, gain the mayor's chair in 1911. Rolph, in charge of local arrangements for the 1909 festival, was active in organizing Portolá events throughout the city. In 1911, endorsed by both the Democratic and the Republican parties, he unseated McCarthy as mayor, the first elected office for which Rolph had ever run. "Sunny Jim" Rolph remained in the public eye as San Francisco's mayor for nineteen years. By all accounts Rolph was a master urban showman and politician. As the self-proclaimed "mayor of all the people," he continued to associate himself with popular spectacle as well as with the interests of downtown businesses.[37]

But Rolph presided over just one more Portolá Festival, despite festival organizers' intentions to make the affair an annual event on the order of New Orleans's Mardi Gras or Pasadena's Tournament of Roses. In 1913, the downtown merchants managed to raise enough funds for a second festival, justifying their expenditure as part of the publicity campaign for the upcoming Panama Pacific International Exposition of 1915. The Portolá Festival of 1913 was not created solely for the consumption of the national mass media, but its organizers made motion pictures of the Portolá Week events available throughout the United States. Further cementing the connection among the Portolá Festival, publicity for the exposition, and a program of municipal improvements, alongside the impersonator of Gaspar de Portolá there marched in 1913 another historical figure, Vasco Nuñez de Balboa, who laid the cornerstone for a new city hall during festival week. The parade line-up in 1913 was similar to that of 1909; liberal use of carnival imagery and newspaper descriptions of the "polyglot, cosmopolitan crowd" and a "unity that left none outside its circle" obscured the fact that again organized labor did not participate (figure 23).[38] The 1913 festival lost even more money than the one in 1909, and the dismal financial record of these events doomed proposals to revive the festival in 1922 and 1928[39]—although the city government did help subsidize a month-long

Fig. 23. "Balboa Discovers the Joy Ocean." This editorial cartoon representing the urban public as an undifferentiated mass united in celebration appeared on page 10 of the San Francisco *Call* on October 22, 1913.

series of events under the name of "Portola Festival" in 1948. Significantly, in this latter festival—when Chicanos were a greater presence in the city—the accent was dropped over the "a" in Portola, and the complexion of the dancer on the cover of the official program was lightened up considerably, emphasizing the purity of her Spanish or American, rather than Mexican, ancestry (figure 24).[40]

TODAY, AT the turn of another century, city governments continue to promote the urban experience to tourists, and representations of the urban crowd assembled in celebration remain an important part of that civic imagery. Urban businesses collaborate with city governments in the production of giant festivals designed to lure tourists and suburban residents downtown, where they can experience, if only temporarily, the

Fig. 24. Souvenir program for the Portola Festival of 1948. Compared with the program for the festival in 1909 (see figure 16), the complexions and features of the principal figures have been anglicized. Note also the prominent place assigned to new symbols of San Francisco: the Golden Gate Bridge and the city's professional football team. San Francisco History Center, San Francisco Public Library.

sense of excitement that comes from being part of a joyous urban crowd. Chambers of commerce cultivate this imagery of the city as festival in downtown shopping districts with historical themes, such as Baltimore's Harborplace, New York City's South Street Seaport, and Boston's Faneuil Hall, where the selective marketing of ethnic and cultural diversity in the food courts symbolizes the implicit assumption that in this state of festivity the everyday battles of urban life can be pushed aside.[41]

Another heavily subsidized public venue in which the urban crowd united in celebration has come to be regarded as representative of the city's historical character is the sports arena. Newspapers rhapsodize about how professional sports teams—especially winning ones—heal social divisions both inside the stadium and out, while local politicians, like San Francisco's Jim Rolph in the 1910s and 1920s, are quick to associate themselves with these successful teams as a way to gain popular support. Like the municipal iconography of urban festivals at the turn of the century, team names often recall romanticized folk characters associated with the city's past—Yankees, Celtics, Knickerbockers, Padres, Forty-niners. The private business persons who own these teams are considered to have a public responsibility; the team stadiums are considered as public spaces, even if not actually owned by the city. The players are treated as public figures representing the city as a whole, and those who remain more than a few years—Ted Williams in Boston, Brooks Robinson in Baltimore, Julius Erving in Philadelphia—are viewed as important figures in the city's history, despite being professional entertainers in no sense representative of the local population. Newspapers describe the behavior of the crowds watching the athletes perform as somehow representative of the character of the city—even though many of those in the stands are affluent suburbanites who want nothing to do with urban life. Like the businessmen, professional entertainers, and newspaper reporters who collaborated in the creation and interpretation of urban carnivals at the turn of the century, the professional sports enterprise is engaged in the business of civic representation, with clear political overtones.[42]

CIVIC CELEBRATIONS, like city spaces, remain full of references to history. At the neighborhood level, such histories serve as anchors for local community identity in environments often undergoing wrenching physical and demographic transformation. But at the citywide level, the politics of "collective" historical representation become even more apparent. Though historians of American cities have emphasized the rational aspects of changes in urban politics since the turn of the century—the press for economic advantage, the expansion of municipal services, the restructuring of urban government—the cultivation of an irrational attachment to "the city" and the channeling of that attachment into particular political allegiances has also been an important part of the century's political transformations. Alongside the creation of large bureaucratic systems to bring municipal order out of chaos, a carefully cultivated, conspicuous sense of disorder has played a role in the process of urban governing. As public display began to eclipse public debate as a staple of urban politics, as the economic health of cities such as San Francisco began to depend less on what local residents produced than on what visitors consumed at the various sites and experiences developed for their pleasure, new citywide "collective" histories, communicated in the style of commercial popular culture, have addressed urban resident and tourist alike as members of fun-loving crowds. Carefully selected historical imagery has obscured existing social distinctions and the memory of recent political struggles while paying the way for a new kind of antidemocratic politics. If the carnival tradition as it developed in Europe and America over the years entailed social inversion and criticism, then the businessmen behind the Portolá and other urban historical festivals at the turn of the twentieth century inverted the inversion by depicting the urban public as happily accepting their enlightened political and economic leadership. The Portolá Festival encouraged the working people of San Francisco to participate in the public life of their city as consumers of a shared commercial popular culture, as members of an undifferentiated, fun-loving crowd, but not as members of organized groups competing for control of city government. The festival's historical imagery, and more important, the interpretations of that imagery and descriptions of crowd behavior that appeared in local newspapers, attached political and commercial significance to an aura of the city as a fun place. Throughout the twentieth century, urban residents have been governed not only by their economic and administrative systems but also by public displays of history in celebrations that cultivate the powerful emotion of rooting for the home team.

# 4

Watching *The Civil War*

# THE CIVIL WAR

VALENTINE MUSEUM

A Film Series by Ken Burns
Produced by Florentine Films and WETA-TV

THE MARRIAGE OF history and popular culture that was evident in San Francisco's Portolá Festival has existed throughout the twentieth century, and not only in civic celebrations designed to communicate a political message to the public. Rest stops along highways are full of racks brimming with brochures for historical attractions designed primarily to make money, which live or die depending on how many visitors they draw through their gates. My morning newspaper displays ads for television and motion picture productions "based on a true story," trying to amass enough viewers to make a profit for their sponsoring studios or advertisers. History offers a nearly inexhaustible source of tales that can be reworked to maximize their mass appeal.

Wars especially seem to furnish stories that make for popular history. The residents of towns such as Orange encounter reminders of past wars not only in the monuments they have placed in countless memorial parks but also in their local movie theaters and on their television screens. Virtually every American war—the Revolution, the Indian wars, the Alamo, World War II, Vietnam—has been the subject of popular commercial films. Yet perhaps no historical film in recent years has had such impact as a nonfiction documentary created for public television, Ken

Burns's *The Civil War*. Burns's film lies at the intersection of academic and popular history, and, as we will see, personal and public history as well. Through close analysis of the public's response to the film, we can explore a number of questions about the place of the past in American life, and how the mass media history we encounter diverges from the conventional ways in which we think history is communicated.[1]

Popular historical productions such as *The Civil War*, aimed squarely at attracting the largest possible audience, often make historians uncomfortable. In the division between highbrow and lowbrow, as it emerged in the late nineteenth century, the study and writing of history has always been considered a genteel rather than popular art, the product of educated judgment rather than of mass taste. Since the 1920s and 1930s, folklorists and oral historians have ventured beyond traditional elite or professional histories to consider other images and uses of the past, but these studies have scrupulously avoided mass media histories, preferring instead to focus on the indigenous tales of groups seemingly out of the mainstream, such as Appalachian whites, recent immigrants, or former slaves, and thus free of the corrupting outside influence of commercial popular culture. While American studies scholars in the 1950s and 1960s took historical imagery in commercial popular culture seriously, analyzing dime novels, melodrama, and pulp fiction as evidence of the broadly shared myths that held American society together, today we dismiss these scholars' works as hopelessly out of date, unable to account for the diversity of a multicultural society in which every group is its own historian. The traditional view among scholars is that mass-produced versions of the past homogenize and destroy an authentic sense of history rather than serve as a means for its communication.[2]

Professional historians have been especially hard on popular historical films. Reviews of films in professional journals such as the *American Historical Review* often take the form of warnings that the public is being deluded by what it sees. As Robert Sklar notes, historians watching films about the past feel most comfortable playing the "cop" role, applying the same historical standards they use for books and articles to judge how badly filmmakers such as Oliver Stone have distorted the historical record. Only occasionally have they gone beyond this role to analyze how a film communicates its message about the past, examining how the film was created, how it embodied themes and values typical of the larger culture, or how it was received by reviewers.[3]

But even the most discerning analyses have not examined how the people viewing popular historical films actually interpret what they see and hear. We can assume that people watching a popular historical film, like any other popular culture product, do not all see the imagery on the screen in the same way. Rather, they actively place it in various contexts according to their social background and previous knowledge and experience. These contexts determine, in effect, the meaning of what they see and hear. By focusing on viewer response, rather than only on the intentions of the filmmaker, we can begin to go beyond the history that the filmmaker wanted to make and explore the history that viewers saw and understood.[4]

In many important ways, Burns's film departs from the Hollywood history that professional historians often deride. It is a nonfiction film, and it relied for two-thirds of its funds not on a few investors seeking to make money but on an assortment of educational foundations seeking to give money away, which required the use of academic historical consultants as a condition of their participation. *The Civil War* was made for public television with no expectation of commercial theatrical release or of selling advertising time during the broadcast—even though General Motors underwrote the other one-third of the production costs and reminded the public frequently of its association with Burns and his film. But from the beginning, as Burns tells us, despite the lack of commercial intentions, he aimed to create something that would compete successfully with Hollywood productions in keeping the average "eighth-grader" glued to his or her chair. His ambition was to reach the million, to create a new popular history of the Civil War, one of epic proportions.[5]

Burns tells us that he first got the idea for the Civil War film in 1984 after reading a best-selling novel, Michael Shaara's *The Killer Angels*, about the battle of Gettysburg.[6] Already an award-winning documentary filmmaker, Burns parlayed grants from the Corporation for Public Broadcasting, the National Endowment for the Humanities, the Arthur Vining Davis Foundation, the MacArthur Foundation, and General Motors, as well as his contacts in the historical profession from previous films, to assemble a large production team, including twenty-four historians as consultants.[7] As he describes it, text and image research proceeded on parallel tracks; it was more or less at the final stage that he, his brother Ric Burns, and writer Geoffrey Ward synthesized text in need of images or images in need of text into a single script that was then edited and revised.[8] Burns's stated goal, as he explained in interviews after the initial screening, was to convey the emotional reality of the war, to "make the past come alive," and to "place the audience in that time and place."[9] He told Bernard Weisberger in *American Heritage* shortly before the series first aired, "Film goes directly to the emotions without translation."[10]

Burns also had a second goal—to create a national epic that would explore the question "What does it mean to be an American?" He repeatedly described the Civil War as "the great traumatic event in our collective childhood" and, quoting Lincoln, hoped that his series would remind Americans of the deep and affecting " 'mystic chords of memory' that connect us all as Americans."[11] Early on he found a kindred spirit in the novelist Shelby Foote, who gave Burns exactly what he wanted—evocative comments about the experience of soldiers, Northern and Southern, that mirrored Burns's own vision of the war as a family conflict pitting brother against brother.[12] Echoing Foote's remark that his three-volume work *The Civil War: A Narrative* had been consciously modeled on the *Iliad*, Burns told interviewers about his own aspirations for *The Civil War* film to become an American *Iliad*, told over a week across the nation to audiences gathered around the electronic hearth of television.[13]

Thanks in large part to advance publicity, the series attracted an unprecedented number of viewers for public television. Nearly 14 million tuned in on the evening of its first broadcast in September 1990, and the series's initial 12.9 percent ratings share declined less than 1 percent over the remainder of the week. During the week of its initial broadcast, 40 million individuals in over 24 million homes—nearly one-sixth of the total United States television audience—saw at least one segment of the film.[14] Within a year, the companion volume to the film had sold three-quarters of a million copies, while Time-Life Books sold over one hundred thousand videotape sets.[15] Since 1990, *The Civil War* has been rebroadcast on PBS stations again and again, especially during pledge drives, and teachers show episodes to their students in schools and colleges across America.

Even before *The Civil War* aired, viewers opened up their newspapers and magazines to find overwhelming praise for Burns's accomplishment. Press response largely echoed Burns's assessment of what he had tried to do, which is not surprising considering the money that GM poured into advance publicity for the series, sending Burns on a promotional tour crisscrossing the nation for interviews. Burns's extensive interviews in the national media immediately before the series aired, as well as his on-camera interviews with newspaper reporter Charlie McDowell on each evening of the initial television showing, in which Burns advanced his vision of the Civil War as a "family drama," provided a forum for instructing his audience about what he was trying to accomplish and how to view his film.[16]

The only group that did not seem to appreciate Burns's accomplishment, according to himself and the press, were professional historians. At a time when historians were under attack for ignoring audiences outside the academy, the popular press treated *The Civil War* as a tonic, demonstrating that history when done right could attract a large and interested public. The enthusiastic popular reaction to the series seemed to say that Americans really did care about their history, once free of the ways that professional historians usually presented it to them.

In fact, *The Civil War* attracted not only a huge popular audience but also the attention of the historical profession, more than any historical film before or since. Historians showed segments of the film in their classrooms, invited Burns to public forums on their college campuses and professional meetings, reviewed the film in their scholarly journals, and even published a book of essays analyzing the film. By and large, they did not like what they saw. Reluctant to share their authority for interpreting the past, the historians attacked Burns for his focus on military history (though some criticized him for focusing on the wrong campaigns), for all but ignoring immigrants, and for "a wholesale neglect of women."[17] Criticism focused especially on what historians saw as Burns's scant treatment of black emancipation and the aftermath of the war, which they attributed to his overreliance on Shelby Foote as a commentator. Quoted in *Newsweek* in October 1990, just after the series aired, Michael Thelwell of the Afro-American Studies Department of the University of Massachusetts Amherst stated that Foote "looks like he should be sitting in front of a Southern courthouse with tobacco juice running down his face."[18] Several months later, in a forum at Hampshire College, Burns's alma mater, Thelwell's colleague John Bracey wondered aloud why the film had been so popular with white America—and asserted that black Americans had seen the film more critically than whites.[19] In April 1993, eight hundred people attending a conference in Boston on film and history heard the historian Leon Litwack compare Burns's series with D. W. Griffith's *Birth of a Nation*, arguing that the lack of attention in *The Civil War* to the costs that blacks paid along the road to sectional reunion had unwittingly echoed the racist climate in 1915 which had produced Griffith's film.[20] In separate articles, historians David Blight and Eric Foner agreed, attacking Burns's uncritical use of footage from the veterans' reunion at Gettysburg in the final episode as a pernicious recapitulation of the racism underlying national reconciliation at the turn of the century. Blight reminded his readers, "White supremacy was a silent master of ceremonies at the Gettysburg reunion."[21] Historians expressed concern that in depicting the heroism of both sides, Burns had led his viewers, like the veterans at Gettysburg, to lose sight in a haze of nostalgia of the causes for which the war had been fought.

Burns replied to these criticisms by stating that historians simply did not understand how films are made and had a hard time coming to grips with any medium for history other than print. His decisions of what to include and how to tell the story were those of a visual artist, not a text-bound academic. Burns explained that Shelby Foote appeared on camera so often because he spoke in short sentences that evoked the emotional experience of the war, while most of the history professors Burns filmed spoke in lengthy abstractions. Even in an eleven-hour series, Burns noted, it was impossible to cover Reconstruction; his film was about the Civil War, and from a dramatic point of view, everything that had happened after Lincoln's assassination was anticlimax. Besides, Burns told Thomas Cripps in an interview published in the *American Historical Review*, he had to stop somewhere. Occasionally his spirited defense of his work came in the form of a counterattack. Appearing at the same Boston conference as Litwack, Burns finally remarked, exasperated, toward the end of a question-and-answer session on his work, "The one thing we really haven't said is how much history has been murdered by people who are professionally employed as historians."[22] He repeated this charge, along with a call for the public to "rescue history from the academy," in an interview with David Thelen for the *Journal of American History* the following year.[23]

Burns's principal rebuke to his critics, however, has been to point to the thousands of letters that he received in response to the series. In an

interview in the *American Historical Review*, Burns declared that professional historians such as Leon Litwack "need only to pore through the
letters" to realize that their criticism of his treatment of black emancipation "misses the point."[24] At the Hampshire College forum, Burns
countered John Bracey's charge that blacks viewed the series more critically than whites with the claim that he had received many letters from
blacks who liked the series. Over and over in public appearances such as
at the Boston conference, in interviews published in the *American Historical Review* and *Journal of American History*, and in a rejoinder published at the conclusion of Robert Brent Toplin's anthology *Ken Burns's
Civil War: Historians Respond*, Burns quoted the same letter from an
African American viewer eloquently expressing how Burns's film had
prompted him to consider the necessity for racial reconciliation. For us
truly to be free, the writer concluded, "white America must abandon its
racial conceits and I must abandon my hate."[25] Similarly, in support
of Burns's view of his film as a great Homeric poem of national self-
definition (and his own self-definition as an epic storyteller to the nation), he repeatedly quoted a letter referring to the series as an "American Bhagavad Gita."[26] As proof that he appealed to Americans North
and South, to all classes and races, Burns also declared that 98 percent of
the letters he received "approved" of the series, with the remaining 2
percent equally divided between complaints that the film was pro-
Union or pro-Confederate.[27]

But how representative were these letters of the people who had
viewed Burns's film? How representative were Burns's quotations and
generalizations of all the letters that he received? During March 1991,
Kim Crawford, a University of Massachusetts graduate student, and I
visited Burns's studio in New Hampshire and read through his mail in
response to *The Civil War*. Our systematic examination of the letters
allows us to get beyond the debate between Ken Burns and his critics to
discover, to some extent, how Burns's viewers understood what they saw
and heard. What did Americans see when they watched *The Civil War?*
What did they learn from the series? In what contexts did they place the
series? What did the images of the past flickering across their television
screens remind them of? Was the Civil War film that the majority of
Burns's viewers thought they saw a different one from what professional
historians thought they saw, or even a different one from what Burns
thought he had made?

Before proceeding further, remember that the following analysis characterizes not the 40 million Americans who saw at least some of *The Civil War* during its initial broadcast week in the fall of 1990, but rather a special group—those who chose to write to Burns about his film. We took a random sample of 750 letters (the first 50 letters from each of fifteen folders), and reduced the sample to 444 by omitting resumes, invitations to speak, proposals for new projects, and general letters of congratulation or complaint that did not mention why the writer liked or disliked the series.[28]

Despite Burns's claim that he received letters from all classes and races—at the Boston forum he declared that 30 percent of the letters he received were from blacks—we simply do not know the race and class of the men and women who wrote to him.[29] We do have a PBS audience research report stating that 97 percent of those watching *The Civil War* were white, 54 percent were male, 61 percent were between the ages of 35 and 64, 56 percent had annual household incomes over $40,000, and 37 percent held professional/managerial jobs while 18 percent had skilled/semi-skilled ones.[30] But again, it is important to remember that the letter writers may not have been representative of those who saw the series, either demographically or in their opinions.

We were, however, able to analyze the letters Burns received by region. Burns claims to have received an equal number of letters from North and South; while this is not literally the case, it is true that the amount of letters he received from different regions of the United States was roughly proportional to their populations. Approximately 59 percent of Burns's letters came from the North (defined as former Union states, minus California), 18 percent from the South (defined as former Confederate states), 7 percent from the West (former territories), and 12 percent from California. The remaining 4 percent were from Canada and overseas or had no return address. Of course, we do not know how long the letter writers had lived in the regions from which they were writing; in an era when Americans frequently move between regions, a great-granddaughter of the Confederacy is as likely to live in Los Angeles as in Montgomery. Nevertheless, the letters Burns received offer a glimpse into how, if at all, region might still matter in how Americans understand their past.[31]

We were also able to analyze the letters Burns received by sex. Burns is essentially correct in his assertion that nationwide, he received about the same number of letters from men as from women. But as we can see from the table on page 98, the national count obscures the fact that the total includes a disproportionate number of letters from northern women and southern men. Probing this unequal response further, and the different topics men and women mentioned in response to the film, offers a glimpse into what difference gender might make in how popular history is viewed and understood.

The following analysis, then, tracks by region and sex what topics were most frequently mentioned by letter writers in connection with the film. These were the memories that Burns's film evoked, the contexts in which viewers placed the film which gave meaning to the images and sounds that appeared on their screen. In what contexts did the letter writers view *The Civil War?*

One context was that of other television shows. Many letters praised *The Civil War* as quality television. A man from Washington praised it as evidence that a program need not have "car crashes and mindless violence" to attract millions of viewers. Public television viewers describing their favorite programs often claim "I never watch television . . . ," but, in fact, the film may have attracted a significant number of people who rarely watched TV—one broadcasting industry publication in 1990 estimated that as many as 4 percent more homes watched television on the first evening that *The Civil War* was broadcast than normally did so on a Sunday night.[32] Other letter writers noted that the spectacular quality of Burns's film equaled that of commercial television and movies. A man from California remarked, "I think your productions exceed those of Spielberg." Several writers mentioned how they were glued to the screen during the series—and compared the experience of watching *The Civil War* night after night to evenings spent two decades earlier watching television coverage of the Vietnam War. Another man, from Texas, wrote, "I have not had an experience like this with television since the week-end of November 22, 1963 and the assassination of President Kennedy." To these letter writers, the series primarily evoked memories not about Civil War history but about television watching (which also has a history).

Another context was that of contemporary politics. In the fall of 1990, with the Vietnam conflict still in living memory and an impending war in the Persian Gulf, a few letter writers drew lessons from Burns's film for America's contemporary foreign policy. A woman from San

Letters to Ken Burns concerning *The Civil War*, fall 1990:
Percentages mentioning various items, by region and gender

| Distribution of letters by region[d] | All 100 (444) | | | North[a] 59 (261) | | | South[b] 18 (82) | | | California 12 (53) | | | West[c] 7 (32) | | |
|---|---|---|---|---|---|---|---|---|---|---|---|---|---|---|---|
| | Men | Women | Both | Men | Women | Both | Men | Women | Both | Men | Women | Both | Men | Women | Both |
| Distribution of letters by gender[e] | 48 | | 50 | 44 | | 54 | 63 | | 34 | 45 | | 53 | 50 | | 50 |
| Items mentioned:[f] | | | | | | | | | | | | | | | |
| Emotion/direct reality | 26 | 29 | 27 | 27 | 27 | 27 | 13 | 36 | 21 | 33 | 43 | 38 | 38 | 19 | 28 |
| Civil War ancestors | 20 | 26 | 23 | 18 | 24 | 22 | 29 | 29 | 29 | 21 | 32 | 26 | 6 | 19 | 13 |
| Civil War buff in family | 8 | 6 | 7 | 9 | 8 | 8 | 2 | 7 | 4 | 8 | 4 | 6 | 19 | 0 | 9 |
| Letters/diaries | 16 | 26 | 21 | 19 | 22 | 21 | 12 | 36 | 20 | 13 | 21 | 17 | 19 | 38 | 28 |
| Music | 13 | 14 | 14 | 12 | 15 | 14 | 10 | 11 | 10 | 17 | 7 | 11 | 19 | 19 | 19 |
| Photographs | 8 | 13 | 10 | 11 | 15 | 13 | 4 | 7 | 5 | 0 | 11 | 6 | 6 | 13 | 9 |
| Shelby Foote | 9 | 12 | 11 | 10 | 14 | 12 | 10 | 7 | 9 | 13 | 14 | 13 | 6 | 6 | 6 |
| Barbara Fields | 4 | 3 | 4 | 5 | 1 | 3 | 4 | 7 | 5 | 0 | 4 | 2 | 6 | 6 | 6 |
| Additional fact(s) | 12 | 8 | 10 | 10 | 11 | 11 | 17 | 0 | 11 | 13 | 7 | 9 | 6 | 0 | 3 |
| Error(s) of fact | 7 | 5 | 6 | 7 | 6 | 7 | 4 | 7 | 5 | 8 | 4 | 6 | 13 | 0 | 6 |
| Error(s) of interpretation | 7 | 2 | 5 | 6 | 1 | 3 | 10 | 11 | 11 | 0 | 4 | 2 | 13 | 0 | 6 |

a States that remained in the Union, except California (CT, DC, DE, IA, IL, IN, KS, KY, MA, MD, ME, MI, MN, MO, NH, NJ, NY, OH, OR, PA, RI, VT, WI, WV).

b Former Confederate States (AL, AR, FL, GA, LA, MS, NC, SC, TN, TX, VA).

c Territories during the Civil War (AK, AZ, CO, HI, ID, MT, ND, NE, NM, NV, OK, SD, UT, WA, WY).

d Percentages are of the total number of letters in the sample; the remaining 4 percent were mailed from Canada, overseas, or unknown places. Figures in parentheses are of absolute numbers.

e Percentages are of the number of letters in the sample from the region concerned. The figures do not sum to 100 as a small proportion of letters (2 percent overall) was from persons of unknown gender.

f Percentages are of the number of letters from men, women, and both genders in the region concerned.

Francisco thanked Burns for "a beautiful, gut-wrenching eloquent anti-war film." But overall there was surprisingly little reference to current events or to issues of war and peace.[33] Though we might have expected the film to prompt comments on war in general or recollections of military service, only 4 percent of the letters mentioned a war other than the Civil War.

The relative scarcity of letters connecting Burns's film to contemporary political issues applies to race relations as well. The letter that Burns frequently quotes in public from the African American praising *The Civil War* as a call for racial reconciliation was exceptional, though in our sample we found a letter from a self-identified white woman from New York who stated, "I do not believe that the Civil War will be over until we admit as a nation that we are racist." If *The Civil War* is suffused with the issues of the civil rights movement and the Vietnam War when Burns came of age, as some critics have observed, few viewers who wrote to Burns in the months immediately after the film premiered seem to have noticed.[34]

While Burns's film inspired relatively few writers to comment on issues of war and peace or race relations, many more were prompted to discuss the shortcomings of history education in the schools. Approximately 7 percent of the letter writers contrasted Burns's emotionally compelling film with what they remembered as the dull history classes they endured in school. A woman from Annapolis declared that she had learned more in eleven hours of *The Civil War* than in sixteen years of schooling. Another writer from Maryland remarked, "It may be that public broadcasting will have to pick up the instruction where public schools have failed." A man from Chicago exclaimed, "Yahoo! Let's have some more of that American history! Yum Yum! Why did it taste so bad in *school?*"

Indeed, why did Burns's recipe for presenting the past taste so much better than the previous versions that viewers had been fed? What did viewers like about the history they saw in Burns's film?

More than one out of every four letter writers (27 percent) praised Burns for offering them a sense of direct, emotional connection with the past. A woman from California wrote, "I feel as if I had actually been there. I could smell the dust and hear the cannon long after the program had ended." Another woman, from New Jersey, wrote, "I truly feel as if I know Sam Watkins, Elisha Hunt Rhoads, Nannie Haskins, Mary

Chesnut, Barbara Fields, and mostly Shelby Foote." The effortless slide between historical and contemporary figures mentioned in the above letter mirrored Burns's technique of using familiar contemporary voices to read the words of historical characters. When a letter states, "I was able to call up the clear, crisp, and refined images of the war, similar to the way one recalls a visit to a familiar place," it was largely because the scenery, stories, and above all, the voices were in fact familiar to many contemporary viewers. Fifty years from now, when the voices of Charlie McDowell and Garrison Keillor will be as unknown as those of the radio stars of the 1930s and 1940s are to us today, the sense of familiarity the film conveys may diminish.

Over and over writers praised Burns for making an emotional impact that the earlier histories they had encountered in school or books or movies had not, and they equated that impact with a sense of reality, of experiencing what the Civil War was really like. A woman from Lynn, Massachusetts, confessed, "The series affected me emotionally. Many times tears streamed down my face. I felt as though I had gone back in time."[35]

Certainly the use of still photographs, not only of generals and famous individuals but also of ordinary people who might show up in the viewer's family album, contributed to the reality effect. Although Burns constantly altered the perspective of the historical photographs he filmed with his moving camera, all were from the period. Many writers compared Burns's nonfiction film favorably with, in the words of a woman from Maryland, the "Gone with the Windy historical perspective" of other popular histories. Comparing *The Civil War* to the television miniseries *Blue and Gray* and *North and South*, a woman from Vermont concluded, "None of them had the impact your film had. In the movies you are reminded of the real thing but you know as soon as the order 'cut' is given that all the 'dead' soldiers are going to get up and go home. With your authentic photographs the reality is brought home in a way it never has been in a reenactment." In interviews, Burns reminded his audience of his painstaking research, winnowing sixteen thousand original photographs from 150 archives into the three thousand images he presented on film. Burns did not mention that many of the historical photographs of camp scenes and battlefield dead he used had originally been staged, according to the conventions of Civil War photography.[36]

But what most persuaded Burns's viewers that the history they saw was real were his present-day scenes of battlefields such as Antietam and Gettysburg. In a November 1996 interview, Burns described his style as having three parts: the investigation of still photographs, the inclusion of voices from diaries and letters, and "going to the places where the past happened and listening for ghosts and echoes of the event."[37] Testifying to his faithfulness to the historical record, Burns told the public in interviews that, as much as possible, he filmed his contemporary footage at exactly the same location, season, and time of day as the important historical event he was narrating. Every image, he assured his viewers, came from the "right" place, even if not from the right time; he would not use a picture of soldiers from Antietam to illustrate Gettysburg—though he would use images from Gettysburg Day 1 to illustrate Gettysburg Day 3. Photographs of actual battlefields—places that viewers could visit—grounded the reality of Burns's presentation. What Burns tells us must have really happened because the places where it happened still exist, even if the people are gone. For all of Burns's poetic and artistic license, and his romantic invocation of spirits and ghosts, he made sure that his viewers knew that they were seeing the actual places where the Civil War had been fought, and it paid off in letters from viewers who insisted that Burns had not only captured the reality of the war but also given them the feeling that they had "actually been there."

Interestingly, this feeling may have been strongest among viewers less likely to have actually been there. The percentage of letters mentioning Burns's film as making history real varied somewhat by region. Thirty-eight percent of letters from California mentioned that *The Civil War* made history seem real, compared with only 26 percent of letters from northern states and 21 percent of letters from southern states, where most of the battlefield scenes were filmed. With fewer opportunities for physical acquaintance with the Civil War landscape, perhaps the west coast viewers were more likely to believe that the televised images they saw were the real thing.

Shelby Foote's repeated presence on camera also contributed to viewers' belief that they were seeing the real war. Approximately 11 percent of those writing to Burns mentioned Foote by name, most praising his seemingly limitless store of information. Foote emerged as a star of the series in large part because Burns cast him as a genial battlefield guide offering additional details about the conflict's colorful soldiers and statesmen, and kept his comments interpreting the war's origins and after-math to a minimum.[38] Letters applauded Foote for sticking to the facts. By contrast, many of the 4 percent of the writers who mentioned the historian Barbara Fields, Burns's second most used on-camera historian, identified her contribution to the film as a "black female" viewpoint on the war. A woman from Arizona exclaimed, "Foote was excellent, as was the black woman professor."[39]

Given the overwhelming sentiment that Burns had captured the real war, it is not surprising that the majority of those writing to Burns believed that he had stuck to the facts rather than presented his own interpretation of events. A letter from an Illinois woman declared that Burns "simply stated the facts—told it like it was—and left it to [the] audience to reach whatever conclusions they wished." While only 4 percent of letter writers specifically mentioned Burns's objectivity, many more praised Burns for offering what they believed was an unbiased picture of the conflict. When viewers praised Burns for sticking to the facts, they meant that they saw nothing with which they could disagree. And by and large, unlike recent histories of the Civil War by profes-sional historians, the way that Burns related the events of the war did not upset viewer expectations or conventional categorizations. Burns never considers, for example, that when black residents of Mississippi are in-cluded, more Mississippians fought for the Union during the Civil War than for the Confederacy.[40] Burns's inclusion of all the familiar generals and political figures—in contrast to the turn away from great white men and toward social and women's history among professional historians—must have been comforting to some viewers. For even though many of those writing to Burns dismissed the previous sources through which they had learned about the Civil War, from *Gone With the Wind* through school textbooks, these sources still formed the framework through which they judged whether or not Burns's account was true.

To the letter writers, real history consisted of facts, dramatically pre-sented. Many of those writing to Burns successfully placed his film within the context of their previous knowledge of the war not only by accepting what he presented as "real" but also by offering him more facts or correcting the details that he got wrong. Sixteen percent of the letters addressed Burns as a fellow Civil War buff, chiming in with additional facts about the war that Burns missed, or else correcting a detail, such as Lincoln's age at death (fifty-six, not fifty-four) or the caliber of the bullets used (.58-inch, not .53-inch). While these knowledgeable viewers caught Burns getting a few details wrong, few challenged his interpretation of the war—or even acknowledged that he had an interpretation or thought that interpretation had a place in history. Burns's elaborate artifice by and large succeeded in making his view of the war appear simply as the natural one.

The relatively few letters—approximately 5 percent—that challenged Burns's interpretation were not equally divided by region. Only 3 percent of the 261 letters from writers living in northern states in our sample challenged Burns's interpretation, while 11 percent of the 82 letters from writers living in southern states did. Echoing charges in the southern press that the film opened "Old Wounds with Old Lies," and the judgment of the Sons of Confederate Veterans in Atlanta that Burns was a "northern-born producer, blinded by sectional prejudice," individual southern men and women wrote to Burns to uphold the honor of the Confederacy.[41] In the words of a man from Mooresville, North Carolina, Burns presented a "decidedly Union view of the war." Another North Carolina man confessed, "I can overlook the bias you are showing the North since you are a Northerner yourself. But my pride in my Southern heritage will not permit me to overlook your verbal slander of our great general Robert E. Lee." An Atlanta man, while enjoying the "marvelous anecdotes delivered in a charming style by Shelby Foote," denounced Burns for "bias and revisionism" in making slavery the primary cause of the war. Letter writers protesting that the film gave too much weight to slavery as a cause of war and not enough to economics and states rights likely based their criticism largely on the interpretations of the "war between the states" that they had learned in southern schools. These were the same sentiments that reporter Tony Horwitz found among white Civil War reenactors in the South—that beyond the fun of playing soldier, they identified strongly with the politics of the Confederate "cause."[42] Interestingly, male and female Southerners were equally likely to write to Burns that his interpretation was in error, while in the North, men were much more likely than women to complain that Burns had gotten it wrong.

Criticism that the film was too easy on the Confederacy, common in academic reviews, rarely appeared in the letters. We might expect that black viewers would be more likely to lodge this complaint, as John Bracey asserted. Again, it is impossible to know the race of the letter writers, but evidence from the small number of self-identified black viewers in our sample is equivocal. Several praised Burns for telling white America about the important role that African Americans played in winning the war, but others criticized Burns for allowing Shelby Foote to go on at length praising the Confederate general Nathan Bedford Forrest, the man responsible for the Fort Pillow massacre and later a leader of the Ku Klux Klan.

The distinctive response to Burns's film evident in letters from the former Confederate states suggests that regional identity, though perhaps not as strong as earlier in the century, is still passed down in families and communities and can surface in surprising ways. One man born and living in Arkansas, who had married a woman from Mississippi, confided to Burns that for most of his life, especially in the era of segregation, he had opposed all that being southern stood for, but that in watching *The Civil War* he had discovered that he was in fact a "real Southerner. When Richmond fell, I almost cried. When Lee surrendered, I did cry." The film could evoke a sentimental attachment to the region and its Lost Cause even among those who opposed it intellectually.

As well as prompting latent expressions of southern regional identity, *The Civil War* elicited viewer expressions of national identity too—though not as often as Burns claimed. Only 2 percent of all the letters mentioned feelings of nationalism explicitly, though many more praised Burns for his sympathetic depictions of both sides in America's "family conflict." A woman from Texas found watching Burns's film "a profoundly moving experience, one that gave us a deeper sense of the scope of the war—the heroism, the suffering, the noble aspirations on both sides. We now have an even deeper sense of pride in being an American."[43]

Above all, however, those writing letters to Burns placed *The Civil War* in the context of the history of their families. Fully 23 percent of the letters Burns received mentioned Civil War–era ancestors, often including additional material or requesting more information from Burns about them. A woman from Massachusetts wrote, "Your film helped me to gain insight into the character and personal priorities of my great-grandfather . . . who was a Union army veteran." Another woman, from

Montana, reported that the series had changed the way she looked at the photographs of her ancestors who had fought in the war: "Your film allowed me to truly feel the experience of the war as I never had before." The film helped fill in the gaps in family stories. A woman from Florida declared that the film "brought my ancestors to life—my family comes from Tennessee and Mississippi—and for the first time everyone just seemed so real."[44]

Another 7 percent of the letters to Burns mentioned family members of a later generation, relatives who were Civil War buffs and had given the writers an early and powerful acquaintance with the war. To these writers, Burns's film explained not only the war but the passion of their relatives. A woman from California wrote, "As I sit in my den writing this I look over at a picture of my great-grandfather who died in the battle of Gettysburg and recall growing up hearing my mother singing 'Rally Round the Flag' and other Civil War songs." One man from Vermont sent Burns a lengthy reminiscence of visiting Fords' Theater in Washington with his father, who had died shortly after *The Civil War* series aired. Another letter, from a woman in Seattle, deserves quoting at length for its expressiveness:

> Every summer of the late '40s and early '50s my father packed the suitcase and gently herded my mother, my sister and me into the Ford and drove out of Detroit, headed south. The itinerary varied but his intent was the same—year after year. He believed that history was best learned by touching the ground over which it passed, by seeing first hand the artifacts housed in a myriad of museums, by running your hand over cold metal cannons resting silent on far away battlefields. The Civil War was a history he knew well and wanted the same for us, his children. Before I was 15 I had trampled, scurried and crawled over scores of battlefields. The circular mural of Cyclorama was as familiar to me as the pictures of presidents that hung over our school's blackboards. I learned and remembered yet sadly, then, never truly understood the depth of emotion those experiences held for my father until experiencing your masterpiece, *The Civil War*.
>
> I can vividly recall standing in a hot dusty Gettysburg field, listening to him re-narrate a battle fought there. I still see him pointing over to Little Round Top explaining yet again the assault. I hear his faltering voice crackling with emotion, tears rolling down his cheerless face. It embarrassed me then and I hoped no one else saw the man I idolized behave so.

But from the opening segments of your film to its poignant close, I finally felt what he had those years ago. My only regret is not being able to tell him; my father died in 1974.

For 11 hours of a brilliantly orchestrated history lesson and a deeper appreciation of the dominant figure in my life, I thank you, thank you, thank you.

For viewers of *The Civil War*, clearly family history served as a lens through which to understand the nation's history (especially among people already highly knowledgeable about their family history), and the nation's history served as a lens through which to understand more about the history of their families.

The interplay of letters and diaries in the film made this bridge between public and family history easier. The star of the series was not Abraham Lincoln or Robert E. Lee but a common Union soldier, Sullivan Ballou. His moving letter home to his wife Sarah, recited at the close of the first evening's segment, became so popular that facsimile copies soon blanketed the nation, offered as premiums for donating to public television stations. While 10 percent of the letters to Burns commented on his use of still photographs and 14 percent of his use of music, 21 percent of those writing to Burns praised the way he incorporated diaries and letters into his film; of those, three-quarters mentioned Sullivan Ballou. Writers from every region of the country were equally likely to mention the film's letters and diaries, but there was a big gender difference. Many more women than men singled out the letters (26 percent of all letters to Burns from women, 16 percent of all letters to Burns from men), suggesting their greater identification with how the majority of women at the time experienced the war—in letters. Of course, all of the viewers in our sample were predisposed to letters as a form of communication or they likely would not have written to Burns at all.

The tremendous success of *The Civil War* as popular history can be tied to the fact that Burns's interpretation of the war did not challenge that of his national public television audience, as well as to the sheer emotional power of words and images and music artfully combined. But the film's success also was the result of Burns's combining the stories of famous military figures and places with those of ordinary families whom the audience could imagine as their own ancestors. He presented contemporary scenes of places that his viewers could visit, and historical photographs and quotations from people who looked and sounded like his viewers, or resembled people who could be found in their own family albums. Burns's slow, careful attention to photographs taught the public how to look at their own family photographs in a new light, while the structure of diaries and letters invited viewers—particularly women—to insert their family history into the story of the nation and to view the national past in the context of their families.

Watching *The Civil War*, most viewers did not see the same film as professional historians. While historians criticized Burns for his interpretive omissions, such as the lack of a discussion of Reconstruction or the Free Soil ideology, most viewers were unlikely to comment on what Burns did not choose to show. Instead, they praised the series for sticking to the facts, on the one hand, and for providing a surprisingly emotional educational experience on the other, one that ultimately helped them to understand their families as much as their region and nation. When letters from viewers did complain about an error of interpretation, it was generally Southerners mourning the absence of the familiar economic and states rights interpretations that they had learned in school.

Based on our sample of the letters that Burns received, clearly most Americans who watched *The Civil War* saw not an interpretation of the past to accept or reject, as an academic historian might, but rather a vast, colorful album that they could fill with additional information about the war that they had collected previously from watching other television programs and films, from visiting museums and historic sites, from sitting through history classes in school, and most of all, from hearing stories told in their families. The album's pages were not entirely open, of course; Burns requested that his viewers fit their stories within his romantic nationalist vision of the Civil War as one of brother against brother. But even though Burns remained firmly in control of the history that his viewers saw and heard, those writing to Burns suggest that his technical artistry—the blend of word, image, and music, letter, diary, and photograph—made them feel close to the process of making history, not passive and removed. *The Civil War* demonstrates that a mass media product can carry deeply personal meanings, and can serve as a vehicle for communicating a sense of history, especially as it prompts conversations around family photographs. But Burns's film also demonstrates the limitations of such history. *The Civil War* connected profoundly with a mass audience by playing to our craving for the experience of the past.[45] It did not challenge most viewers' understanding of the Civil War, or of history, but rather allowed them to confirm, on a more emotional level, what they already knew. As other filmmakers and museum professionals mimic Burns's style in the hope of duplicating his enormous success, the expectation that popular history first and foremost must offer the public a dramatic emotional experience, one that simulates the sensation of actually "being there," will likely affect the presentation of historical topics in films, museums, classrooms, and books for years to come.

# 5

# Place and Placelessness
# in American History

Fig. 26. Making music on a Sunday afternoon in August 1940 under the soldiers' monument in Provincetown, Massachusetts. Photo by Edwin Rosskam; Library of Congress, Prints and Photographs Division, Farm Security Administration–Office of War Information Collection, LC-USF34-012709-D.

THE DESIRE of those watching *The Civil War* for a connection, if only through a television screen, with the actual places where their ancestors had been, reveals the importance of emotional attachments to particular places as a vital component of Americans' sense of history. We professional historians have a hard time understanding this because our own professional education inculcates an indifference to place. Unlike many professionals who can choose where they will live and work, our historians in training, especially those seeking a position teaching college, soon learn that they stand a slim chance of ever winding up in a part of the country where they want to live. We teach them, by our example and the discipline of the job market, to regard the places where they will spend their future careers as more or less interchangeable. The assumption that place does not matter permeates our work—not only how we are trained but how we do history.

Indeed orientation to place separates academic from public history, the research of the professional historian from that of his or her neighbors. Historians begin their inquiries into the past by identifying a particular social or political process, then looking for the places where it happened; the public begins with a place that it cares about and then asks, "What happened here?"

"What happened here?"—a common enough question—gets at the heart of the role that history and memory play in how we come to value our local environment. It is through the histories we tell that we define the boundaries of our backyard, the territories that matter, from those of others around us. Communication about the past is inextricably intertwined with communication about particular places; we attach histories to places, and the environmental value we attach to a place comes largely through the memories and historical associations we have with it. The remaining chapters of this book explore the connections between Americans' sense of place and their sense of history. The chapters demonstrate how a greater awareness among historians of how Americans have identified with the particular places where they have lived and worked can strengthen our research into communities of the past, as well as our efforts to preserve historical sites that are meaningful for the present. Historians have important roles to play in helping our fellow citizens to protect the environments that they value. But first, we must be able to look at the American past and the society around us, and see more than the reflection—or the inverse—of our own geographically mobile images.

My observations concerning the importance of place attachments in American life stem not only from my own experiences and research but also from a burgeoning scholarly literature in environmental psychology, folklore, and cultural geography, as well as history and nature writing. The resurgent interest among scholars in place and region— greater than at any time since the 1930s—reflects trends in the larger culture as we enter the twenty-first century, the contemporary suspicion of the nation-state and the search for a smaller, more manageable scale of human affairs. By and large historians and naturalists who have written about place have used the term as a proxy for the physical environment, the natural setting where the events they are describing unfold. A sense of place, especially for nature writers, springs naturally from a society's long interaction with its physical environment.[1] Yet in fact the sense of place of the residents of a locale is no more a natural product than their sense of history. And just as in earlier chapters of this book we have explored the making of historical consciousness—how ideas about history have been created, institutionalized, disseminated, understood, and changed over time in conjunction with war memorials, civic celebrations, and popular film—we can explore the making of place consciousness, what scholars in environmental psychology, cultural geography, and folklore call "sense of place."

## Place

What do we mean by sense of place? At the most individual of levels, it concerns the organization of environmental stimuli into meaningful cognitive structures. Rather than investigating how a particular setting produces a particular behavior, psychologists have found it more useful to employ a humanistic, developmental model that explores the role of the physical environment in the formation of individual identity. Not only does this model help us to consider how individuals over time develop their unique way of looking at the world, it also helps us to understand the evolution of feeling and how children form emotional attachments to places as they grow.[2]

Psychologists theorize that children form attachments to places in a manner similar to the way they bond with their parents. In the early stages of life infants take the mother for granted as a supplier of needs, not even recognizing the independence of her existence until they mature and become conscious of a relationship to her; similarly, children take their local environment for granted and only form a relationship to it as they develop. Place attachments emerge through children's active exploration and manipulation of their environment. By age three, children begin naming places and categorizing them: the most intense bonding to place occurs between ages six and twelve, when children are most active in exploring and learning to manipulate the physical world with same-sex friends. Psychologists believe that children's early experiences gaining control over nearby spaces—feeling ownership of a place, something they can call theirs—are crucial to the development of their positive self-identity as adults.[3]

Childhood place attachments continue to exert an influence in adult life. Adult memories of childhood places remain a crucial anchor for personal identity; we anchor a sense of self in the places of our past, and echo our relationship with those places in the dwellings we choose as adults, in the places we call home, in the places we are fleeing from. The psychologist Claire Cooper Marcus observes that in making a home, adults often try to reproduce favorite childhood places; this takes the form of choosing familiar house types and garden plants, and of putting inherited furniture in a home to provide a sense of continuity with the past.[4] Adults often intertwine their life stories with stories about favorite childhood places. Cooper Marcus has found that these special places of memory tend to be outdoors more often than indoors—environments associated with a sensation of range and freedom where as children they could hide from the control of elders. Interestingly, when psychologists interview older children (as opposed to adults) about their favorite childhood places, they also list outdoor sites—children as young as twelve engage in environmental nostalgia, wistfully recalling where they played as kids. Memories of childhood places also are shaped by economic status. Affectionate memories tend to be attached to places that a family owned, or else to public places that no one owned; by contrast, ambivalent or negative memories tend to be attached to places where, often because of poverty or racism, a family experienced unstable connection with a place.[5]

Although our sense of place reflects the imprint of childhood environmental attachments, it is developed and reinforced by the social networks we participate in as adults. Place attachment is often the product of habituation and social interaction. Long-term residence substantially increases sentimental ties to a locale by increasing the likelihood of local social ties. The longer we live in a place, the more likely we are to associate it with our friends and kin, as the environment becomes saturated with memories of our significant life experiences.[6]

Psychologists have studied not only the development of emotional bonds between individuals and places but also the emotional consequences when those bonds are broken, the grieving for a lost home that occurs among the elderly or exiles forcibly deprived of a familiar environment. In an often-cited study, the psychologist Marc Fried interviewed over five hundred residents of the West End of Boston shortly before, and then after, their forced relocation to make way for an urban renewal project in the 1950s. He discovered that approximately one-half of the former West End residents exhibited severely depressed reactions even two years after the move, and compared their mourning for the loss of a place to mourning for the loss of a person. Fried explained that the identity of many working-class residents was tightly woven into the social networks that pervaded the neighborhood; as a result, they suffered the impact of the destruction of this bounded social world more than the neighborhood's middle-class residents.[7] In passing, he noted that places such as the West End possess an intelligibility in memory that they may never have had in experience—a destroyed collection of streets gained coherence as a single "neighborhood" primarily through the memory of its destruction.

Psychological studies of place attachment remind us of the enormous influence that memories have upon how we see our environment.[8] When we recall places, we recall emotions and activities and not merely the physical setting.[9] The memory of a place becomes a language through which we recall our past social networks and emotions. We remember places as the settings for past social experience, and these places, as we remember them, can have even more emotional impact on us than our experience of them at the time.[10] One implication of this is that our sense of place, largely a product of memory, does not necessarily decrease in response to changes in our physical environment; in fact, living in an urban environment constantly reshaped by a fast-changing mass culture may produce as powerful feelings of place attachment as living in a more slowly changing rural environment.

The connection between remembered places and personal identity in America—between where we grew up and who we are—is especially articulated in the work of writers such as William Faulkner, Toni Morison, Louise Erdrich, and Wallace Stegner. Each create powerful identities for themselves through the act of remembering particular places. For each author, writing about the past places in their lives serves as a form of self-discovery. Toni Morison considers the significant places in her past the source of her artistic inspiration; she begins each work by recalling a specific place, then depicts the emotional reality of that place for her readers.[11] Erdrich insists that writing about a particular environment that she knows well enables her to encounter the reality of the human condition, providing a frame of reference for the stories she tells, a grounding for her parables of life.[12] Even nonfiction works that purport simply to describe a place—whether the nature writing of a John Muir or John McPhee, or the social documentary journalism of a James Agee—are deeply rooted in the writer's environmental preferences and memories and direct the mind's eye to some landscape features but not others. Of course, environmental historians also tell stories about places; as William Cronon notes, histories of the Dust Bowl have been highly selective narratives, as much shaped by the personal backgrounds and political ideologies of their writers as any work of fiction.[13]

Visual artists' representations of place are also highly selective. By arranging the environmental features they see into a "landscape," painters such as Thomas Cole or photographers such as Ansel Adams and David Plowden have communicated their personal identity and values as much as the lay of the land.[14]

When the descriptions of places by artists and writers are widely disseminated, they help others to see the environment in a certain way (as the individual artist and writer does). Artists and writers have the power to make places for others, to transform otherwise ordinary environments into "storied" places.[15] Wallace Stegner notes, "No place is a place until the things that have happened in it are remembered in history, ballads, yarns, legends, or monuments."[16] Stegner's reference to monuments reminds us again of the commemorative landscape of Memorial Park in Orange and that the making of an ordinary space into a special place is a profoundly social and political process as well as a psychological one. Our perceptions of the environment are shaped by our personal experiences and memories but also by the products of our larger culture, its art and literature, its commemorative ceremonies and historical markers. Environmental perceptions are also shaped by our conversations with family and friends. Psychologists, artists, and writers contribute to our understanding of how early encounters with the environment influence the development of our place attachments and landscape preferences as adults, but clearly our sense of place is also influenced by larger patterns of group communication and collective memory.

In the words of Kevin Lynch, places "furnish the raw material for the symbols and collective memories of group communication."[17] The collective memories attached to places emerge out of dialogue and social interaction, as individuals discuss their different perceptions of place with one another and discover common ground. Folklorists have been the most active in examining what Mary Hufford terms "genres of place," the stories about local characters, about the weather, about work, through which a community explains the environment to itself and makes spaces into places.[18] Tracing the various ways that place-knowledge is communicated within social groups, and how various residents of the same area attach different meanings to the same space, folklorists demonstrate how culture and communication guide environmental perception.

Much of the research examining collective memory and place in America has focused on relatively isolated rural areas such as Appalachia, where folklorists raced to identify and document the native's distinctive "spirit of place" before it was lost to outside influences. But more useful for American historians are folklore studies that examine the impact of tourism on these areas, and the interaction between outsiders' and residents' perceptions of the environment. In one study, Tim Cochrane characterizes the sense of place of the local fishing community of Isle Royale, Michigan, as embedded in its various traditional practices. But then Cochrane observes that "visitors' overriding interest in the aesthetics of their tourist experiences stimulated fishermen to be more articulate about their sense of Isle Royale's beauty and unique character." Cochrane contrasts the sense of place of the raconteur-fishermen who can tell place stories to tourists with that of other local residents lacking the language skills or interest to represent their place to outsiders.[19]

As we saw in connection with civic celebrations, public representations of a place not only express local residents' feelings of attachment to their environment but also consist of images directed to outsiders that can affect how local residents perceive where they live. This leads us to question "collective memory" as the principal source of a community's sense of place. Rather, there are conflicts with political implications over the meanings attached to places; San Francisco's Portolá Festival in 1909 exemplifies how the invention of a "collective" sense of place, like the invention of a public history, reflects the struggle for power among various groups and interests. In the cultural studies lingo of geographers Denis Cosgrove and Mona Domosh, "landscapes" are no more than "readings of texts on the part of dominant individuals or groups who inscribe these readings into their transformations of the natural world and then naturalize such readings/writings through their ideological hegemony."[20]

To understand the ideological aspects of place-making, we must supplement psychological and folklore studies of the subjective experience of place with a critical geographical analysis of the social production of space—how the environments in which we live have been molded by larger social, economic, and political forces. Clearly the largest factor determining spatial arrangements and land use in America has been modern capitalism; in addition, the distribution of impoverished slums and wealthy suburbs, and who gets to experience which place, reflects the force of racism in society. At both the global and the regional levels, differences in the look and feel of particular places make manifest the social production of inequality.[21] The geographer Ed Soja defines the study of place as an exploration of "how relations of power and discipline are inscribed into the apparently innocent spatiality of social life."[22] Looking at the American past, in settings such as a colonial New England village, an antebellum Southern plantation, or a late nineteenth-century Pennsylvania company town, we can see how patterns of spatial relations and social hierarchy seem mutually determined. Each locale impressed upon the majority of its inhabitants a coherent, if oppressive, sense of place. By contrast, the spatial patterns produced by America's contemporary political economy defy environmental sensibilities inherited from our agricultural and industrial past. In Los Angeles, for example, various and unrelated land uses exist side by side, and local residents commute from their homes in the center to their ever-shifting workplaces on the periphery, rather than to a central downtown, as some economic nodes decline while other ones boom. Such spatial arrangements, when adjoining land uses are not visibly related and nothing is where we expect it to be, challenge our traditional senses of place and compel us to fashion new ones.[23]

## Placelessness

Many critics assert that it has become virtually impossible for Americans immersed in a world of mass media images, the Internet, and multinational corporations to develop and sustain an authentic sense of place (figure 27). If individuals can experience a sense of place, they can also experience a sense of placelessness—the feeling of belonging in no particular place. Critics argue that in the modern global economy anything can come from anywhere, eroding our perception of the uniqueness of places. They distinguish between an authentic sense of place that has evolved through the interaction of local residents with a distinctive built environment that visibly demonstrates continuity with past land uses, and a place identity that corporate leaders or the mass media have arbitrarily assigned to a standardized, interchangeable, instant landscape. The latter, in the words of the geographer Edward Relph, are "pseudo places," environments directed to visitors, not local residents.[24] Relph's

Fig. 27. This photograph was taken alongside Route 9 in Hadley, Massachusetts, in June 2000. Photo by the author.

criticism has been echoed by others who characterize postmodern architecture's penchant for historical pastiche as no more than "variations on a theme park," with period reconstructions that seemingly change with the season, mirroring the continuous transformations of consumer capitalism.[25] Critics denounce both the sleek international-style modern building and its postmodern eclectic successor as making neither intellectual nor emotional sense to local residents; neither architecture can nurture a distinctive sense of place.[26]

In fact, complaints that the standardization and commercialization of the environment under modern consumer capitalism have diminished Americans' sense of place extend back well over a century. Contemporary concerns with placelessness have antecedents in philosophical, sociological, and historical treatises at the turn of the century that lamented the decline of "community." Essays by Josiah Royce, Edward A. Ross, and Frederick Jackson Turner warned that as the centralization of economic and political authority under the modern corporation and the nation-state weakened local economic and political control, and improvements in transportation and communications technology demolished the boundaries of local residents' social world, the distinctive features of local community life would disappear. Fear that America's provincial customs were endangered resurfaced in another generation of writers in the 1920s and 1930s who sought to identify and preserve the distinctive character of American regions.[27] Many of the regionalist writers were historians, though few taught in colleges or universities. Along with attacks on modern progress for the destruction of distinctive landscapes and places in the 1920s and 1930s came the romanticization of displaced peoples—Yankee farmers, Southern sharecroppers, Native Americans—as being close to the earth. The same critique of modernity and romanticization of native people's relationship with the land has pervaded environmentalist thought of the past decade as well.[28]

Critics of placelessness over the past century have viewed it as not only a modern problem but a peculiarly American one. They attribute Americans' disregard for place to unique features of both American history and American historical consciousness. The high degree of geographical mobility evident throughout American history—the pioneer always in motion leaving behind deserted villages and depleted soils in search of economic opportunity—has been both the cause and the result of our inability to value where we live.[29] This restlessness has in turn led to America's lack of historical consciousness. Americans lack a sense of place because they lack a sense of history and commitment to community; they lack a sense of history because they are too geographically mobile to develop a sense of place. In the nineteenth century, Alexis de Tocqueville and Charles Eliot Norton made similar observations. Both noticed the lack of old homes in America—that Americans always on the move developed no attachments to place and thus no sense of historical connection with the land; that the American built environment seemed uniformly new, bereft of evidence of the passage of time that could make places distinctive by reminding Americans of past generations. In the 1940s, the sociologist Fei Xiaotong, visiting the United States from China, pronounced that Americans lived in an eternal present, a "world without ghosts."[30] Contemporary observers such as Michael Wallace and Edward Relph echo earlier critics when they claim that Americans are not only "historicidal," denying the relevance of their past for the future, but also "placeless," living in "anonymous spaces and exchangeable environments."[31] To these critics, placelessness is a historically American condition that is now being exported throughout world.

Criticisms of American placelessness certainly remind us that our sense of place is affected by powerful external economic and political forces and is not purely subjective or communal; but it is important to recognize the limitations of this approach. One problem with associating feelings of placelessness with the onset of industrial capitalism and modernity is: whose sense of place are we talking about? Obviously for Native Americans, African Americans, or recent immigrants from overseas, feelings of displacement began long before industrialism. Placelessness becomes a problem only when middle-class Americans begin to experience a loss of control over space—when a newcomer ethnic group takes over a neighborhood or an ancestral farm becomes the site of a shopping mall. But these displacements are minor compared to the changes Native Americans experienced when Europeans arrived.

The argument that feelings of placelessness are exacerbated by modern transportation and communications technology, which compresses Americans' sense of time and space, ignores all those who do not experience that technology or who experience it differently from a globe-trotting corporate executive or academic. Within the same city are people who work at the pace of fax machines and the Internet, while others travel by bus. The old, the young, and the poor are relatively immobile groups whose social world is often extremely bounded.[32] The amount of one's economic, social, and political power affects one's sense of place—we experience place differently depending on where we are in society, as well as how much control we have over where we are. A genteel, back-to-the-land farmer has a different sense of place from a farmer tied to the land by debt. And as we see in the next chapter, a young white suburban couple moving into an inner-city neighborhood to restore a historic house has a different sense of place from a black family unable to leave the neighborhood because of racism and poverty. Attributing American placelessness to the nation's historically high degree of geographical mobility does not acknowledge the differences in power that shape perspectives on place between the industrial worker who moves from Detroit to Arlington, Texas, to pursue a manufacturing job and the corporate executive who moved the job there.[33]

Finally, those who contrast place and placelessness frequently romanticize and oversimplify the aspirations of the "folk" living on the land. Artists, writers, and social scientists identify a sense of place with social stability and permanence, with people and landscapes that seemingly remain the same, unaffected by the modern world. These places, of course, can only exist in memory; for in reality, places continually change, their residents engaging with the larger society. The same observation applies to the way that Americans think about history. Writers of letters to Ken Burns about *The Civil War* believe that history consists of facts and experiences that cannot be changed and that offer a stable anchor for personal, family, and national identity—in contrast to academic historians' insistence that the past is a social construction that changes over time in response to present needs.

Despite the limitations of "placelessness" as a concept, the term reminds us that, in the words of the folklorist Henry Glassie, there is a difference between a portable past made of paper and a stationary one made of dirt.[34] The new electronic communities of communication can never supersede place-based communities as creators and conservators of environmental value. Though contemporary writers who call for a return to such communities, such as James Howard Kunstler, Scott Russell Sanders, Gary Snyder, and Kirkpatrick Sale, tend to have a romanticized view of the past, they are essentially right that the American economy has long been based on the interchangeability of places, and that our institutions and land use decisions rarely reflect a sense of environmental value other than that of the marketplace.[35] Before turning in the next chapter to a discussion of how historians can help their neighbors to identify and protect the special places in their communities, I first summarize what we have learned from our brief excursion into the scholarly literature on sense of place in America.

## Six Axioms for Thinking about Place in America

*1. A sense of place does not spring naturally from the environment.* Although the meanings we give to a place are rooted in its physical setting and location in the world—the residents of an inner city, a mining town, or the neighborhood built over the Love Canal encounter certain inescapable environmental realities—these meanings are not intrinsic to it. Individuals understand places differently depending on how they have experienced them, and this experience in turn is shaped by their social characteristics such as age, gender, race, class, and physical condition. When New Yorker Tony Hiss waxes eloquent about the sensation of walking alone in Prospect Park or Grand Central Station, without mentioning any fear of crime, he ignores the way that his age and sex shape his experience of place—the degree of freedom he feels in these environments is likely different from that of an elderly person or a woman.[36] How would his experience of these places differ if he were a black teenager closely watched by the police? Or in a wheelchair, or blind? Moreover, as we saw in the earlier chapter on civic celebrations, our perceptions of place are also shaped by public representations of "community identity" or "town character" that business leaders and politicians use to interpret our environment to outsiders. Local residents create and have created for them different images of their environment—"friendly small town" vs. "tough inner-city neighborhood"— and have different amounts of say in how these "collective" representations are articulated.

2. *Places, in the end, are not interchangeable with other places.* Once the residents of Orange created a memorial park there was only one site that would do for a doughboy statue, and Ken Burns had to shoot the contemporary footage for *The Civil War* on the right battlefield at the right time. But even the most ordinary of landscapes can become a special place. We make places first by building upon nature to create a house, a factory, or a shopping mall; by shaping nature to create a farm, a garden, or a park; or by preserving nature to create an open space or a wilderness area. Then we remake those places by attaching our memories and meanings to them. In one sense, a shopping mall destroys a local sense of place by obliterating evidence of past land uses on its site—most malls are built on former farmland, but it is hard to visualize that agriculture ever took place on them. But in another sense, even the most undistinguished-looking mall or fast-food restaurant can become a site where a distinctive sense of place and history is created in the community. This sense stems not from a standardized historical facade, such as the Mission-style exterior of a Taco Bell restaurant, which only recalls "history" in a generic way, but from its status as a gathering place for older people to walk around and swap memories, or a provider of childhood memories of shopping trips with grandparents, soccer team victory celebrations, and hanging out with friends. To those living outside a community, a franchise restaurant there is interchangeable with any other; to local residents, it is a particular place where conversations about the local past occur, where time is passed and becomes "past."

3. *Place values are rooted in the material world.* Our evaluation of a place is shaped by our personal background and by social and cultural

norms, but it is difficult for us to value what cannot be seen. In America, the "land without ghosts," environmental features that have a material presence are easier to perceive than features that have to be imagined. My father can tell my children about his forty-plus years working at a General Electric plant in southwest Philadelphia, but his stories would mean more to them if they could still see the massive building where he worked, which was long ago leveled. Public activities such as holding a commemorative ceremony, erecting a monument, and marking a historical site or district makes places visible by linking what ordinarily cannot be seen—a community's values and reminiscences, its history—to features in the physical environment.

    4. *We experience places as overlapping locales with permeable boundaries.* At first glance, our attachment to place seems to weaken as the size of the place increases. Do we care more about local, national, or global history? But, in fact, in different situations the "place" with which we identify most intensely might be a nation, region, town, neighborhood, or household.[37] For many of us, the significant places in life are in multiple locales: we live in one town but also identify with another— root for its sports teams, follow its weather. It may be that the high rate of geographical mobility in American history has resulted not in a sense of "placelessness," as critics assert, but rather in an acute sense of attachment to multiple places. The letters to Ken Burns demonstrate how family history in America often plays out in a succession of places rather than a single locale; as the writers told Burns about their Civil War ancestors, they traced the path from their current residence back to the towns in Illinois or Georgia or Massachusetts where their ancestors had lived. What constitutes a distinctively "American" sense of place, perhaps to a greater extent than with any other nation, is the simultaneous feeling of being in a place and caring about somewhere else. I wonder if this multiple place consciousness accounts in part for the popularity of the Weather Channel, and the fact that in California, where more than one-half of all residents were born out of state, television stations report the weather "back" east far more often than eastern stations report the weather "out" west.

    5. *We articulate a sense of place in dialogue with others.* Though talented artists and writers can produce evocative memoirs of significant places in their past, for most of us a sentimental attachment to place remains

subconscious and only emerges in conversations with others, usually only when the places important to us are threatened. Conversations about places establish the intersubjective "reality" of our local environment, bringing life to space and space to life. Through these conversations, we form an active sense of ownership of where we live that allows for action with our neighbors on the issues that affect it.[38]

   6. *Our sense of place and of history are inextricably intertwined.* Every sense of place is also a sense of time; at the individual level we describe space as time (something is thirty minutes away) and time as space (the past is near or distant). We can perceive different times in the same place, as we move to a new housing development and fill our homes with family heirlooms, or look at a field and remember what used to be there while imagining what will be there in the future.

   Perceptions of place and history are also intertwined at the cultural level. One example of this is the evolutionary ideology, inherited from the nineteenth century, that arranges each world culture on a scale from "primitive" to "most advanced." Peoples living far away from Europe, where this ideology originated, are perceived as living in another age, distant in time as well as in space. This ideology also assumes that the direction of history is toward global economic integration, more individual human freedom, and more technological conveniences; we perceive places with less evidence of these attributes—like contemporary Amish communities—as living in the past. Another example still with us is the perception that America's East is somehow older than its West. Despite the continuous presence in the West of Pueblo and Spanish settlements established well before those of Jamestown and Plymouth, the prevailing ideology of the nation's "expansion" prompts us to give priority to places settled by the English in the East. Ironically, in western states such as Arizona evidence of the passage of time, such as layers of exposed rocks, fossils, and the remains of pre-Columbian structures, is more visible on the land than in the humid East, yet because of the recent explosion of the Anglo-American population there, we think of the state as "new," a place of virgin land and a boundless future. Geographers claim that the accretion of human traces adds value to a landscape, but clearly it depends on which humans they are.[39] The antiquity of a site matters less than the clues we are culturally conditioned to see.[40]

   In the words of Henry Glassie, "History is the essence of the idea of place."[41] We live in landscapes dense with both histories and memories, idealized images of the past that compete to become the standards we use to evaluate and shape our present environment. Personal recollections of past places stand against a flood of place images created for us, from guidebooks and maps published by local civic organizations that recognize some "historical" places in our community but not others, to the generic images of past American landscapes and smalltown life by Currier and Ives or Norman Rockwell reproduced in the calendars on our kitchen walls. History in all its varieties guides our sense of where we live, contributing to our perception of the traditions that make our places distinctive.[42]

WE HAVE MUCH more to learn about the cultural processes through which Americans come to identify their personal and family histories with one or more special places. Historians can contribute to this knowledge by researching the history of past placemaking activities and environmental perceptions. Rather than taking place as a given, the backdrop for historical activities, we can study placemaking as a historical activity in itself, an essential element of the interaction of humans and nature in a particular environment and time. We can investigate the multiple perceptions of place in a past locale, and the politics of how some perceptions became advanced as the public one as in the Portolá Festival, or institutionalized through preservation legislation, as we will see in chapter 6, concerning New England "town character." We can examine the development, whether by government or private entrepreneurs, of tourist attractions such as scenic wonders, probing how the meanings for these special places were established and interpreted.[43] And we can look behind the language of cultural amnesia and placelessness to explore the actual relationship between place attachment and population migration in the American past, reevaluating our view of the restless pioneers by focusing on their early efforts to impart a settled quality to their environment by designating certain places as historical. Chapter 7 traces this place-making process in California during its first century of statehood.

Historical research into how Americans have made the places where they live and work part of their individual and communal identities can illuminate important issues in the American past, such as the impact of population migration and changes in environmental values. It has even more profound implications for historians who work directly with the public in historic preservation agencies, local historical societies, and museums. The next chapter demonstrates how an understanding of the ways that memories attach to places can help historians to create meaningful historic preservation strategies and public programs that support local residents' efforts to define and protect the special places in their community.

# 6

# Rethinking New England
Town Character

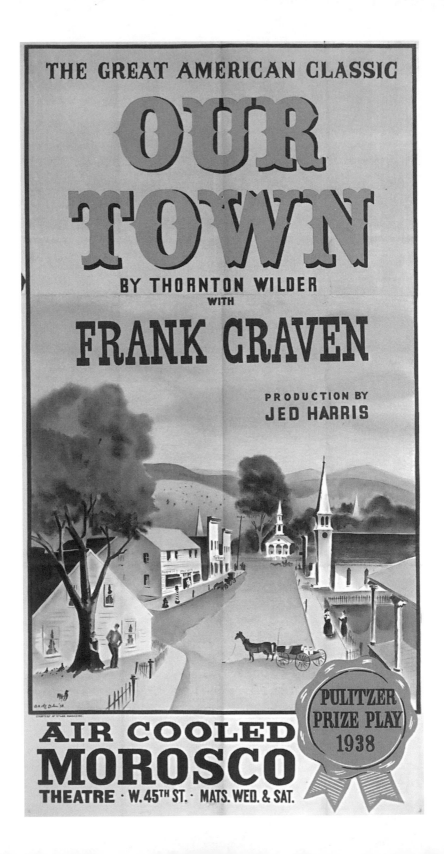

Fig. 28. Adolf Dehn's poster for *Our Town* in 1938 depicted an idealized New England village at the turn of the century. The Harvard Theatre Collection, The Houghton Library.

W HEN CHRISTOPHER Kenneally interviewed Ken Burns for *USAir* magazine, he traveled to Burns's home in Walpole, New Hampshire, which he described as "a small quintessential New England village on the banks of the Connecticut River."[1] Keneally's words bring to mind a picture of white houses clustered around a church and common, of Burns and his family taking their place in the community alongside a set of sturdy characters who have just stepped out from the Thornton Wilder play *Our Town* or a Norman Rockwell painting. There is a certain timelessness implied in Keneally's vision of the New England village as well—as if, should he have visited Walpole 50 or 100 or even 150 years earlier, it would not have looked or felt substantially different from today. The essential character of the town had been established in the colonial era, when its first English settlers laid it out.

If the landscape of Walpole and countless other New England towns at the turn of the twenty-first century have a historical look and feel, it is the result of the activities of recent years as much as those of the past. In fact, many of these towns look much more colonial now than they did 150 years ago. And in the face of pressure for new development, many residents of the towns are more determined than ever to keep this historical character intact.

Notions of town character exert a powerful influence on the way that New England residents look at and consequently shape their environment. In 1990, the Massachusetts Special Commission on Growth and Change listed preserving "community character" at the very top of its list of goals for guiding future development in the commonwealth, declaring, "We need help in keeping the identity of our communities intact."[2] The following year in Boston, the Northeast Regional Office of the National Trust for Historic Preservation issued a four-page "report card for protecting community character."[3] As in other regions of the nation, city governments in New England attempt to improve the character of "slum" neighborhoods, and that of their residents, by encouraging their renovation into historic districts that attract a new urban gentry. Suburban developers seek a market edge by investing their instant neighborhoods with historical "character" by means of design details that suggest a distinctive feel. And various public and private initiatives are under way to control development in agricultural areas and preserve their rural character.

What do New England residents mean when they talk about the "character" of their town or neighborhood? What gives a town or neighborhood its distinctive look and feel? How do residents with different ideas of what constitutes the essence of their town or neighborhood decide what characteristics are most vital to enhance and protect?

Through close examination of the meaning of town character in three New England communities, we can learn more about the role that notions of history play in the creation of a sense of place. We have already investigated the many different perceptions of history present in places such as Orange, Massachusetts, and San Francisco, and the politics of how some versions of the past became the public history; here we will explore the many different senses of place in a locale, and the process through which some representations of place become the prevailing ones. The making of a public history in a community and local residents' senses of place are inextricably intertwined. Individuals attach histories to places, and perceive places differently when they are designated as "historic"; similarly, public debates over land use often reveal conflicting perceptions of local history.

Our rethinking of New England town character will raise not only questions of historical interest—when did idealized images of the colonial past come to dominate the New England landscape, who promoted these images and why, how have they changed over time?—but also important questions of professional practice, especially for historic preservationists. While implicit notions of town character have influenced development patterns in New England throughout its history, making such ideas explicit and investing government with the power to re-form the landscape according to them has only emerged with the profession of city and regional planning in recent years. Town character is a terribly amorphous concept, but it has real consequences when various public agencies and private organizations, with the help of historians, invoke it to shape the environment through zoning, master plans, and preservation ordinances.

ANY DISCUSSION of town character in New England begins with a discussion of the New England town. The historical geographer Joseph Wood has shown that most of the English colonists who settled in New England, like their counterparts in other regions of North America, lived in widely dispersed agricultural communities. The medieval settlement pattern of common fields surrounding a village of tightly grouped homes, which the Puritans sought to revive in North America when they crossed the Atlantic in 1630, never became very widespread. Within a generation, the demand of new arrivals and the grown-up children of the founders for nearby land outstripped the ability of most towns to provide it. The nucleated settlement pattern we see in much of New England today, and which we assume dates back to the colonial era, in fact did not develop until the early nineteenth century, when merchants in places such as Walpole built new stores in close proximity to the local meetinghouse, creating commercial centers for the surrounding farms.[4]

Even at the time, notes the historian Stephen Nissenbaum, these new commercial villages were being romanticized as embodiments of the ideal family-centered industrious democratic community. In 1796, Timothy Dwight looked down from the summit of Mount Holyoke on the Connecticut River and saw a mature, harmonious working landscape of farms and villages that stood in stark contrast to the explosion of disorderly frontier settlements in the West. By the mid-nineteenth century, novelists such as Harriet Beecher Stowe had made this image of the New England town as the crucible of American moral development into a staple of popular culture, used to trumpet the superiority of Northern civilization in the Civil War era.[5]

Later in the century, as the sons and daughters of New England farmers moved westward and cityward, idealized images of the towns from which they came assumed a new meaning. The New England town took on an aura of home, a sentimental association that was promoted by the towns themselves during "Old Home Week," when they invited former residents and their descendants back to visit as tourists. The image of the New England town as America's home place appeared across the nation in a variety of media, including popular art, fiction, and exhibitions. The Chicago World's Columbian Exposition of 1893 featured twenty-one replica colonial buildings in the section devoted to the states, while on the Midway, the section of the fair devoted to amusements, a "New England kitchen" staffed by women in colonial costume served food to hungry tourists. A group portrait of these women appeared in the souvenir book *Midway Types* alongside ethnographic portraits of women of other nationalities. Not coincidentally, Thomas Hovendon's *Breaking Home Ties*, a nostalgic portrait of a farm boy leaving his family, was voted the most popular painting at the fair (figure 29). The romanticization of the New England town as home was part of larger literature of regional nostalgia in America at the turn of the century, one in which the authors invariably wrote about where they used to live rather than their current place of residence. In popular culture, at least, the New England town, all but abandoned by its sons and daughters, achieved a certain picturesque, if shabby, stability; the more Americans broke home ties and moved westward or cityward, the more the New England town was depicted in art, literature, and popular song as staying the same.[6]

By the late nineteenth century, art and literature idealizing the New England town as a repository of important American traditions dating from the colonial era began to have an impact on the look of actual New England towns, as residents sought to remodel where they lived in accordance with this ideal. The residents of these towns not only put up new colonial-style homes and public buildings and redecorated the halls of their old ones according to their ideas of what colonial interiors must have looked like, but also remade the surrounding landscape. In rural and suburban towns, village improvement societies sought to restore the old commons in their town centers, or more often, as with Memorial Park in Orange, to build new ones where the early settlers had forgotten to put them originally. The town of Litchfield, Connecticut, remodeled its entire downtown in 1913 to make it look more "colonial."[7] The craze for the colonial placed familiar local environments in a new-old light, as various groups sought to attach long histories to otherwise ordinary places. Through civic celebrations and historical pageants, campaigns for historic preservation, and sets of roadside historical markers such as accompanied the Massachusetts Tercentenary of 1930, self-appointed guardians of local tradition highlighted the places that testified to the essentially colonial character of their all too modern towns—a character formed before the onset of industry, immigrants, and suburbia.

Perhaps nowhere was this transformation from the Victorian to the colonial more complete than in Deerfield, Massachusetts, which became virtually a museum village as early as 1900. Even though some sections of Deerfield experienced a manufacturing boom in the mid–nineteenth century, the oldest part of town, containing the homes of its first families, stagnated. But when a local merchant suggested that this part of town, known as "the Street," needed new commercial development, his ideas were rejected by a group of residents associated with the

Fig. 29. *Breaking Home Ties*, by Thomas Hovendon, 1890. Philadelphia Museum of Art. Gift of Ellen Harrison McMichael in memory of C. Emory McMichael. Photo by Will Brown.

Fig. 30. The Center for Rural Massachusetts at the University of Massachusetts, Amherst, offered this sketch as a model for how a parcel of land could be developed in ways that encourage the "traditional tightly knit character" of New England towns rather than suburban sprawl. It appeared in many publications, including *Dealing with Change in the Connecticut River Valley: A Design Manual for Conservation and Development* (Amherst: Center for Rural Massachusetts, 1988), p. 21.

local historical society who believed that the key to Deerfield's economic revitalization lay not in updating for modern commerce but rather in remaking the town into a haven from it. By emphasizing "Old Deerfield's" colonial character, playing up the sentimental images of New England's agricultural past and village life popular in the Gilded Age, they could entice the wealthy descendants of the town's first families to purchase their ancestral properties as summer homes. Local women especially played a vital role in the rehabilitation of several historic properties, the establishment of an arts and crafts society that sold handmade needlework to tourists visiting by trolley from Springfield, and (dressed in colonial-era costume) the production of several historical pageants. By the 1920s, Frank Boyden, headmaster of Deerfield Academy, was restoring houses on the Street to use as dormitories for his students, using the colonial ambience to entice children from wealthy families to his school. Henry and Helen Flynt, the parents of one such student, were so taken with the colonial townscape of "Old Deerfield" that they purchased and restored the Street's remaining available houses and established Historic Deerfield, Inc., in 1945.[8]

Alongside the creation of these new historical environments in New England in the first half of the twentieth century came a new idealization of the New England town among intellectuals interested in regional planning. More than a century after Timothy Dwight praised the pattern of compact villages and surrounding farms of the Connecticut River valley as a civilizing influence, Lewis Mumford and Benton MacKaye, founders of the Regional Planning Association of America in the 1920s, described the New England town in much the same way, holding up its "traditional" settlement pattern as exemplifying manageable scale and the perfect integration of humans and nature, in contrast to modern urban-industrial sprawl. Mumford and MacKaye's ideas were echoed by a new generation of regional planners in the 1980s and 1990s who promoted cluster zoning mimicking the "traditional" New England village as the best way to preserve the character of rural and suburban areas facing new development (figure 30).[9]

THE NOTIONS of town character we have discussed so far have been largely those of artists, writers, entrepreneurs, and regional planners, each advancing their particular vision of the ideal relationship between landscape and people that they associate with New England communities of the past. But how do the contemporary residents of these communities view the character of their towns?

In 1991, with the support of the Massachusetts Foundation for the Humanities, I began an investigation of how notions of town character were defined and used in three western Massachusetts communities: Northfield, Wilbraham, and the McKnight Historical District of Springfield. The methodology used was similar in each place. In Northfield, in late spring, I teamed with Kathleen Nutter, Deborah Taricano, Carolyn Spencer, and Rosa Johnston, members of the local historical society and historical commission, to conduct a series of five public meetings. At each meeting, held in a different area of town, we asked local residents to describe the places that they thought contributed the most to Northfield's special character. In Wilbraham and McKnight, I teamed with preservation consultant Gregory Farmer of Springfield in leading a study group composed of academics, land use professionals, and residents of the two communities under study. The group included Daniel Horowitz, a Smith College historian; Arthur Keene and Ellen Pader, anthropologists from the University of Massachusetts; and John Pearsall and Robert McCarroll, city planners from Wilbraham and Springfield respectively; Christine Thompson, a University of Massachusetts planning graduate student; Stan Sherer, a photographer from the University of Massachusetts; David Tebaldi, a philosopher, former McKnight resident, and executive director of the Massachusetts Foundation for the Humanities; and Larry Duquette and Linda Fuller, both Wilbraham residents active in local history. We believed that two residents of McKnight had agreed to be part of the study group, but the only meeting they attended was one that we held in McKnight. Meeting on six evenings—approximately every other week—during the fall of 1991, we discussed our various and often conflicting individual perspectives on what the concept of town character meant. Then we moved into the two communities, with daytime site visits and evening public meetings. In each public meeting, we showed slides that Thompson and Sherer had taken of different local sites, and recorded the conversations that each photograph evoked. The results of the investigations in the three communities challenge the assumption that the unique character of a New England town comes primarily from its "colonial" settlement pattern of clustered development around a church and common; that a town's character is primarily a product of its physical setting; and that local residents experience this physical setting more or less in the same way.

## Northfield: Everyone Remembered the Places They Missed

Northfield, Massachusetts, is a town of approximately 2,400 located on both sides of the Connecticut River just below the Vermont border. In many ways it is a postcard New England town, and was featured in *Yankee Magazine* in 1987. Founded in the 1670s, Northfield retains traces of the "colonial" settlement pattern also evident in Old Deerfield, of houses clustered along Main Street and fields off to the sides (figure 31), and boasts an impressive historic district of early nineteenth-century houses at its center. If anywhere, we would expect the residents of this small town to agree on the features most essential to its character, and indeed at the public meetings we heard many local residents indirectly discuss the importance of maintaining the town's historic settlement pattern of village and field. But we were also struck at these meetings by the enormous differences in the views of Northfield expressed by different neighborhoods and generations, as well as in the wide range of places associated with the past that local residents mentioned as making Northfield distinctive, places that bore little relation to the officially designated historic sites of Main Street.

Our first public meeting was in the south of Northfield, in a neighborhood known locally as "the Farms." We met in the Field Memorial Library, a tiny, antiquated building that still served several days a week as a branch of Northfield's main public library, headquartered at the opposite end of town. The conversation that night was dominated by older residents who expressed a strong sense of continuity with the land; their families had occupied the same houses for years, and the places that they felt made Northfield special were the ones where their relatives had lived. When asked to draw a special place on a giant hand-drawn map that the group created on a roll of blank paper we spread across the old library table, one man sketched a feature that he labeled the "Aunt Hill"—a hill where all of his aunts had lived while he was growing up. These elderly residents spoke less of Northfield's historical sites than of the places they remembered personally, mostly homes and natural features that existed before the 1930s but were now gone. Relatively recent additions to the neighborhood landscape, such as the Northfield Mountain electric power plant, a huge physical presence, never made it onto the map.

Our second public meeting was in the north end of town, in an area known locally as "East Northfield." The Northfield–Mount Hermon

Fig. 31. Northfield, Massachusetts, from the air. Northfield Historical Society.

Academy, a prestigious private secondary school, is located in this part of Northfield, and we met on the academy grounds in the former home of Dwight Moody, the prominent nineteenth-century evangelist. When asked about Northfield's special places, not surprisingly the group mentioned nearby historical features such as the Moody home and the academy's architecturally distinguished buildings. But some members of the group hinted at how these grand structures held different meanings for the wealthy outsiders who sent their children to the school and the townspeople who worked on campus. After the meeting ended, an elderly man walked up to me and bitterly recalled how little he had been paid to cut the grass during the Depression.

The next meeting was in an area of Northfield known locally as "the Mountain." True to its name, it was a heavily wooded hillside south and east of the town center. Unlike in the first two "neighborhoods" in which we held public meetings, the houses were newly constructed and far apart, and were occupied primarily by young families who had moved there for the opportunity to build an affordable home. The conversation that night took place in a classroom of the Linden Hill School, a private institution for the education of dyslexic children (figure 32).

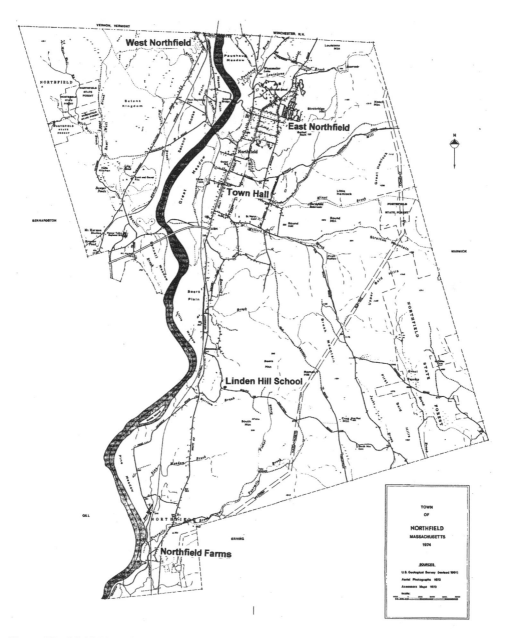

Fig. 32. Northfield, Massachusetts. This map originally appeared in "Pathway to Tomorrow: A Master Plan for Northfield" (1977) and has been altered to show the locations of the five neighborhood meetings we held in spring 1991. Planning Board, Town of Northfield.

When asked what made Northfield special, Mountain residents described the all but hidden places that they had discovered in their new surroundings, including cellar holes and other remains from what had been a thriving logging community a century earlier. To these Northfield residents, history meant not the continuous nearby presence of generations of their families, as in the Farms, or the experience of living in the shadow of a dominant institution, as in East Northfield. Rather, those living on the Mountain associated history with the evidence in their backyards of their unknown predecessors on the land.

The fourth meeting was in West Northfield, the part of town located across the Connecticut River, in a clubhouse maintained by the West Northfield Playground Association. The conversations of the residents in this area seemed pervaded by feelings of loss, as if little special remained about where they lived. Northfield's main railroad station had once been on their side of the river, but it had long been closed. Much of the farmland in the area had turned to brush in the past two decades as working farms went out of business. The Schell Bridge connecting residents to the rest of Northfield had closed six years earlier, turning a short walk across the river to the post office or the grocery store into a twelve-mile round-trip drive. With the loss of the railroad station, the bridge, and many local family farms, the biggest landmarks in West Northfield were the sand and gravel operation of a local construction company, and two trash transfer stations managed by the town, which West Northfield residents cited as evidence of their "second-class status" compared with their neighbors on the other side of the river.[10]

Only at the last of our meetings, held in the basement of the town hall in the center of Northfield, did the participants identify as essential elements of their community's distinctive character places with officially recognized historical significance. Compared with what we had heard in the four public meetings conducted in the other parts of town, relatively few of the special places mentioned at this gathering were associated with personal and family history or memories. Meeting on the edge of the downtown historic district, those present neglected nearby sites associated with the history of more recent, non-English immigrants, such as the Polish Catholic church. Nor did the residents of the town center remember as a special place the house at 88 Main Street that had been Northfield's first post office in 1795—but had become the run-down home of a religious commune in the early 1970s and been demol-

Birnam House. Northfield, Mass.

Fig. 33. The Northfield "Chateau" was built in 1902 and demolished in 1963. Northfield Historical Society.

ished following a fire in 1978. Unpleasant memories of the historic building's controversial final years, left unmentioned at the public meeting, effectively erased the place from the map.[11]

To the residents of Northfield, the special character of where they lived existed not only in the early nineteenth-century houses that stood in the historic district in the town center but also in their memories of cherished sites from childhood that had been lost within their lifetimes. Residents recalled the West Northfield Railroad Station; "The Chateau" (figure 33), an impossibly oversized home in East Northfield from 1902 to 1963 that its builder had modeled after the Hotel Château Frontenac in Quebec City; and the Northfield Inn, a hotel that had also served as the site of many local dances and high school graduation ceremonies. They remembered the family farms that had reverted to brush, and natural features largely unknown to outsiders, such as "Garnet Rock," the "Ice Cave," and "Wanamaker Lake" (figure 34), a favorite swimming hole that had long been drained. In all five neighborhood conversations about what made Northfield special, residents talked about the views that they saw, of the mountains and woods visible from the backdoors of their houses, and of the bend in the Connecticut River and the cluster of buildings on Main Street as seen from a hillside. The town's "colonial" settlement pattern continues to have meaning in the lives of local residents, not necessarily as a reminder of the town's historic past but as a way of ordering nature.

One year after completing the project, I attended a public meeting in the Northfield Elementary School cafeteria to listen to residents discuss proposed revisions to the town's master plan. The moderator, Dick Parsons, a former farmer from West Northfield, soon turned to the problem that town expenses for important public services such as schools and fire and police protection had increased much faster than the local tax base. He asked, "Do you want to keep the town as it had been with its same number of people and same kinds of businesses, or do you want the town in its official activities to encourage the building of new businesses or new homes?" The debate that evening over whether or not to encourage new development in Northfield was intense, with some residents expressing fears that new industries and people moving in would alter the "character" of the town.[12] Seeking to define and protect

Fig. 34. Northfield residents remember "Wanamaker Lake" as a favorite swimming place, though it has been drained since the 1970s. Northfield Historical Society.

Northfield's special character, local residents contemplated not only an arrangement of physical structures but the memories and social relationships that they had embedded in the landscape.

## Does Wilbraham Have a Center?

Wilbraham is a community of 12,600 located immediately east of Springfield. The population is 97 percent white, affluent, and mature—in 1990 the average age of its residents was forty. We thought of Wilbraham, which had developed largely since the 1940s, as a typical postwar commuter suburb—though one Wilbraham resident insisted that it was more a rural farm village (there were still several working farms in town). At first, we intended to examine only the center of Wilbraham, but a visit to the town led us to question whether such a center existed (figure 35). Wilbraham residents had rejected the creation of a central retail district called for in a 1960s master plan, as well as the establishment of a central historic district near the Wilbraham Academy, a building already listed on the National Register of Historic Places. In contrast to Memorial Park in Orange, the small common at the geographical center of Wilbraham was empty, and seemed underused. Indeed, to outsiders like ourselves, accustomed to the look of New England towns such as Northfield, the layout of Wilbraham appeared to be inside out; the post office, town hall, police station, and commercial buildings we expected to find in the town center were instead located on the northern and western periphery (figure 36).

Wilbraham residents, however, vehemently insisted that there was a center to the town. At an evening public meeting in the town hall, hosted by the Wilbraham planning board, local residents responded derisively to our comments that we had had difficulty locating a well-defined town center. One woman retorted, "I live in the center of town and it surprised me to hear you say that there isn't anything in the center of town. You academics have the gall to say 'It's an ill defined center' as if there is nothing in the center. The post office isn't there, the police station isn't there, the town hall isn't there. But that has nothing to do with whether there is or isn't a center. We feel that there is."[13] Other residents spoke glowingly about the benefits of the dispersed pattern of development that had emerged in Wilbraham as it grew after World War II. They credited this pattern—which to us looked like sprawl—

Fig. 35. The center of Wilbraham contains little of the commercial or government activity expected in New England towns. Photo by Christine Thompson.

with keeping traffic, commercial nuisances, and high-density development such as apartments and condominiums on the edge of town, leaving the middle quiet and uncluttered. Those attending our public forum insisted that longtime residents of Wilbraham could describe the boundaries of their town's center, even if newer residents could not.

As we showed Stan Sherer's slides of various people and places from throughout Wilbraham, the fifty or so residents in the room had much to say about the increase in local traffic as more land was developed for high-priced housing and the town's population grew. But they had little to say about changes in the town's social patterns, or about the special places where they liked to meet. Those present, mostly older, longtime residents, mentioned the dump, the library, the churches, and the schools as places where they often saw one another. They also mentioned the former post office in the town center. Pictures of the former post office, and of the new colonial-style one on the edge of town (figure 37), prompted intense discussion about whether the sense of community had diminished as a result of the move. Residents also questioned whether Wilbraham's prevailing housing pattern—homes developed around a cul de sac—also fragmented a sense of community since it made it virtually impossible to walk around the block to visit neighbors.

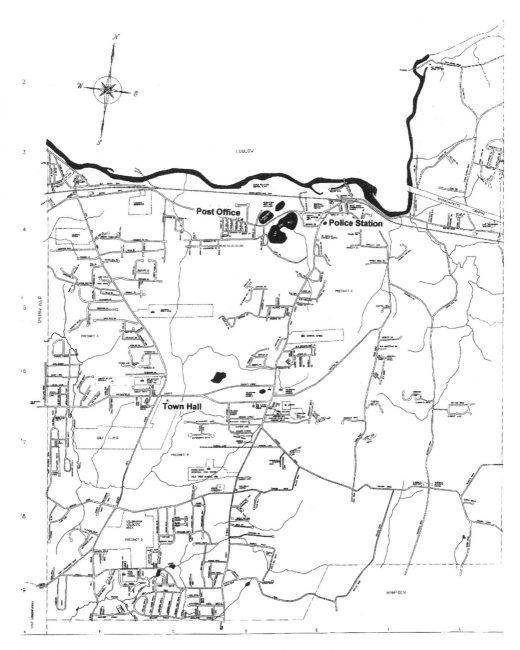

Fig. 36. Wilbraham, Massachusetts. This map was originally prepared by the Wilbraham Engineering Department and has been altered to show the locations of the town hall, police station, and new post office. Engineering Department, Town of Wilbraham.

Fig. 37. The new Wilbraham post office. Photo by Stan Sherer.

But overall, those attending the public forum in Wilbraham considered the new post office, the increased traffic, and the new streets that barely connected with one another as minor annoyances in an otherwise friendly and coherent environment.

The debate over Wilbraham's center was really a debate over the social as much as physical character of Wilbraham. Local residents believed that they had the strong sense of community they associated with a traditional New England town, while those of us from outside of Wilbraham were unwilling to believe that such a sense of community could exist in a sprawling postwar commuter suburb lacking a concentrated pattern of settlement. The public dialogue in Wilbraham demonstrates how little the physical characteristics of a town observable to outsiders contribute to local residents' sense of connection to their environment and one another. Also evident in the public meeting that night, though left unsaid, was how much Wilbraham's sense of community derived from its residents' virtually identical social characteristics as upper-middle-class whites, in contrast to the less affluent whites, African Americans, and Puerto Ricans living immediately to their west in the city of Springfield.

## The Meaning of the Tapley School

Our public meetings in the McKnight district of Springfield (figure 38) also made us question our assumptions about the relationship between

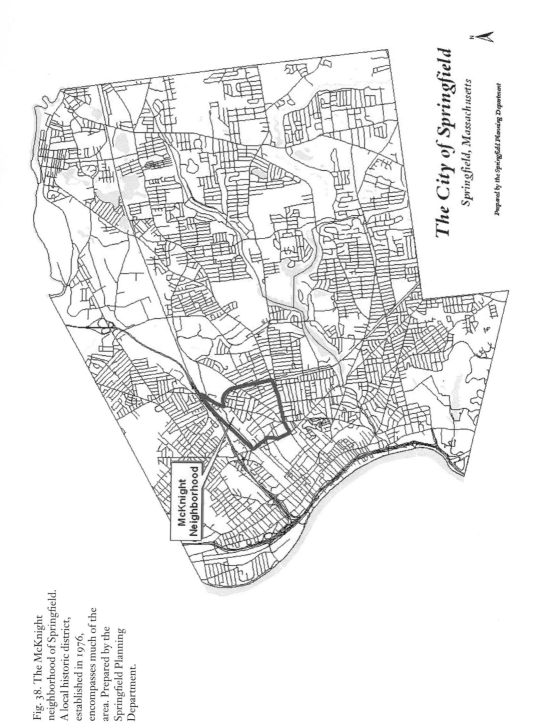

Fig. 38. The McKnight neighborhood of Springfield. A local historic district, established in 1976, encompasses much of the area. Prepared by the Springfield Planning Department.

McKnight Neighborhood

The City of Springfield
Springfield, Massachusetts

Prepared by the Springfield Planning Department

N

the physical characteristics of a neighborhood, its social characteristics, and its residents' sense of history and place. McKnight was among the largest planned residential neighborhoods built in late nineteenth-century America. Developed for the upper middle classes of the booming manufacturing city, McKnight's large homes housed some of Springfield's most affluent families through World War II. But when African Americans, displaced by urban renewal in the city's North End, began moving into McKnight in the 1950s, many older white residents moved out; by 1990 the district's population of 5,200 was nearly 60 percent African American, 18 percent Hispanic, and young (average age thirty). More than half of the housing units in McKnight in 1990 were rented, rather than owner-occupied. Clearly the character of McKnight's population had changed in the postwar era, even as another movement was emerging, to restore the neighborhood's unique physical characteristics. With many of its Victorian exteriors still intact, in 1976 McKnight became a historic district, listed on the National Register of Historic Places and recognized by local preservation ordinances. Alongside the African American majority came a new generation of whites who moved into McKnight to renovate its nineteenth-century homes. Pulling off aluminum siding and taking down chain-link fences, replacing dull exterior colors with vividly painted polychromes, McKnight's newest residents worked hard to bring the old neighborhood's Victorian character back to life, and regularly displayed the results of their efforts in historic house tours that attracted architecture buffs from throughout the region (figure 39). We allowed a local realtor active in these tours and other efforts to promote the neighborhood to organize our first public meeting in McKnight; not surprisingly, the only residents who attended were white, relative newcomers to the neighborhood. This prompted us to organize a second public meeting, this time with the help of Marjorie Guest, an African American who headed the McKnight Neighborhood Council, a multiracial organization that had been in existence since 1957. With the Neighborhood Council's participation, the second public meeting drew an equal mix of white and African American residents.

We showed identical slides of the neighborhood, in the same order, at the two public forums. While significant differences existed in the comments evoked by the slides at the two meetings, there was one strong similarity. On both evenings, emotions soon focused on the pictures of the Tapley School (figure 40). Built in 1887 and closed by the city in the early 1970s, it had been the neighborhood elementary school, which black and white residents alike had fought unsuccessfully to have re-opened. Still owned by the city in 1991, the Tapley School was deterio-rating, and the slides of it provoked strong expressions of outrage that McKnight's children had lost their neighborhood school and were now bused throughout the city. A woman at the first public meeting declared, "I think it's a sin if you can't educate students in a building that looks like that instead of some institutional monstrosity. When I went to grade school I went to an old school. I really miss it. It has healing propor-tions."[14] Outrage over the closing of the Tapley School also surfaced in response to our showing a picture of a new citywide magnet school being built on the edge of the neighborhood. Looking at the image on the screen, another woman at the first forum insisted, "That is not a neighborhood school. It will never be the focus for any particular com-munity."[15] A black man at the second public forum stood up and ob-served, "A school is not a good alternative to economic development that can uplift a community." He then went on to give a short history of

Fig. 39. The vivid colors and McKnight banner of this restored Victorian home proclaim the owner's pride of place. Photo by Christine Thompson.

Fig. 40. The Tapley School in the McKnight Historic District as it appeared in 1991. It has since been turned into apartments. Photo by Christine Thompson.

the magnet school site, charging that although the vacant lot, located on "the most traveled street in the city of Springfield," was a prime commercial location, local banks and the Springfield Chamber of Commerce preferred to court "white developers" of the downtown office buildings rather than encourage businesses to locate in minority neighborhoods. Strong feelings of being discriminated against by the powers that ran the city also surfaced when, in response to the Tapley School slide, Marjorie Guest informed the group about a new proposal to turn the Tapley School into apartments (a proposal that later came to fruition). Everyone in the room roundly attacked the idea as yet another example of subsidized housing being forced on their neighborhood. "Why should our neighborhood become the concentration in Hampden County where only poor people live, where only minorities live?" The brick structure of the Tapley School seemed to symbolize for all their sense of powerlessness and frustration in the face of the city and state bureaucracies.[16]

Indeed the sense of place expressed in the two public meetings in McKnight—especially in contrast to the forum in Wilbraham—was that of a neighborhood fighting for its survival. It was not surprising to hear the two members of our group who lived in Wilbraham declare that McKnight, despite its elegant Victorian housing stock, was a scary place. But McKnight residents—especially those attending the first public forum—also communicated their fears, along with their day-to-day struggles to board up broken store windows, discourage drug dealers, and pressure city government to improve police response time and trash pickup. Those white McKnight residents attracted by the opportunity to restore the neighborhood's buildings to their Victorian heyday seemed to share a pioneer mentality, telling stories of their battles to reclaim the urban wilderness.[17] While they valued the cultural diversity in the neighborhood, they also vehemently defended its identity—and by extension, their own—as middle class, and indicated that the badge of that status was the ability to maintain their home. At the first public forum, someone greeted a picture of a house in poor repair with the comment, "That's a rental house, no?" to which another voice responded, "No. They just act like it's a rental." When shown a picture of a nearby housing project, the group launched into a long critique of how its architecture did not fit in with its surroundings, before one woman finally confessed, "I think maybe it's not so much that we don't like the architecture, it's that we don't like the people that were there."[18]

Significantly, the African American residents who attended the second public forum also vehemently defended McKnight's middle-class character. The slides we showed of the commercial establishments on the edge of McKnight in Winchester Square, a predominately poor neighborhood, prompted fond memories of the block's economic heyday in the 1940s and 1950s, but also a pointed reminder to us that these now struggling businesses were outside of the neighborhood boundaries, that this was not McKnight. The African American residents' pride of place was also evident in their response to our pictures of various houses in the neighborhood. Like the white residents at the first public forum, they did not hesitate to tell us their aesthetic judgments— which houses they liked or disliked, which color looked best—as well as their moral judgments concerning which owners did or did not seem up to the task of keeping their property in good repair. As one man put it, "I sincerely believe the reason why you have a good integrated community here is because of the houses. That's the primary thing, what both blacks and whites are here for."[19]

Although both the black residents of McKnight attending the second public forum and the white residents of McKnight attending the first one shared a firm belief in the importance of keeping up middle-class appearances, as well as frustration with the city's closing of the Tapley School, there was one significant difference between them. In the first forum, discussion of the neighborhood's history focused either on the Victorian era, when most of the homes were built, or on the 1980s, when whites began moving into the neighborhood to restore them. By contrast, in the second forum, African American residents talked mostly about the 1950s and 1960s, when Springfield's black community first began to make McKnight its home. Black residents responded at length to slides of the neighborhood's now boarded-up commercial strip, recalling the arrangement of each store in its heyday in the 1940s and 1950s—a drug store, a meat store, a small grocery market—an era that ended abruptly in 1968 in the aftermath of the assassination of Martin Luther King. Memories of these busy decades were also prompted by slides of the Faith Baptist Church, built in the 1960s (figure 41).

The two public forums in McKnight revealed how many different

Fig. 41. Faith Baptist Church, McKnight. The original church burned to the ground and was rebuilt in the 1960s. Photo by Christine Thompson.

senses of place can indeed inhabit the same space. For the white middle-class residents who attended the first public forum, the McKnight neighborhood seemed to offer affordable homes with historic "character" in a compact, culturally diverse setting that they perceived as more neighborly, even if more dangerous, than the postwar suburbs in which many of them had been raised. For the African American middle-class residents who attended the second public forum, McKnight's nineteenth-century homes and cultural diversity seemed less important than its meeting places, such as churches and commercial establishments, that dated from the 1950s and 1960s. These were the years when an African American community first began to flourish in McKnight, and the neighborhood continues to be the place where middle-class African Americans move from less affluent areas of Springfield. In both public forums, McKnight residents defined their local environment in terms not only of where it was but also of where it was not. For whites, McKnight was not the impersonal suburbs; for African Americans, it was not the ghetto of Winchester Square.[20]

By and large the different histories attached to the McKnight district, the white residents' story of a reclaimed Victorian heritage and the African American story of postwar economic progress, coexist peacefully. Clearly, however, when whites move into the neighborhood and "restore" its Victorian character by stripping away elements, such as chain-link fences and aluminum siding, that were added after World War II, they are also removing evidence of the African American presence there (figure 42).

Looking at our experience in all three communities, it is striking how little the physical characteristics observable to outsiders seemed to correspond with local residents' sense of connectedness to their environment and one another. Northfield's tightly clustered "colonial" settlement pattern and central historic district belied an incredible diversity of environmental perceptions and values in its different neighborhoods. Wilbraham possessed a dispersed physical settlement pattern, yet perhaps as a product of its homogeneous social characteristics, its residents seemed to possess a coherent sense of town identity: they knew who they were and why they were living in Wilbraham. McKnight, although more physically coherent as a local historic district with strict ordinances governing the exterior look of buildings, appeared more socially

Fig. 42. Teens meet on the corner in the McKnight neighborhood. The Victorian home behind them retains the aluminum windows and chain link fence added by later residents. Photo by Stan Sherer.

divided between those residents struggling to restore Victorian facades and those struggling to preserve the neighborhood social institutions developed after World War II.

These profiles of the relationship between perceptions of history and place in different Massachusetts locales suggest that we should rethink our use of the term "town character." Too often we hear it invoked by powerful interest groups seeking only to fix a community's identity in time by maintaining the local landscape in accordance with their exclusive, idealized vision of a particular historical period. Or the term appears in highly politicized situations, as when the merchants of San Francisco described the "character" of the city at play shortly before the mayoral election of 1909. If the concept of town character is to be of any use, we need to stretch its meaning to accommodate the many different environmental perceptions in a community, the social networks that make a place distinctive as well as the physical settings, and the fact that a community's identity is dynamic, changing over time. Rethinking town character in these ways not only will help us to write better local histories—reminding us to look for the multiple senses of place in a past locale, and the reasons why some environmental perceptions but not others came to prevail in local land use practices—but also will help us to develop better preservation strategies for identifying and protecting the special features of our contemporary communities.

## Historians and the Making of Historic Places

Historic preservation—known professionally as "cultural resources management"—organizes the environment into historic and nonhistoric spaces. Just as whiteness is defined by blackness, a historic district defines and is defined by its nonhistoric surroundings. Forms for nominating a historic district to the state and national register of historic places require that applicants carefully distinguish the structures that contribute to its historical significance from the "noncontributing" ones. As we have seen, however, the histories and values attached to a locale by government officials, tourists, and local residents differ. Managing cultural resources is inevitably also an effort to manage the multiplicity of memories and meanings of a place; when historians bound and mark certain places as "historic" and distinguish them from ordinary places, or decide to stabilize, to restore, or even to remodel a place "in character," which (and whose) version of community, place, and character will prevail?

We must go beyond the "science" of documenting the historical significance of places by acknowledging that the meanings of a place are socially created, multiple, and change over time. Preservation plans that plot the distribution of historic structures as patterns on the map, each contributing to the distinctive character of an area, fail to question critically the diverse meanings of the structures for local residents; too often each place and building is treated as having a single history.[21] Efforts to employ "objective" criteria when compiling an inventory of "significant" cultural resources or a register of "historic" places ignores the larger political question of adjudicating different place-values within a locale, as well as the differences between local criteria of significance and those of larger polities.

By investigating senses of place at the neighborhood level, we can identify and protect a community's memory sites as well as historic sites. Memory sites are the product of social interaction—the social networks people create that habituate them to certain places, as well as determine the flow of information about those places. Places become "memory sites" as personal and family memories attach to them via day-to-day interaction—and are validated through conversations with others. In contrast to historic sites such as those in the center of Northfield honoring the town founders, or ones that the federal government designates as important to the rise of the nation-state such as battlefields and presidential birthplaces, or the ones that local chambers of commerce designate as appealing to tourists, memory sites are places that local residents associate with their personal and family past. We discovered that even places that had undergone a dramatic physical transformation, such as the former site of the Northfield Inn, the old post office building in the "center" of Wilbraham, or the Tapley School in McKnight, continued to have a vivid presence in the minds of local residents. Randy Hester, a landscape architect and planner, describes these places made special by popular practice, rather than official designation, as "subconscious landscapes of the heart," the places that local residents feel are part of the "sacred structure" of their community.[22] Yet there is a paradox, evident in our work in all three towns: although the local residents may prefer to preserve the places associated with events that they remember personally rather than those of the remote past, historic preservation—both in legislation and practice—emphasizes the distant over the immediate past.[23] By developing new practices, such as investigating local residents' perceptions of the special places in their community, preservationists can identify and protect a category of temporary sites that connect with living memory as well as permanent ones that connect with "history."

Our efforts to define and maintain town character through historic preservation strategies must recognize the many different senses of place within a town; examine the social environment as well as the physical one; and consider town character as dynamic, incorporating change, rather than as fixed at some point in the past. We need to discover not only the historic sites that a community designates, but also the memory sites usually left unmarked—places so woven into local residents' daily lives that their special qualities remain unarticulated until it is too late to protect them.

Developing new preservation strategies that recognize the multiple senses of place in a locale is especially important when we consider the tourist relationship to the historic sites that we produce. By and large tourists look for novelty in an environment—for what they cannot see back home—while local residents look at the same environment for traces of past experiences with family and friends.[24] We must ensure that the landscapes we restore, full of the unique historical character that delights visitors, do not overwhelm the landscapes that local residents have created through their own labors over time.

## Public Programming and the Representation of Place

Public programs that foster dialogue about history and place can help local residents to articulate their environmental values and thus better protect what they value about where they live. By feeling more knowledgeable about their physical and social environment, they can enter early on into the land use planning process and help to shape where they live according to their conception of the kind of place where they would like to live. In the process, they create pressure to make planning and land use decisions more open and democratic. Public forums such as those in Northfield, Wilbraham, and McKnight offer opportunities not only for public officials to explain what they do but also for various elements of the community to speak and, ideally, for the planners and government officials to listen.

In designing public programs to elicit the memories attached to local places, we must ensure that the multiple voices of the community be represented; even in apparently homogeneous towns or neighborhoods, the residents have many different senses of place. The different neighborhoods of Northfield offer one example of this; so do the different black and white perceptions of McKnight, and the differences between longtime residents of Wilbraham who lived close to the quiet town center and more recent arrivals living in condominiums near the commercial strip on Route 20—a neighborhood not even represented in the pictures we took. Preservationists can go well beyond what our study group accomplished by exploring further the diverse views of town character among different populations. How might interviewing children, young parents, or recently settled residents in Wilbraham have yielded different results? What do renters, the majority of McKnight residents, think about their neighborhood?

Photography is an incredibly powerful tool for discovering environmental values and underlying historical associations in a community. Since most local residents are unaccustomed to articulating their environmental likes and dislikes, a series of photographic images, with as much variety as possible regarding season, time of day, and content, helps to evoke their preferences. Demonstrating the tenet that sense of place is not intrinsic to an environment but the product of social interaction, the photographs that prompted the most conversations at our public meetings were ones that included people as well as buildings. Stan Sherer shot half of his images of McKnight in black and white, explaining, "In black and white you begin to see the people more than the place" (figure 43).[25] Photographers should pay particular attention to the places where local residents gather. Instead of using a professional

Fig. 43. Dancing children, McKnight. Photo by Stan Sherer.

photographer for this purpose, historians might organize a community photographic project in which local residents are loaned inexpensive cameras (or handed disposable ones) to take pictures of the sites they regard as important in their town or neighborhood. The residents could then share and compare these images at a public meeting. At the same time that project organizers collect the cameras to develop the images for the meeting, they can offer to copy any older photographs the residents might have of memorable places that no longer exist. Displaying a combination of older and newer images allows those present at the public forum to consider how their town or neighborhood has changed over time.

Public programs such as photographic projects emphasize that a community's sense of place and history are actively made, not passively received. Among the other kinds of activities that can make and remake places are schoolchildren's interviewing older residents about the local past; neighborhood walking tours led by local residents; and public art projects such as Boston's "Arts in Transit," in which neighborhood oral historians collaborated with artists in developing the public art that was installed at each station along the MTA's Orange Line.[26] Historians may find that the challenge of depicting the history of a place—how to present multiple points of view in a single narrative—may be more easily met through the creation of public programs that involve various local groups than through the writing of books or journal articles.

But is it enough to devise public programs that simply evoke the multiple senses of history and place in a community? Or do historians have a role in actively shaping how the residents think about the places where they live and work, to help them understand where they live in a political sense as well as an emotional one? We cannot forget that the various senses of place in a community reflect not only its residents' emotional attachments to the local environment but also their position in a larger economic and political system. In the public forums in the three communities, there emerged an underlying sense that perceived threats to town character—whether new development in Northfield, the runaway post office in Wilbraham, or the vacant Tapley School in McKnight—resulted from actions beyond local control.

Representing the powerful outside forces that shaped what local residents have come to think of as their backyard should be as integral to historians' public programs about place as recording and presenting local residents' memories. In 1992, the Bostonian Society opened an exhibition, titled "The Last Tenement," that in addition to evoking fond memories of Boston's West End in the 1920s and 1930s, critically examined the public policies that had resulted in the neighborhood's destruction as part of an urban renewal project in the 1950s. The exhibition explored why the West End was demolished, as well as how the social connections among its former residents have been kept alive by their memories of the neighborhood.[27] In Los Angeles, the "Power of Place" project of the mid-1980s identified and marked sites associated with the achievements of local women, non-Anglos, and the working class, and then developed public programs, brochures, and guided tours that located the sites in a larger social and political history of the city. Dolores Hayden, the project's director, explained that such public programs make visible previously obscured spaces and the history they represent as well as interpret the built environment in terms of a "dynamic, aesthetic, social, and economic history of the production of space."[28] Public programs about local history should strive to encourage a progressive, forward-looking sense of place rather than merely evoking a nostalgic and reactionary one, helping local residents to expand their environmental perception to include not only the multiplicity of memories that inhabit the landscape but also the political, economic, and social relations that created it. The powerful relationships that transform environments often remain invisible because they are seen as "natural" forces, or originate outside of the confines of neighborhood or town.[29] Historians can participate in the process of placemaking and contribute to local residents' sense of place by adding a critical sense of location to local residents' sentimental sense of emotional attachment, helping residents to see what ordinarily cannot be seen: not just the memories attached to places but the larger social and economic processes that shaped how the places were made.

Public historical programming can even explore the larger social, economic, and cultural processes that have made some places "historic" but not others. Throughout the twentieth century, the desire to promote tourism as a tool of economic development has exerted pressure for towns to create more historic sites. Rather than simply signing off on all of these sites, historians might examine with the public why towns seek tourism in the first place. If there were still a vibrant textile industry in Lowell, Massachusetts, would the mill complex have been set aside as a historical attraction? Just as in the late nineteenth century Yellowstone became a national park because the railroads made the case that its land had greater economic value as a scenic attraction for tourists than as a source of timber and minerals, so too the hundreds of historic sites that Americans established in the century that followed have been subject to the market forces that determine how land is used in America. Public programs interpreting "points of historical interest" could investigate with the public not only the points and their histories but also the interests involved in their creation. Why, and for whom, did this place become a historic place?

In a time when real estate developers and local chambers of commerce invite us to think about the character of where we live primarily in terms of the edge it can offer in marketing our community to outsiders, we can develop histories that encourage local dialogue about the nonmaterial value of particular places. Through such dialogues about history and place, incorporated into public programs and preservation strategies, Americans can become more aware of their own particular connection to the local environment and one another. Beyond that, dialogue about history and place can expand our fields of perception to recognize the different senses of place and history of our neighbors, as well as to discover the common ground that will allow us to act on environmental issues of common concern.

# 7

# Making Places in California

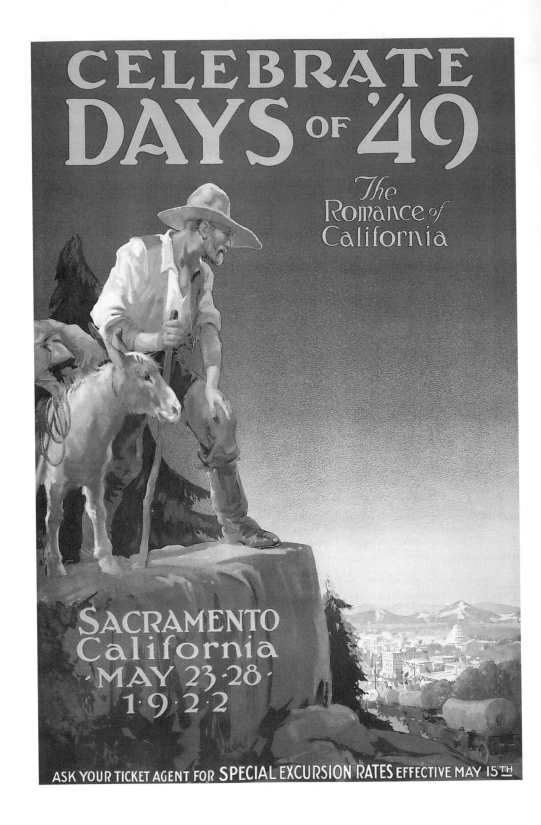

Fig. 44. Poster for the "Days of '49" celebration in Sacramento in 1922. Courtesy of the California History Room, California State Library, Sacramento.

ONE YEAR after completing my report to the Massachusetts Foundation for the Humanities on town character in New England, I moved to the Central Valley of California. This was where I wanted to be. I was married to a Californian, and thanks to a one-year fellowship from the National Endowment for the Humanities and the hospitality of the history department at the University of California at Davis, our children finally would be able to spend time near their maternal grandparents, who lived in Grass Valley, just on the other side of Sacramento. I wanted to expand my research and writing about the relationship between Americans' sense of history and place, and I looked forward both to reading and reflecting on my past public history projects (and writing this book) and to conducting a new special places project in California similar to the ones that I had undertaken in New England. As I surveyed my new surroundings in the fall of 1993, two sites attracted my attention. One was Old Sacramento, a restored historic area downtown that, like the McKnight district of Springfield, had gone through a number of physical and demographic changes in recent years. The neighborhood was formerly Sacramento's Chinatown, and the Sacramento Museum of History, Science and Technology was developing an exhibition on the history of Chinese immigrants to Sacramento scheduled to open in April. I anticipated that the oral histories that would be conducted as part of the research for the exhibit could give me fascinating examples of how memories attach to places. The other potential site was Nevada City, a small town near my in-laws in Grass Valley. Nevada City was an old mining town, a compact, postcard-perfect representation of the old West, and had an active preservation organization that kept it that way. I thought that like Northfield, it would be a good place to explore the differences between the senses of history of local residents and the history presented to outsiders.

Initial interest on the part of local institutions, however, did not develop into projects that I could join. The Sacramento museum turned over the development of the exhibition to a committee of prominent local Chinese Americans, who made "The Legacy of Gold Mountain: A History of the Chinese in Sacramento" into a marvelous celebration of the progress that their families had made as they moved out from the cloistered city neighborhood to the surrounding suburban metropolis. But the exhibition organizers showed little interest in exploring the history of the neighborhood they left behind. The members of the Nevada City Historical Society felt that they already knew where the community's special places were and did not need to hold public meetings or neighborhood conversations to find out. Initially disappointed, I decided to focus my research instead on a question that did not depend on the cooperation of contemporary communities—that, in fact, contemporary communities took for granted: how did the historic places in California towns such as Sacramento and Nevada City get to be historic in the first place?

Looking for history-mindedness in California cuts across the American grain. After all, for much of American history, California has represented a land of new opportunities, a place where Americans move to escape the past, not to find it. And if length of residence and the age of physical surroundings—time to have memories of significant life experiences attach to places—is crucial to a sense of history, then statistics bear out the thinness of California's soil for nurturing historical consciousness. For most of its history, less than one-third of California residents were born in-state, compared with the two-thirds or so of Massachusetts residents.[1] While long periods of economic stagnation in the twentieth century have left much of the Massachusetts landscape dense with abandoned farms turned to forest and textile mills turned to empty shells, Californians live in environments constantly remade in the near-constant boom times since World War II. The unique character of the New England town appears to embody centuries of tradition; by contrast, the California landscape appears to have sprung up yesterday, the material expression of a people rootless, placeless, always in flux.[2] These circumstances, along with the tendency to date history from the first English settlement, contribute to Massachusetts's reputation as an "old state" whose residents purportedly have a large number of historic sites and place attachments, and to California's reputation as a "new state" whose residents purportedly have a scrambled sense of history manifested in a paucity of historic sites and places to anchor their memories. Even Joan Didion, a Sacramento native whose family has lived in California for generations, admits that she grew up feeling that history always happened somewhere else. "In California," she recalled in 1993, "we did not believe that history could bloody the land, or even touch it."[3]

Still, many aspects of the place of the past in California resemble that in Massachusetts and the rest of the United States. We have already seen how at the same time that cities in the East and Midwest used public celebrations to underscore the English and Protestant heritage of their communities amid an influx of Irish, Italian, and eastern European immigrants, San Francisco's business leaders launched a Portolá Festival that celebrated the aristocratic Spanish colonial past in reaction to labor unrest and the influx of Asian and Mexican immigrants to the city. In the 1940s, at the same time that the Wells family in Massachusetts created Old Sturbridge Village, a collection of early nineteenth-century buildings brought to a site near Route 20 to ensure easy access for automobile tourists, Bakersfield and San Jose developed new "pioneer villages" alongside the freeway featuring collections of historic buildings rescued from their booming downtowns—and of course, Walt Disney's historic Main Street USA was under construction in Anaheim. Contemporary Californians enjoy participating in Civil War reenactments and watching historical films such as the Ken Burns series as intensely as their counterparts in other regions of the United States.[4]

Between 1850 and 1940, as elsewhere in America, Californians came to identify certain otherwise ordinary places in their environment as historic. Tracing the development of historic space in California reveals much about the unique place of the past in California on which Joan

Didion and so many other writers have commented. It also reveals something of the racial politics of the state, as "Anglo" Californians from a variety of northern European backgrounds assumed the power to define particular environments as "historic" for the rest of society, and came to identify themselves with a "white" pioneer heritage.[5] And, despite California's reputation as the "great exception," it reveals much about the way that a sense of history has been embedded in the American landscape in other places and times.

## Pioneer Memories

When the forty-niners arrived in search of gold, there were no recognized historical places in California. The Spanish missions cultivated memory gardens and maintained cemeteries that reminded priests and parishioners of their religious predecessors, and Miwok and other Indians knew of sites such as Chaw'se, a massive grinding rock containing physical evidence of aboriginal use over many centuries.[6] But in the minds of the newcomers, these places did not count. Certain that they were in the vanguard of the nation's westward expansion, voyagers to California at midcentury saw themselves in a "new land," one that, in the words of the historian Elliot West, was "no past and all possibilities."[7] They recognized other people's history on the land only selectively, as when the purchasers of large Mexican rancherias defended the titles of the land's former owners against federal officials who would have opened them for homesteading.[8]

The newcomers saw the California landscape as barren of history, but their mental world was full of places elsewhere that they remembered. The forty-niners' sense of place included an intense consciousness of where they were not, as well as of where they were, and from time to time, they gathered to celebrate the history of these other, now distant places. As early as 1847 the Sons of New England held a Thanksgiving dinner in San Francisco; in 1850 they dined in Sacramento, where they petitioned the new state government to make Thanksgiving a California holiday. The following year in December they celebrated "Forefathers' Day," the anniversary of the landing of the Pilgrims. A newspaper reported that the assembly lingered in thought "among blessed scenes of childhood" as well as honored the great names of the *Mayflower*.[9] Such events made the memory of home places far away the basis for a new social bond.

Another California organization, the Society of California Pioneers, appealed to its members' growing attachment to their new locale. The society first appeared in August 1850 when a group of fifty "earliest residents" marched as a unit in a procession upon the death of President Zachary Taylor. The society's constitution distinguished these early residents from the forty-niners who followed, assigning first-class status to those arriving before 1849 and second-class status to those arriving before 1850. Although the society's constitution mentions historical purposes of the organization, and the duty of members to "collect and preserve information connected with the early settlement and subsequent conquest of the country"—like those of pioneer societies established in the Midwest and the plains in this period—there is little doubt that the primary purpose of the society in its early years was social.[10]

The sense of geographic isolation in the 1850s and 1860s was palpable; away from their family members in the East, the main order of business of the pioneer societies, like other fraternal organizations in California, was for their members to bury one another and provide for one another's relief. The bylaws of the Sacramento Society of California Pioneers, founded 1854, required members to attend one another's funerals.[11] The pioneer societies played an important social role in perpetuating memories of the departed, and their cemeteries often became the first designated memorial spaces in a community.[12]

Still, but for the scattered pioneer graves, California Gold Rush communities offered little evidence of having a past. At least that's the way Professor Josiah Royce of Harvard recalled the Grass Valley of his childhood during the 1850s and 1860s, a "community that had no history behind it, except the history of the individual fortunes of its members and of their families." Writing in 1909, Royce theorized that the many different people drawn to California by the Gold Rush lived uninfluenced by local memories; there had been "little social memory in the community." "The community as an organized body was unable to form an idea of a past that it could call its own." Royce attributed this to the fact that "one's memories, and usually one's hopes, lay elsewhere." "Home was not here." Royce's essay celebrated the rise of "provincialism" in California, the gradual process through which the settlers who decided to remain in towns such as Grass Valley eventually developed distinctive customs and a sense of community with a shared local history.[13] These were the settlers who planted orchards instead of extracting gold and moving on, who replaced the disreputable social world of the miners with morally sturdy family farms, who labored mightily to make great changes in the land and later would proudly identify themselves and their history with those changes.[14]

But the first Californians to visualize Gold Rush towns as historic were not the ones that Royce celebrated, who put down roots and transformed the land, but rather native sons and daughters like Royce himself who left and remembered how the towns used to be. Historic sites first existed in the minds and conversations of former Gold Country residents and their families, a substantial segment of the state's population in the 1870s–1910s. California's ever-upward curve of population gain conceals that between 1860 and 1870 nearly one out of four California counties lost population. Calaveras County plummeted from 16,299 to 8,895; Tuolumne from 16,229 to 8,150; El Dorado from 20,562 to 10,309. Though the population of these counties declined less precipitously in the 1870s and 1880s, and even increased somewhat in the 1890s, it dropped sharply again in the years 1900–1920. Calaveras County fell from 11,200 to 6,183 between 1900 and 1920; Tuolumne dropped from 11,166 to 7,768; Nevada from 17,789 to 10,850; Amador from 11,116 to 7,793; El Dorado from 8,986 to 6,426. The end of the Gold Rush and the migration from town to city, created a landscape of abandoned homes and depleted towns. Remembered by former residents in the stories they told their children, the places became, as for Royce, historic: material embodiments of memories and social ideals rather than the sites of contemporary activities.

Stories of the old Gold Rush towns circulated during the regular reunions of their departed residents. Former residents of Tuolumne County began holding annual picnic reunions in the San Francisco area as early as 1867; in 1869, eighty met in Alameda Park and organized the Tuolumne Pioneer Association (formally incorporated in 1876). Former residents of El Dorado County met to organize the Pioneers of El Dorado County in 1870; those from Placer County began meeting in 1871; the Old Calaveras Association began in 1872; former residents of Nevada County began annual reunion picnics in 1876. Bay area papers remarked that the annual reunions at Badger's Park in Oakland drew residents scattered from throughout the state, who gathered to hear speeches, renew acquaintances, and share stories about where they used to live. "Here and there might be seen groups of men and women of the older sort, occupying some shady grass plot, recounting the scenes and events of the early days in the mountains, and many a thrilling adventure, long since forgotten, was dragged up from the weary recesses of failing memories to become prominent features in the nursery tales of their posterity."[15] Places were given an existence in memory at these gatherings that they may never have had in the past, and certainly did not have in the present.

The pioneers' memories of the Gold Rush were colored not only by the passage of time but also by the popular literature of the period. Indeed, through the 1870s and 1880s, the literary efforts of former residents, especially Mark Twain and Bret Harte, played an important role in fixing certain places in the Mother Lode in the memory and imagination of those who had left (or had never been there). So did the works of the San Francisco author and publisher Hubert Howe Bancroft. Bancroft's agents collected "Dictations" from pioneers, which he employed throughout the latter volumes of his *History of California*, published between 1884 and 1890.[16] But widespread attempts to visit and mark these "storied" places as historical would not occur until a later generation.

Indeed, unlike the former residents of rural New England towns who returned for annual visits during Old Home Weeks, the members of the California pioneer societies seemed much more comfortable celebrating their old haunts from a distance, away from the physical settings where so many had earlier gone bust. In 1890, the Society of California Pioneers of New England, a Boston-based organization consisting of "the men or the children of the men who went to California prior to 1860" (figure 45) insisted on chartering an excursion train to the sites of their former western adventures. Consisting of twelve Pullman cars, two dining cars, and 150 passengers (90 men and 60 women), the group began its California visit by joining the local pioneer societies in San Bernardino and Los Angeles in acting out rituals recalling the Gold Country where they had used to live. In Pasadena, mimicking the Bret Harte stories, they participated in a "Roaring Camp" in which they dressed as old miners, panned for gold in the Arroyo Seco, purchased "drinks" in a "saloon" with "gold dust," and settled a mock dispute over a poker game with six-shooters.[17]

But after the warm ritual recollections of the Gold Rush with their fellow pioneers in southern California, the trip north to Sacramento and the actual sites of former activities was more than a little disturbing. The

Fig. 45. *New England Associated California Pioneers of '49*, by George G. Spurr, ca. 1890. Toned lithograph, 22 15/16 x 18 1/8 in. Amon Carter Museum, Fort Worth, Texas, Acc. no. 1978.11. The relationship between this group, organized in Boston in 1889, and the Society of California Pioneers of New England, organized in Boston the previous year, remains unclear.

men vainly searched for their old camps and cabins; they marveled at the enormous physical changes wrought by agriculture, and remarked consistently that they could not recognize where they were. Nicholas Ball rode out to Rattlesnake Bar to view the claim he had mined forty years earlier but could not find it; "only one thing looked natural—a rock in the [American] river near the bar, from which I shot many an otter in 1850 and 1851." Charles Stumcke wrote his son that when he tried to visit his old diggings near Auburn, he could not find anyone left who had lived there in 1849 or 1850. Another New England Pioneer, riding the train through the same area on his way back East, remarked on how the landscape looked totally unfamiliar. Hills formerly covered with chaparral and black jack oak had been washed away by hydraulic mining, or else were now covered by fruit trees, vineyards, and fields of grass and grain. The Pioneers experienced at the end of their journey in northern California feelings not of homecoming but of displacement—that the material basis of their memories had all but disappeared.[18]

It was this sentiment—that the physical world they had once known was disappearing along with the comrades who had shared their memories—that propelled the members of the California pioneer societies' first historic preservation efforts. In 1890, the same year as the New Englanders' visit, the California societies dedicated a permanent monument to James W. Marshall in Coloma, the site of his famous gold discovery (figure 46), and launched a campaign to protect Sutter's Fort in Sacramento from the extension of a city street through the site.

## Native Sons and Daughters

But the biggest push to preserve Gold Rush memories as marked historic places in California came not from the men of the pioneer societies, but from their children, organized into chapters of the Native Sons and Daughters of the Golden West. The Native Sons was organized in 1875; chapters quickly formed throughout California, with the largest membership in the Bay area, among men who knew the Gold Country primarily through their parents' stories. The Native Daughters, founded in Jackson, Amador County, in 1886 (figure 47) soon counted twenty-four local "parlors" (chapters) stretching down to Los Angeles and San Diego, with over half in the Bay area. Membership in the Native Daughters climbed steadily, from less than 2,000 in 1890 to over 5,000 by 1904, and over 14,000 by 1928.[19] Like the Society of California Pioneers, both the Native Sons and Native Daughters of the Golden West functioned primarily as fraternal organizations with elaborate rituals and regalia, at the same time that they tried to keep alive the memory of their parents' deeds.

Fig. 46. With an appropriation from the state legislature, California pioneer societies erected this monument to James W. Marshall in 1890 near the site of his gold discovery at Coloma. Courtesy of the California History Room, California State Library, Sacramento.

Fig. 47. Native Daughters of the Golden West dedicating a plaque on the building where the organization was founded, Jackson (Amador County), California, 1932. Courtesy of the California History Room, California State Library, Sacramento.

The Native Daughters launched the first statewide effort to locate and mark historic places. At their "Grand Parlor" (annual convention) in 1898, the Daughters resolved to begin functioning as "local history and landmarks clubs" and to make "preserving landmarks" a principal activity along with collecting California legends, facts, pictures, and mementos. By the following year the Daughters had appointed a Historical Landmarks Committee chaired by Eliza D. Keith, a schoolteacher from San Francisco, which appealed to each local chapter to mark the historic spots in its community with a monument, tablet, or tree. And in 1901 the Native Daughters launched a survey, asking the local parlors to list not only any residents of their county "who may justly be considered historical personages, that is, who in the early days helped to make or to form history," but also any "historical landmarks." Keith's instructions were quite specific: "If there be landmarks, state whether they are natural features or artificial. In case they are natural features, say whether they are trees, hills, or what; by whom now owned, what traditions cling to them, and on what authority. . . . If the landmarks be artificial, give the character of them, whether monuments, houses, churches, etc.; by whom owned, state of preservation, cost of acquisition, etc."[20]

Of the eighty or so Native Daughters parlors in existence in 1901, twenty responded, and Keith mentions three in her 1902 report. As with women's organizations in other parts of the United States, the Native Daughters saw landmarks work as part of an overall program of town improvement; in Ventura, preservation activities went hand in hand with planting shade trees and placing rubbish boxes along Main Street. Few of the survey respondents noted natural features—the Santa Barbara parlor singled out the San Ynez mountains as memorable because General John Charles Frémont and his men had passed across them during the Mexican War. Several other parlors in the southern part of the state mentioned missions, which since 1896 had become the object of preservation efforts by Charles Fletcher Lummis and the Historical Landmarks Club of Southern California. In response to the call for historic personages, many chapters simply sent in Pioneer Society membership rosters; the twenty-five living persons mentioned by name in Keith's report included twenty-one men (such as Juan de Mata Pico of Santa Barbara, identified as "the connecting link between the old days and the present") and four women—Jessie Benton Frémont, the widow of John Frémont, and Patty Reed Lewis, Eliza Donner Houghton, and Frances Donner Wilder, the three surviving members of the Donner party's ill-fated passage over the Sierra in the winter of 1846–47.[21]

The preservationists' sense of urgency stemmed from the fear not only that the material props for remembering their ancestors would disappear but also that new and different memories would inhabit these places. In 1909, one Native Daughter lamented that despite the presence of the Marshall Monument in Coloma, the site of the gold discovery was unknown by the present generation of residents: "We wander into the vale of Coloma today and what do we see? Practically a sandy cobbly waste, on the outskirts are possibly a half-dozen rose embowered cottages, occupied by no more than a score of people, the half of whom are black. . . . We ask the denizens to direct us to the site where once stood the historic saw mill, white nor black, not one of them could do it."[22] New residents, unappreciative of the former settlers, were transforming the environment and bringing new and different memories to the sites.

To raise the visibility of their efforts, in 1902 the Native Daughters and Federation of Women's Clubs joined with men's organizations to form the California Historical Landmarks League (figure 48). As with many reform societies in the Progressive era, the formation of a gender-mixed organization marked the organization's passage from a primarily fraternal and sororal function to one of public action. Despite the central role of the Native Daughters, women were only two of seven officers and five of eleven members of the board of directors of the new organization. Eliza Keith shrewdly noted the sexual division of labor that had arisen in history work; while women could "mold public opinion," men had the business and political connections for effective fund-raising.[23]

Many of the powerful men Keith referred to belonged to the Native Sons of the Golden West, and its Historical Landmarks Committee, chaired by Joseph Russell Knowland. Gold Rush and family history certainly intersected for Knowland, who was born in Alameda in 1873, the youngest child of Joseph Knowland and Hannah Bailey Russell. Knowland's father had arrived in the goldfields of Placer County from Long Island at age twenty-four in 1857 but soon moved to San Francisco and entered the lumber business; Hannah Russell, born in Maine, had followed her sister to California in 1863.[24] In a memoir written in 1961, Joseph Russell Knowland traced his interest in California history to hearing the stories his father and mother told in his early childhood, remarking that he could not remember a time when Gold Rush history was not part of his life. Knowland joined the Native Sons at age eighteen, a decision that clearly served his political ambitions as well as his love of history; his rise in the Native Sons paralleled his election to the California State Assembly at age twenty-five, the State Senate at age twenty-nine, and the U.S. Congress at age thirty-one, where he served until 1914. Unsuccessful in his campaign for the U.S. Senate that year, Knowland returned to Oakland and purchased the *Oakland Tribune*. All the while, despite his duties in Washington, he chaired the Native Sons' Historical Landmarks Committee and in 1910, at age thirty-seven, served as Grand President of the entire organization. Knowland remained chair of the Historical Landmarks Committee for the next fifty years, and in this and other capacities would be the single most influential figure in the making of historic places in California.

Not surprisingly, the Native Sons and Daughters first sought to identify and mark places that honored their parents' generation, the Pioneers. In the 1890s, besides building the Marshall Monument in

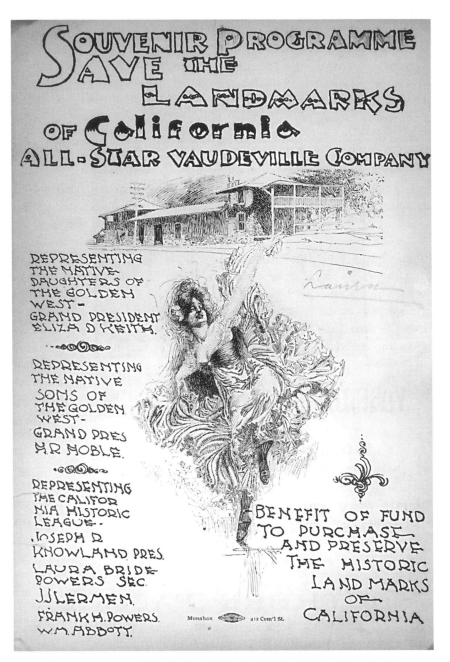

Fig. 48. Souvenir program of a fund-raiser held by the California Historic Landmarks League in 1903. The building depicted is the Customs House in Monterey. California Historical Society, North Baker Research Library, California Ephemera, FN-32081.

Coloma and restoring Sutter's Fort in Sacramento, Native Sons began raising funds for a massive Pioneer monument in memory of the Donner Party, a project not completed until 1918 (figure 49). Most of their markers were more modest, such as a monument in Rich Bar, Plumas County, dedicated "In memory of the pioneers, especially Nancy Ann Bailey, pioneer mother who died in 1851." They placed a historical marker bearing the words "In memory of the bravery of our pioneer officers" near Placerville at "Bullion Bend," the site of a stagecoach robbery in 1869. The Native Sons and Daughters' efforts stimulated others to mark sites as well. In 1909, tourists at the Kirkwood Lodge in Amador County contributed money to erect a monument at a nearby site known simply as the "Maiden's Grave." They believed it was the burial place of Rachel Melton, who had died in 1850 en route from Iowa in a covered wagon. Subsequent research has shown that the particular grave they marked was actually that of a young man.[25]

The Native Sons and Daughters not only marked places corresponding to their parents' pioneer stories, but also sites that linked the political history of California to that of the nation. Like other hereditary organizations in the 1890s, such as the Daughters of the American Revolution, the Native Sons and Daughters emphasized American nationalism and flag worship, and enthusiastically joined in send-offs and welcome-homes for California units that fought in the Spanish-American War. Admission Day, a holiday originated by the Pioneer societies to commemorate the anniversary of California statehood, became the occasion for ever more elaborate public celebrations every September. The Native Sons and Daughters' burst of nationalism in the 1890s gained spatial expression throughout California: of the first fifteen places that received historical markers from the Native Sons, seven related to the Mexican War and the state's subsequent admission to the Union. In 1896 the NSGW erected a monument in front of the Customs House in Monterey where Commodore John Sloat first raised the American flag in 1846, and in 1905 they placed a plaque on the building. Even natural features could be remembered as Mexican War sites; as noted above, the Santa Barbara parlor of the Native Daughters had reported that the San Ynez mountains derived their historical significance from Frémont. Perhaps the Native Sons and Daughters' emphasis on Mexican War sites was to make up for the lack of Civil War and Revolutionary War sites in California. Patriotic and hereditary so-

Fig. 49. The dedication of the Pioneer monument at Donner Lake, June 1918. Standing at the base of the monument, between governors Emmett Boyle of Nevada and W. D. Stephens of California, are Patty Reed Lewis, Eliza Donner Houghton, and Frances Donner Wilder, three survivors of the Donner party. Photo by E. Hess, 1918; © California State Parks.

cieties across America in the 1890s felt the challenge of making citizens feel a part of the nation, but perhaps more so in California than in New England or the mid-Atlantic states, regions less physically removed from the sacred sites associated with events of national history. On the 119th anniversary of the Battle of Lexington, April 19, 1894, the San Francisco chapter of the DAR placed a "Liberty Tree" in Golden Gate Park, planting a sequoia in soil gathered from Lexington and other Revolutionary War battlefields as well as from the grave of Lafayette.[26]

## Padres and Indians

When the Daughters of the American Revolution erected their first historic monument in California, however, it was neither to remember descendants of Revolutionary War soldiers who had emigrated west nor to glorify California's role in the history of the nation. On June 17, 1914, members of the Copa de Ora chapter dedicated a marker in Lincoln Park, Alameda, to the memory of 450 Indians whose remains had been discovered six years earlier when a burial mound of shells one thousand feet to the west had been leveled to provide fill for roads (figure 50). Speaking at the monument dedication was Thomas Waterman, an anthropologist from the University of California, who brought along Ishi, a Yahi found living in the wild three years earlier, to unveil the marker.[27]

It was not unusual in this period for "Anglos" like the women of the DAR to mark historic places connected with events before their ancestors' arrival. Besides Indian burial grounds, the most celebrated of these places were the missions, which Californians sought to preserve as part of a larger Spanish colonial revival at the turn of the century. The mission movement in southern California actually predated the Native Sons and Daughters' preservation efforts in the Mother Lode by a few years; Charles Fletcher Lummis, editor of the magazine *Land of Sunshine* and a tireless promoter of the romantic charm of the "Spanish" southwest, founded the Historical Landmarks Club of Southern California in 1896. In 1904, Mrs. A. S. C. Forbes of Los Angeles, chair of the California History and Landmarks Department of the state Federation of Women's Clubs, organized the El Camino Real Association to place mission bells along the old coastal highway that linked the missions.[28] Tourists seeking the places they read about in Helen Hunt Jackson's popular novel *Ramona* (1884) also raised the visibility of the missions. In 1910 the St. James Hotel in San Diego restored "Ramona's Marriage Place" and marked it with an iron sign.[29] Joseph Russell Knowland and the Native Sons, though primarily interested in Gold Rush history in the north, also raised money for mission preservation through their involvement in the California Historical Landmarks League, aided by publicity and dollars furnished by the newspaper publisher William Randolph Hearst.[30]

The preservationists were not above using economic arguments for creating historic places. In arguing for the preservation of Mission Santa Inez, Native Daughter Laura Bride Powers noted that "historic spots have an economic value, wholly aside from their ethical or esthetic worth, as the wise old nations of Europe long ago recognized. Picture what France or Italy would be if their places of historical interest were wiped out, would tourists continue to flood them?"[31]

But the preservationists had an ambivalent relationship with California's Spanish and Catholic past. As part of a fund-raising appeal in 1905, the California Historical Landmarks League offered a picture of Mis-

Fig. 50. Daughters of the American Revolution dedicating a plaque in memory of the prehistoric Indians of Alameda, California, on June 17, 1914. Ishi, the Yahi, stands in the center. Courtesy of the California History Room, California State Library, Sacramento.

Fig. 51. Copies of this photograph of Mission San Antonio de Padua taken circa 1903 were sold to raise money for its restoration. Posing in front is Dona Perfecta Encinal, a descendant of the Indians who originally lived at the mission. According to Knowland, Indian laborers participated in the mission's restoration, which began in 1903 and was completed in 1907. From Joseph Knowland, *California: A Landmark History* (Oakland: Tribune Press, 1941), p. 8.

sion San Antonio de Padua in a state of collapse, which it sold for $1.25 each as an artistic view suitable for framing (figure 51). Unlike the Catholic Church, which sought to restore the missions as functional buildings, the Native Sons and Daughters sought to preserve the missions in a state of picturesque, arrested decay. Knowland declared flatly that "It was better to allow the old missions of California to crumble than to attempt modernization."[32]

The preservationists' ambivalent relationship to the Spanish past also was evident in the process of restoring Sutter's Fort in the 1890s. The same newspaper article that lamented the poor condition of Spanish-era adobe buildings throughout the state praised the "true Spanish generosity" of Marino Malarin of Monterey, who ordered the old Olarte building in his city demolished so that its clay tiles could be reused in the restoration of the Sacramento landmark.[33]

## Roots in Nature

Californians sought antiquity in the landscape from another source—the preservation of giant sequoias and coastal redwoods. While advocates for the preservation of big trees followed in the footsteps of John Muir by arguing that they offered Californians an ecstatic communion with timeless nature, the big trees were also celebrated as California's "living link in history." Preservation campaigns referred to the trees as California's ancient inheritance. In 1920, Madison Grant, a prominent nativist who had gained fame four years earlier for his call for eugenics and immigration restriction in *The Passing of the Great Race*, wrote an article for the Save the Redwoods League that compared cutting down redwoods to "breaking up one's grandfather clock for kindling" or "lighting one's pipe with a Greek manuscript." Enos Mills, a prominent nature writer best known for his advocacy to establish Rocky Mountain National Park, declared the sequoia "the earth's oldest living settler—the pioneer of pioneers."[34]

Big trees were named, labeled, and displayed like historical relics.

Fig. 52. After this 300-foot redwood tree fell in Humbolt County in 1987, a cross section was cut and important dates in Anglo-American history were marked across its trunk. Postcard purchased 1994. Photo by Bob von Normann; © FVN Inc., Redcrest, California.

Often, important dates were marked on a cross section of a fallen tree so as to make the tree tell of important events in Anglo-American history: the birth of Christ, the signing of the Magna Carta, the Pilgrim landing on Plymouth Rock, the inauguration of George Washington (figure 52). Such displays, by proxy, established an ancient Anglo-Saxon presence in the land.[35]

The redwoods and sequoias also became associated with the memory of more recent historical events. Many of the big trees on the coast were preserved in the decade after World War I as part of memorial groves commemorating individuals who died in the war. Trees also served as war memorials in the cities; in 1921, to honor World War veterans, the DAR planted a "Victory Memorial Grove" in Elysian Park, Los Angeles, while the Native Sons created a "Grove of Memory" in Golden Gate Park, San Francisco.[36]

In addition, memorial plaques were used to transform Native American burial grounds, Spanish missions, and big trees into historical relics for "Anglo" Californians, offering them an enduring presence in the land that predated the arrival of their biological ancestors. The most important part of such plaques was the name of the organization at the bottom, by which a group marked a site as its own, inserting itself into the history being commemorated. In contrast to the family history integral to the making of Gold Country memory sites, which implied, "Let us present our history to you as your history," the making of big trees, Indian burial grounds, and Spanish missions into historical spaces suggested, "Let us present the history of the land in such a way that we can place ourselves as its possessors and guardians." Stewardship, whether of a Pioneer cabin, a redwood tree, or a Spanish mission, also declared one's possession of a site.

## Bret Harte Country

*The pioneers were the real thing! Yet such is the nature of this topsy-turvy world, the copies will remain, whilst the originals will fade away and be forgotten.*

—Thomas Beasley, 1914

In 1914, Thomas Beasley published *A Tramp through Bret Harte Country*. The travel writer admitted that the title of his account had an ironic quality, because Bret Harte, having left California in 1871, "never realized the transition from mining to agriculture and horticulture as the leading industries of the state." Beasley found Sonora "the center of a prosperous agricultural district," and Coloma "a sweet and peaceful little hamlet" devoted to horticulture. "So far as the *new* Coloma is concerned, Marshall's discovery might never have been made. Nowhere else will you find a spot where gold and what it stands for would seem to mean so little."[37] Yet even though the miners and pioneers had left these areas, the stories about them remained, and Beasley, like other travel writers, used these stories to make visible the Gold Rush landscape that the orchards and ranches had superseded.

In the years since the California Pioneers of New England grand excursion of 1890, accounts of visits to the Mother Lode by train and carriage had become a staple of travel literature. Articles in *Sunset* and *Overland Monthly* narrated travelers' adventures, pointing out what to do and where to stay in a region they commonly identified as "Bret Harte Country." Like Beasley's book, several articles took as their theme the quest for the actual places that Bret Harte had written about in his stories.[38]

On May 19, 1922, the Native Sons' Historical Landmarks Committee embarked on a pilgrimage to "locate and temporarily mark the most noted historic spots . . . made famous by the writings of Bret Harte and Mark Twain."[39] Most of the party hailed from the Bay area, like their leader, Joseph Knowland. Over the next five days, they temporarily marked one hundred sites with wooden signs and numbers, such as "the old Fandango Dance Hall" in the town of Hornitos and the "site of the old Mark Twain cabin" on Jackass Hill near Tuttletown.[40] The group attached the label "old" to sixty-nine of the sites they marked, a renaming that connoted the place's value as well as obsolescence. One member of the party, Harry C. Peterson of the California State Library, reported that when the "pilgrims" arrived in Angel's Camp, they slept "in the very barroom in which Mark Twain heard the story of The Jumping Frog of Calaveras."[41] While the Native Sons paid scant notice to sites associated with Mexican or African American communities of the Gold Rush era, they did mark a half-dozen or more places associated with the Chinese, including four sites in the town of Chinese Camp.[42] Several of the designated sites were natural features, such as the big oak tree from which Oak Flat took its name, as well as the "old" hanging trees in Coulterville, Second Garotte, and Jackson. The pilgrimage ended in Sacramento on May 23 as the city was staging its "Days of '49" celebration featuring various citizens dressed as cowboys, Indians, and miners (see figure 44). Soon after the Native Sons' numbered sites found their way into maps and guidebooks for tourists, and by 1929 the route that they took had gained official designation as the "Bret Harte Trail and Mother Lode State Highway" (figure 53).[43]

The advent of automobile tourism in the 1920s marked another transformation in the environment of the Gold Country. In the 1910s, towns in Tuolumne and Calaveras counties seeking new population and industry fought to escape being labeled "historic"; brochures issued by the Tuolumne County Chamber of Commerce in 1915 emphasized that the county was "an old community with new ambitions" and that "there is a new life in store for Tuolumne." None of the pictures or maps in the brochures were of historic attractions. Instead they highlighted the region's orchards, timber operations, hydroelectric power facilities, and modern quarries and mines (figure 54).[44] In 1923, the Tuolumne-Calaveras Bi-County Federation of Women's Clubs produced a map

Fig. 53. Stetson's Hardware Store, Shaws Flat, along the Bret Harte Trail in Tuolumne County, date unknown. Courtesy of the California History Room, California State Library, Sacramento.

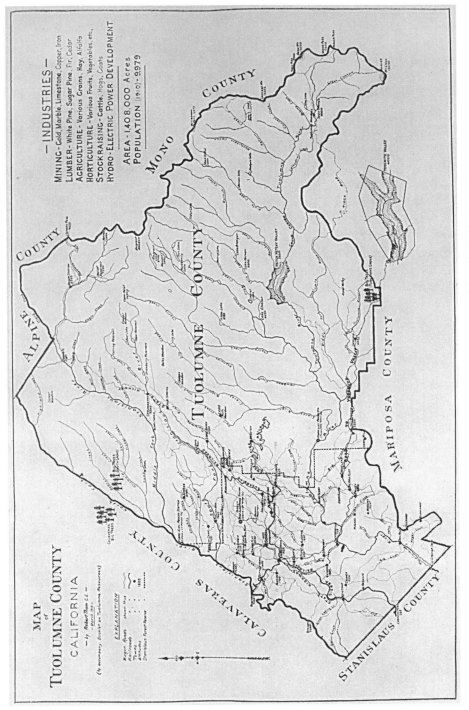

Fig. 54. The Tuolumne County Chamber of Commerce produced this map in 1915 as part of a booklet highlighting the area's natural resources and new industries. Courtesy of the California History Room, California State Library, Sacramento.

renaming the area around Sonora the "Bret Harte and Mark Twain locality," with historic sites recently marked by the Native Sons' pilgrimage prominently shown (figure 55). By 1930, less than a decade after the Native Sons' landmarks pilgrimage, a new Tuolumne Chamber of Commerce brochure highlighted "Historic and Scenic Old Tuolumne" and how the towns had retained their "peculiarities and old time characteristics." A separate section listing historic attractions enticed visitors to towns such as Columbia, "as full of historical reminiscences as a nut is full of meat," or Jamestown, where the buildings contribute to the "old time atmosphere" and "there are always some old timers around who can tell interesting stories."[45] Sites not in keeping with the newly old flavor of the area dropped off the map in favor of historical ones. In 1923, the 540 acres of apple and pear orchards of the John D. Williams ranch outside Sonora were subdivided into summer home lots and renamed "Twain-Harte."[46]

Everywhere, tourists were told that nothing had changed since 1849. An *Overland Monthly* article in 1929 reported that in the Mother Lode "we follow the activities of the pioneers in the identical settings they themselves knew. Nature had seen to it that no changes have taken place since the last coaches thundered out of San Andreas, Angel's Camp, and Columbia. In the Mother Lode mere human progress has given place to the perennial charm and magnificence of nature." The article described how local residents had cooperated in the remaking of their landscape into a historical playground. "Whenever you look in Angel's Camp you see a reproduction of a jumping frog. Pictures of these green frogs in the act of jumping are pasted in the store windows, on the windshields of automobiles, on the side of delivery wagons. Green frogs are also printed on handkerchiefs, on lady's scarves and shawls, and on the caps of school children. Last Spring on the Main Street of Angel's before the hotel there was held a jumping frog contest which was attended by 75,000 people from all parts of the state and country." The author also reported attending a dinner given by the Angel's Boosters where they discussed plans for staging an annual "Mark Twain Memorial and Pageant."[47] Reorienting the representation of their history for tourists, local residents downplayed (or in the case of Twain-Harte erased) the environmental transformations their families had wrought in the previous two generations in favor of an ethos in which nothing that had happened after 1870 was worthy of public recognition.

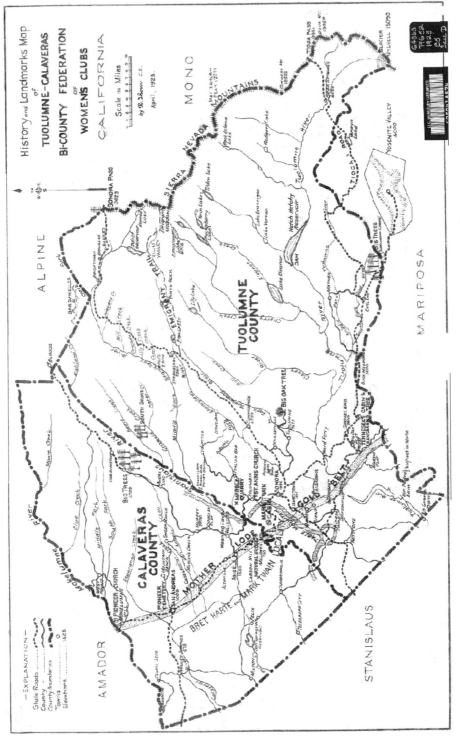

Fig. 55. The Tuolumne-Calaveras Bi-County Federation of Women's Clubs produced this map in 1923 as part of a pamphlet highlighting the area's historical attractions. Unlike the 1915 map (figure 54), this one features the Mark Twain Cabin, Tennessee's Cabin, and Hangman's Tree. Map Collection, University of California, Berkeley.

This included changes in the mining industry, which was still important in many Gold Country towns: the Empire Mine in Grass Valley remained in operation through the mid-1950s. But a dead mining town has more room and incentive to accommodate tourists than one that is still active. Moreover there were ideological reasons for focusing on mining's early years, and the colorful stories of individual prospectors, rather than that of miners' collective struggles to unionize at the turn of the century. While pictures of the Industrial Workers of the World leader Bill Haywood might have a place within the miner's homes, they had no place in the history presented to tourists.[48]

The perception of the Gold Country as a vacation playground was further advanced by a new historical organization, E Clampus Vitus. It was founded in 1931 by a group of San Francisco lawyers and businessmen interested in Gold Rush history, who took the name from a miners' fraternal organization active in the mid–nineteenth century. An all-male organization, the new E Clampus Vitus perpetuated the notion of Gold Rush history as masculine frolic. The "Clampers" marked obsessively, their plaques to the "Ladies of the Night," and "Wall of Comparative Ovations" parodying those of the women's clubs and Native Daughters chapters that often dominated historic preservation efforts at the local level (figure 56).[49]

## White Space

By the late 1920s, the Native Sons, Native Daughters, and Daughters of the American Revolution had developed a network of marked historical spaces representing their version of California's past. As with much frontier history, many of these spaces were points of contact, places that commemorated the acts of pioneer Californians or their Spanish predecessors in first laying claim to the land. Trailblazers and explorers such as Gaspar de Portolá, Juan Bautista de Anza, Jedediah Smith, and Kit Carson had special significance. Increasingly the European colonizers, whatever their national origin, were identified in explicitly racial terms. No matter how many men and women had been on a trail before, the first "white" to pass along it deserved a plaque (figure 57). Historical space in California of the 1920s was also white space, echoing the increasingly strident nativism of the Native Sons of the Golden West in the decade.[50] In 1925, for the first time the six-point credo published on

Fig. 56. This plaque recounting the founding of E Clampus Vitus is shown affixed to the "Wall of Comparative Ovations" in Murphy's, California, in 1994. Photo by the author.

the back cover of the Native Sons' monthly publication *Grizzly Bear* proclaimed the organization's desire not only "to cherish the memory of the pioneers" and "to preserve the historic landmarks of our state" but also "to hold California for the White Race." That year Grand President Fletcher A. Cutler linked the need for scenic and historic conservation to "the retention of the state and its soil for the white race." *Grizzly Bear* editor Clarence Hunt strongly endorsed the new federal immigration laws of 1920s, and quoted approvingly from a speech given in the California state legislature that "we must fight to keep our blood white and the nation white."[51] As racial politics further heated up in California in the 1930s and 1940s, the Native Sons were at the forefront of anti-Mexican and anti-Japanese sentiment.

## Toward a California History

Prompted by private organizations such as the Native Sons, the California state government added its official participation to the designation of historic places in the 1920s, commissioning inventories of sites that could be woven together into a program of public education and tourist promotion through a comprehensive historical marker program. The drive to develop an integrated system of public places for California history out of a congeries of local memory sites paralleled campaigns to promote state history in other states in the 1920s.[52] But government efforts to cultivate the sense of a statewide, California history also may have been stimulated by the feeling of a need to assimilate the enormous influx of migrants to California from other states. In southern California, especially, new state societies proliferated around the idea of memories of one's home state; events such as the Iowa Picnic created an Iowa

ON MARCH 16, 1774, JUAN BAUTISTA DE ANZA, INDIAN FIGHTER, EXPLORER, AND COLONIZER, LED THROUGH THIS PASS (NAMED BY HIM SAN CARLOS) THE FIRST WHITE EXPLORERS TO CROSS THE MOUNTAINS INTO CALIFORNIA. THE PARTY TRAVELED FROM TUBAC, ARIZONA, TO MONTEREY, CALIFORNIA. ON DECEMBER 27, 1775, ON A SECOND EXPEDITION INTO CALIFORNIA, ANZA LED THROUGH THIS PASS THE PARTY OF SPANIARDS FROM SONORA WHO BECAME THE FOUNDERS OF SAN FRANCISCO. TABLET PLACED BY HISTORIC LANDMARKS COMMITTEE, NATIVE SONS OF THE GOLDEN WEST. 1924.

Fig. 57. The Native Sons dedicated this marker at San Carlos Pass in praise of "colonizer" Juan Bautista de Anza in 1924. The photo originally appeared in Knowland, *California: A Landmark History*, p. 66.

of memory in southern California in the 1920s much as the Sons of New England had done in San Francisco in the 1850s.[53]

Before the 1920s, the California state government had only a sporadic involvement with historical activities. In 1915, a California Historical Survey Commission surveyed county historical records statewide; it was succeeded in 1923 by the California State Historical Association under the state Department of Education, which promoted the teaching of California history in the schools. The California State Library had developed a substantial historical collection under the direction of H. L. Peterson, who had accompanied Joseph Knowland on the Native Sons' Landmarks Pilgrimage of 1922. The state legislature had contributed to the Marshall monument and the restoration of Sutter's Fort in 1890, and ever since, private groups had petitioned the state legislature for monetary support, and on occasion turned properties over to the state to maintain. By 1928, California had acquired nine historic properties in this manner (that is, they had been purchased by private subscription then given to the state): Sutter's Fort, Fort Ross, the Marshall Monument at Coloma, the Marshall Blacksmith Shop at Kelsey, the Juniperro Serra Monument at Monterey, the Old Monterey Theatre at Monterey, Mission San Francisco de Solano in Sonoma, the Pio Pico Mansion in Whittier, and the San Pasqual Battle Monument in Escondido, near San Diego. In 1927, when a group of business and conservation leaders seeking to create a comprehensive state park system for California commissioned Frederick Law Olmsted Jr. to compile a statewide inventory of natural and scenic resources, it seemed appropriate to inventory the state's historical resources as well.[54]

The organizer of the statewide inventory of historical resources was Aubrey Drury, the brother of Newton Drury, secretary of the Save the Redwoods League and a leader of the campaign to create a state park system for California. Aubrey Drury was born in Sacramento in 1891, the son of Wells Drury and Elvira Lorraine Bishop, both natives of Illinois. Wells Drury earned his living as a newspaperman and publicist, eventually heading the Berkeley Chamber of Commerce, and Aubrey and his older brother Newton followed their father into the new field of public relations. In 1913, Wells and Aubrey Drury co-authored the *California Tourist Guide and Handbook*. Among the Drury Company's clients in the mid-1920s, besides the Save the Redwoods League, were the Ford Dealers Association, the Southern Pacific Railroad, and many smaller businesses that depended on tourism, such as hotels and steamship lines.[55]

In the preface to his 1928 report, Aubrey Drury observed that historic sites "add to California's scenic background that 'human interest' which is so vital in attracting visitors—as witness the worldwide appeal of Scotland, where scenic grandeur is united with literary and historic tradition. Without such local color and romantic tradition, a region (no matter how beautiful) seems somehow empty and barren, lacking in interest." Drury listed all of the missions as important historical resources, noting that most already were the object of private preservation efforts. Then he listed the handful of historic sites in California already under state, federal, or local ownership. Finally he recommended new sites to be marked that contributed to the "stirring history of the golden state."[56]

Drury's background predisposed him to view historic sites primarily as resources for tourists rather than for local residents, and most of the historic sites he noted were located away from the growing population centers. He saw it as the responsibility of state government to work closely with automobile clubs and local chambers of commerce to put these marked historic places on the map.

In 1931, the California state legislature established a state historical marker program and put Drury in charge. It was a public program in name only; in reality, control remained firmly in the hands of the state chamber of commerce. Local chambers of commerce, with the help of local chapters of the Native Sons and Daughters of the Golden West, forwarded nominations to the state board, which passed on each application, then forwarded it for registration to Joseph Knowland, who remained head of the Native Sons and Daughters Historical Landmarks Committee in the 1930s and also chaired the California Parks Commission (and was active in the state chamber of commerce). The state's automobile clubs furnished directional signs to the registered sites. The only historic landmarks to be registered would be those accessible from the road that offered tourists something to see (figure 58).[57]

California's roadside historic marker program was one of many established across America in the late 1920s and early 1930s in response to recreational automobile travel. Whereas civic celebrations at the turn of the century, such as the Portolá Festival, represented the history of one place as it changed over time, the state historical marker programs involved many places, each representing a single time and event. The system of highway markers constituted an unusual form of historical narration; the public could discern the progression of history over time only by traveling through space.

The fledgling historical programs of the California state government received a boost from the federal government in the mid-1930s when money from the Works Progress Administration funded unemployed writers to produce historical profiles of the more than three hundred landmarks that had been registered so far. Based at the University of California, Berkeley, many of the writers were graduate students of Herbert E. Bolton. California state government also worked with the U.S. Department of the Interior's Historical American Building Survey in the identification of structures of architectural significance.[58]

California state government programs reinforced the ideological and

Fig. 58. Nothing visible remains of either white or native settlements in Irishtown, Amador County, yet its proximity to state highway 88 allowed it to become State Historical Landmark No. 38 on August 1, 1932. Courtesy of the California History Room, California State Library, Sacramento.

commercial biases that private historical organizations had already established in the historical landscape in the previous decades. The state recognized few new historic places; rather, the state programs primarily marked, registered and publicized sites that earlier had been identified as historical by one or other of the private groups. The state historic sites and markers served as props to help descendants of the men and women who had emigrated to California during the Gold Rush to remember their family history; served the ideological purposes of increasingly nativist organizations such as the Native Sons and Daughters; or were developed as tourist attractions by local chambers of commerce.

This was the California history, popularized and embedded in the landscape, taught to the millions of new Californians who arrived in the state during the 1930s and 1940s. Whatever their ethnic background, as long as they were "white," Pioneer history welcomed these new arrivals, encouraging them to understand their often desperate journey from the southern Plains and elsewhere as the ritual reenactment of an earlier westward migration, the quintessentially American story of place and displacement. In 1934, a recent migrant to Los Angeles from Ohio named Leonard Slye decided to both honor this heritage and profit from it by changing his name to Roy Rogers and forming a singing group called the Sons of the Pioneers.[59]

The Gold Rush centennial of 1948–50 further enshrined the conflation of Pioneer and California history. As early as 1944, the state Chamber of Commerce looked forward to the centennial to develop a "love for their adopted state among its recently acquired citizens." The California Centennial Commission was chaired by none other than Joseph Knowland. Among its activities were commemorative ceremonies at existing historic sites and, in concert with the chamber of commerce, the marking and dedication of a fresh batch of historic places in the Sierra foothills (figure 59), including the acquisition and preservation of the entire town of Columbia as a state historic park (see figure 4).[60]

California's official historic landscape would not change until the late 1960s. All along, Native Americans, Californios, African Americans, and descendants of immigrants from Asia and Mexico had developed and maintained memory sites within their communities. Only in the latter decades of the twentieth century, however, did these groups finally

Fig. 59. This sign marking the site of Hock Farm, near Yuba City, was erected as part of the California Centennial Celebration of 1948–50. Courtesy of the California History Room, California State Library, Sacramento.

gain sufficient economic and political power to insist that the state recognize and preserve their special places as well. They began challenging state government initiatives such as the Points of Historical Interest Program, questioning which points were being chosen and whose interest was being served.[61] By the mid 1970s, the state system of historical landmarks and parks included sites such as the Japanese American internment camp at Manzanar and the African American town of Allensworth. Historical sites that had been established earlier, such as those of the Mexican War, were slated for reinterpretation to reflect the new multicultural political realities of the state.[62]

## California, the Great Exception

*Going back to California is not like going back to Vermont or Chicago;*
*Vermont and Chicago are relative constants, against which one*
*measures one's own change. All that is constant about the California*
*of my childhood is the rate at which it disappears.*

—Joan Didion, 1968

In 1850 there were no recognized historic places in California; one hundred years later, a network of California state historic sites was well established. Over a thousand historical markers represented California history in space; concentrated into places such as the Gold Country and missions along the coast, it left the remainder of the state, its most populous areas, as not historic. Not far from Didion's sprawling Central Valley hometown of Sacramento, Gold Country towns were remembered as oases of stability in a rapidly changing landscape.[63]

Tremendous population in-migration and the rapid transformation of the physical landscape have presented Californians in the twentieth century with unique circumstances not found in Massachusetts. In New England history looms nearly everywhere, in the landscape and in the memories of longtime residents. Several years ago, when the historian Mary Fuhrer proposed that a historical marker be placed on a building in Boxborough, Massachusetts, a member of the local historical society told her that the marker was unnecessary because everyone in town already knew what had happened there.[64] Few Californians would make that assumption; historical spaces must be carefully marked in a landscape where few residents remain in place, where for most residents the historical is always somewhere else, where a constant flow of new arrivals come with their own, new memories to attach to the land. From the first Pioneer graves in the 1850s through the latest efforts to rescue historic sites beside the widening freeways, the historical places of California have been carved from a landscape of physical obliteration and demographic upheaval.[65]

Writing at the time of the California Gold Rush centennial in 1949, Carey McWilliams termed his adopted state "the Great Exception."[66] But when it comes to understanding the social and political processes through which historic places developed at the turn of the century, California's story had much in common with other parts of the United

States. The late nineteenth-century migration from the Gold Country echoed the movement from rural areas to cities throughout the United States. Even in New England in the 1870s, men and women who came to work in Massachusetts factories formed place-based societies such as the Sons and Daughters of Vermont, which met regularly in Worcester, Massachusetts, in the 1870s and 1880s.[67] Museum villages, whether Old Deerfield or the California Gold Country towns, arose from the economic needs of depleted rural communities for capital and the emotional needs of tourists for an adopted ancestral home. Throughout America, memories of depopulated areas not only formed the basis for their future designation as historic but also influenced the remaking of these places for mass auto tourism in the 1920s and after. Since the early twentieth century we have come to delineate carefully our historical and nonhistorical landscapes—even our imaginary ones—from Norman Bel Geddes's Futurama at the New York World's Fair of 1939, which established historic preserves for his residents of the city of tomorrow to visit, through the separation of Main Street from Tomorrowland at Disneyland.

We think that once we make a place historic it will not change. But it will. Historic places, supposedly marked for eternity, disappear from view as the markers crumble and surrounding neighborhoods change.[68] The places that remain are reinterpreted by succeeding generations in ways that mirror changing political ideologies and popular tastes. Also new memory sites are created, with partisans who press for their public recognition as historic; in fifty years' time, will the aerospace factories of southern California survive to acquire the patina of old New England mill towns? As we have seen, it is unlikely that such places will be considered historic until they pass into history and are abandoned, because sense of history is connected to sense of place through the process of displacement.

# Conclusion:
# Finding Our Place

If history were thought of as an
activity rather than a profession,
then the numbers of its practitioners
would be legion.

—Raphael Samuel, 1994

Fig. 60. Relics from the Donner party
on display near the Pioneer monument at
Donner Lake. This photo may have been taken
at the time of the monument's dedication in 1918.
Courtesy of the California History Room,
California State Library, Sacramento.

R ETURNING FROM California, I soon find myself back in
the classroom. After the excitement of living someplace new, in
a part of the country with lots of new construction and few
clouds in the sky, it is hard to readjust to the humid East, the stale air of
the crumbling concrete building in which I work, the familiar respon-
sibilities of my job.

This semester, the job includes teaching the required historiography
course, a graduate seminar introducing students to the history of the
historical profession and important historical works of the past century.
The course is designed to impart a sense of history to a new generation
of professionals, and surrounded by a dozen first-year students, I recall
the scene of my own education as a historian. Our seminar table in
Amherst is much less solid than the one at which I sat in Baltimore
over twenty years ago; modern, functional, interchangeable, its peeling
wood-grain Formica not quite concealing the particleboard beneath, it
wobbles. Though my students deserve better, the shaky footing is somehow appropriate for our subject matter.

What will it mean to be a historian in the new century? I surely
cannot tell my students, as I was told, that full-time appointments teaching in colleges and universities await them when they finish their Ph.D.

degrees. Nor can I tell them, as I was told, that their scholarship will form important building blocks in the edifice of History. After the epistemological upheavals of the past two decades, with the distinction between knower and known all but collapsed, with so many multiple perspectives on the past, it is hard to think of historical knowledge as cumulative. Do we really know more about the past, or only different things? Looking around the table, I ask myself what elements of my professional identity, which truths of what I learned was History, do I want to pass on?

I face a similar question in concluding this book, in deciding what I want my readers to come away with from these diverse essays. They weave us in and out of Americans' relationships with the past in the twentieth century, exploring some of the forms through which we commonly encounter history in public, our war memorials and civic celebrations, our television programs and historic sites. But do they add up to anything? Can we understand this series of discrete investigations as more of a history, and discern trends over time likely to continue into the future? What can these chapters tell us about how Americans will think about history in the new century? What do they say about the place of the historical profession in shaping this thought?

It is much harder to trace the evolution of popular notions of history in the twentieth century than the historiography of the profession. While historiography reconstructs the sequence of ideas and influences among a group of professionals who more or less agreed to practice history in a similar way, the sheer diversity of popular approaches to the past, especially in recent years, makes it impossible to narrow the scope of our inquiry. But we can try to identify what the various forms of history have had in common, as they changed over time.

The number of historical institutions and activities has grown steadily throughout the twentieth century. Over the past hundred years, Americans have accumulated a vast collection of public historic sites, museums, monuments, and holiday celebrations, all intended to enhance our sense of history, to remind us of various aspects of our past. More and more places and objects have been set aside as historic, stretching the limits of what we can possibly maintain, in the hope that later generations will find value in at least something that we have saved for them, and not forget about us.

The profusion of historical activities is the result of a number of factors. One is simply that during the latter decades of the twentieth century a growing number of organized groups—racial, ethnic, religious, as well as veterans, women, gays, people with disabilities—acquired sufficient economic and political power to have their special places recognized and preserved in public alongside those established earlier in the century that honored primarily white males of northern European descent. Contemporary politics dictates that each new identity requires a history, demanding public recognition by the larger culture. Another factor is the widespread faith among local chambers of commerce in both urban and rural areas that developing a rich milieu of new historic sites and commemorative activities will attract tourists and reverse the economic decline that has followed the loss of agricultural and manufacturing jobs. As we saw in the case of San Francisco's Portolá Festival, the use of history to boost tourism and promote the aura of the city as a fun place has flourished throughout the century.

But the enormous proliferation of public histories during the twentieth century has been accompanied by a second trend, the narrowing of scale. Many observers would argue the opposite; the historian Pierre Nora believes that ever since the eighteenth century, forms of public history such as national museums, archives, and historical sites have steadily eroded local traditions and memories.[1] And there is no question that, despite claims that we live in a "postnational" era, for many Americans a sense of national heritage remains strong, as demonstrated in the spirited campaign in recent years for the protection of the nation's venerated objects and battlefields.[2] Yet as we saw with the Orange war memorial and *The Civil War*, Americans place the events of national history in the framework of their families and hometowns. Local and family histories are not obliterated by national history; rather, they are the lenses through which that history is viewed.

We use the various histories we encounter in public in intensely personal and familial ways, to understand who we are, where we live, and with whom we belong, and to impart a manageable scale to the flow of experience. When it comes to history, the personal and experiential take precedence over the global and the abstract, whether we are dealing with veterans insisting on a figurative statue to memorialize their deeds, television viewers wanting to feel that they are actually in the locale of a past event, or tourists seeking the real thing in a New England village or California Gold Rush town. As the marketplace through which we in-

teract with the world becomes more impersonal, we want our histories
to become more intimate, with an emphasis on the particular that just
might keep us from becoming overwhelmed.[3]

Especially in a nation of immigrants on the move, where the pasts of
one's family and one's current place of residence seldom coincide, histories that reinforce our sense of particular places, that help us to understand the succession of places in our past, remain important anchors for
personal and group identity. Enormous population movement throughout the twentieth century, as the children of Kentucky coal miners
moved to Detroit, of Mississippi Delta sharecroppers to Chicago, of
Iowa farmers to southern California, of Pennsylvania steel workers to
Texas, of Cuban cigar-makers to Florida, of California aerospace engi-
neers to Las Vegas, has given Americans a distinctive sense of history, in
which an awareness of the places where their ancestors lived possesses at
least as much emotional power as their present surroundings. This distinctive place consciousness affects what Americans think matters the
most about history, prompting the descendants of Deerfield's first settlers to establish a museum village to preserve the homes of their ancestors, or the sons and daughters of the Gold Rush to make historic sites
out of the rural California towns their families had long abandoned. In
the new century, the even greater mobility of people and ideas around
the globe and through the virtual spaces of the Internet will likely only
accelerate the turn to history as an anchor for personal, communal, and
family identity.

For many of us, then, a sense of history means a sense of home,
something we may flee from early in life as we establish our individual
identities, but return to later in life as we age. Other people's history
may be educational and sometimes even entertaining, like a science
museum or amusement park. But the histories that matter most to us are
the familiar ones, populated by our families. We invite ancestors whom
we never met to enter our lives imaginatively through stories and pictures; reunite families dispersed in space and time through the reconstruction of family trees; and make pilgrimages, real or virtual, to the
succession of places where our ancestors lived. We often look to our
ancestors for a sense of community we cannot find among our neighbors. The community of our ancestors—they are the ones who, para-
phrasing Robert Frost, when we have to go there, they have to take us

in. With the aging of the "baby boom" population in the twenty-first century, we can expect this valuation of family history to become an even more prominent feature of American culture.[4]

Over the past century, the historical profession has not only chronicled these changes in American life but also experienced them. In the decades after World War II, the leadership of the historical profession, located in colleges and universities, turned decisively away from the regional affiliations and job networks that had been the norm in the early years of the century. To become a professional historian in the 1950s and 1960s meant to join a nationwide fraternity, ready to move anywhere to pursue a new subject or position, and the great expansion of colleges and universities in those years enabled historians to pursue the main chance wherever it might be.[5] The expansion also meant that historians who chose to remain in their home regions could stay put and still find academic employment. That era ended abruptly in the mid-1970s, when the number of new Ph.D.s so far surpassed the number of available academic positions that the majority of young historians, trained to believe that the only jobs were academic ones, scattered to the four winds—an aspect of professional life likely to continue in the future. Historians eventually might reach some accommodation with where they wind up living, as I have done in cloudy New England, but few pursuing academic careers will enjoy the freedom to live and practice history where they want. The upshot is that over the course of the twentieth century, it has become less easy for American historians to write from a home place, to identify emotionally with the history of a community or region, in the way that Walter Prescott Webb wrote about the Great Plains, Samuel Eliot Morison about New England, or Robert Kelley about California.[6]

As the preceding essays demonstrate, an orientation to the history of one's place, to one's family, to one's region perhaps constitutes the greatest difference between the history that Americans live and experience and the history practiced by professional historians. For professionals entering the new century there is no history, only histories, subject to endless, often intellectually fascinating, reinterpretation and debate. Though Americans sometimes also turn to history for diversion and entertainment, the reason why they care about it so much is because it addresses fundamental, emotionally compelling questions about their past that they need to authenticate and confirm, embedded in a narrative that is theirs, real and true—essential for understanding who they are and where they live.

In considering what to tell my graduate students about what it will mean to be a historian in the new century, I share many of the values of my colleagues striving to maintain continuity with the profession's past; after all, the solid grounding I received around the seminar table in Baltimore has given me the confidence to recognize that historians can change how they approach their work without losing their professional identities. But knowing that the historical profession in which my students will work is far different from the one in which I was trained, it is important for me to pass along what I have learned not only in archives, libraries, seminars, and professional meetings but also in my experiences interacting with the public. Understanding how Americans have approached the past will place a new generation of historians in a better position than their professional forebears to reach the public with their ideas. Learning how to add the critical edge that they bring to the study of history while remaining sensitive to the more emotional and familial uses that the public has for it, acknowledging and not dismissing the personal, emotional power of the past in their own lives, historians can connect with the public in more profound ways, writing histories that the public will care more about because, ultimately, historians will care more about them, too.

In the end, the distance between historians and the public, between the seminar tables of our universities and the kitchen tables of our neighbors, will be bridged not by historians reaching out to "the public," but rather by their reaching in to discover the humanity they share. The distancing from life, the quest for perspective that historians learn in graduate school as the core of the historical enterprise must be balanced by a recognition of our personal needs for the past. Our own experiences, our own families, our own communities, can be the source of historical insights, not because we assume that everyone is like us, but because we can establish who we are only by writing from a place, from a community, from a location in the world.[7]

So what will I tell my students wanting to become historians? Certainly to learn the history of the profession, and the skills necessary to earn a living doing history, whether through teaching or any number of other pursuits. But also to find a place from which to write, and to cultivate a humanity within yourself that allows you to connect with others in that place. To help the residents of your community to see the value of the ordinary places where they live. To help your neighbors to expand their time perspective beyond a single generation or two. And perhaps most difficult, given the tendency Americans have to make histories that exclude others from their life-stories and neighborhoods, to help your fellow citizens to expand their social perspective beyond their immediate families, so that they discover in their quest for a history and place that they can call their own, that they are part of a larger society and environment.

Sense of history is a response to fundamental human questions concerning individual and group identity and our relationship to our environment, to a succession of past and future generations, and to one another. As the new century begins, I hope that my fellow historians, by understanding more about how Americans think about the past, can help them to connect their personal experiences with the historical experiences of a larger community, region, nation, and planet. Understanding that the public looks to history to address these fundamental questions can give additional meaning to our institutions and profession in the new century.

# NOTES

## 1. Sense of History

1. The table is of sufficient totemic value that the Johns Hopkins History Department had it restored in August 1996. "The Seminar Room," Johns Hopkins University History Department *Newsletter* 13 (October 1997): 38.

2. A prominent example from the mid-1980s expressing concern with American ignorance of the past is Diane Ravitch, "Decline and Fall of Teaching History," *New York Times Magazine*, November 17, 1985, pp. 50+. One of the most prominent critiques of professional historians came from the chair of the National Endowment for the Humanities, Lynn Cheney. See her *American Memory: A Report on the Humanities in the Nation's Public Schools* (Washington, D.C.: National Endowment for the Humanities, 1987) and *Telling the Truth: A Report on the State of the Humanities in Higher Education* (Washington, D.C.: NEH, 1992). Mike Wallace's description of America's "historicidal" culture first appeared in "The Politics of Public History," in *Past Meets Present: Essays about Historical Interpretation and Public Audiences*, ed. Jo Blatti (Washington, D.C.: Smithsonian Institution Press, 1987), 37–53. It also appears in the introduction to Wallace's *Mickey Mouse History and Other Essays on American Memory* (Philadelphia: Temple University Press, 1996), ix.

3. On academic historiography, see Peter Novick, *That Noble Dream: The Objectivity Question and the American Historical Profession* (New York: Cambridge University Press, 1988).

4. In many ways, my distinction between academic historians' interpretations of

history and the public's sense of history is similar to the distinction David Lowenthal makes between history and "heritage." See Lowenthal, *Possessed by the Past: The Heritage Crusade and the Spoils of History* (New York: Free Press, 1996).

5. Among the works associated with the "myth and symbol" school of American studies are Henry Nash Smith, *Virgin Land: The American West as Symbol and Myth* (Cambridge: Harvard University Press, 1950), Perry Miller, *The New England Mind: From Colony to Province* (Cambridge: Harvard University Press, 1953), and William R. Taylor, *Cavalier and Yankee: The Old South and American National Character* (New York: G. Braziller, 1961). I discuss the relationship of contemporary studies of memory to American studies scholarship further in "Monuments and Memories," *American Quarterly* 43 (March 1991): 143–56. On artists' and intellectuals' use of the past, see Warren Susman, "History and the American Intellectual: The Uses of a Usable Past" (1964), reprinted in *Culture as History: The Transformation of American Society in the Early Twentieth Century* (New York: Pantheon Books, 1984). On the historical consciousness of minorities, see Lawrence Levine, *Black Culture and Black Consciousness* (New York: Oxford University Press, 1977). Studies of the changing historical reputations of political figures include Merrill Peterson's *The Jefferson Image in the American Mind* (New York: Oxford University Press, 1960) and *Lincoln in American Memory* (New York: Oxford University Press, 1994). For a pioneering investigation of historical representations in political movements, see Richard Hofstadter, *The Age of Reform: From Bryan to FDR* (New York: Knopf, 1955); for a more recent example, see Dorothy Ross, "Historical Consciousness in Nineteenth Century America," *American Historical Review* 89 (October 1984): 909–28. On decision makers, see Richard Neustadt and Ernest May, *Thinking in Time: The Uses of History for Decision-Makers* (New York: Free Press, 1986).

6. Redfield uses "Social Organization of Tradition" as the title for chap. 3 of *Peasant Society and Culture* (1956), reprinted in *The Little Community* (Chicago: University of Chicago Press, 1967), 40–59. One model for this enterprise is the research of Raphael Samuel, who viewed his work as broadening what the historical profession considers as history to include "unofficial knowledge" of the British past. Samuel, *Theatres of Memory* (New York: Verso, 1994).

7. Carl Becker, "Everyman His Own Historian," *American Historical Review* 37 (1932): 221–36. The new scholarship reflects the impact of communications theory, especially as developed by the Birmingham (UK) school of cultural studies. Among the most useful works introducing this literature are the essays in *Channels of Discourse: Television and Contemporary Criticism*, ed. Robert C. Allen, 2d ed. (Chapel Hill: University of North Carolina Press, 1992), and *Culture/Power/History: A Reader in Contemporary Social Theory*, ed. Nicholas Dirks, Geoff Eley, and Sherry Ortner (Princeton: Princeton University Press, 1994).

8. The insight that oral history interviewees usually place themselves at the center of the historical events they are describing appears in Linda Shopes, "Popular

Consciousness of Local History: The Evidence of Oral History Interviews," paper presented at International Oral History Association, New York City, 1994. The term "uchronic dreams" appears in Alessandro Portelli, *The Death of Luigi Trastulli and Other Stories: Form and Meaning in Oral History* (Albany: SUNY Press, 1991), a fascinating book of essays exploring how individuals and communities remember the past. On personal reminiscence as a spontaneous individual activity, see Robert N. Butler, "The Life Review: Interpretation of Reminiscence in the Aged," *Psychiatry* 26 (February 1963): 65–76. On the social construction of individual and collective memories through group communication, see Maurice Halbwachs, *The Collective Memory* (New York: Harper and Row, 1980), and the essays in *Memory and American History*, ed. David Thelen (Bloomington: Indiana University Press, 1990) and *Collective Remembering* ed. David Middleton and Derek Edwards (Newbury Park, Calif.: Sage Publications, 1990). See also the important collection on gender and memory, *Women's Words: The Feminist Practice of Oral History*, ed. Sherna Gluck and Daphne Patai (New York: Routledge, 1991).

9. See S.R. 257, "Relating to the *Enola Gay* Exhibit," 103d Cong., 2d sess., *Congressional Record* 140 (September 19, 1994): S.12968. The controversies over the Smithsonian exhibit on the end of World War II prompted a torrent of writing on the politics of public history; see, for example, "History and the Public: What Can We Handle? A Round Table about History after the Enola Gay Controversy," *Journal of American History* 82 (December 1995): 1029–1144, and *History Wars: The "Enola Gay" and Other Battles for the American Past*, ed. Edward T. Linenthal and Tom Engelhardt (New York: Metropolitan Books, 1996). On the controversies over national standards for teaching history in elementary and secondary schools, see Gary Nash, Charlotte Crabtree, and Ross E. Dunn, *History on Trial: Culture Wars and the Teaching of the Past* (New York: Alfred A. Knopf, 1997).

10. Benedict Anderson, *Imagined Communities: Reflections on the Origins and Spread of Nationalism*, rev. ed (New York: Verso, 1991); W. Lloyd Warner, *The Living and the Dead: A Study of Symbolic Life of Americans* (New Haven: Yale University Press, 1959); Robert Bellah, "Civil Religion in America," *Daedalus* 96 (Winter 1967): 1–21; Michael Kammen, *Mystic Chords of Memory* (New York: Knopf, 1991); Pierre Nora, "Between Memory and History: Les Lieux de Mémoire," *Representations* 26 (Spring 1989): 7–25. For a superb critical assessment of Nora's work, see Nancy Wood, "Memory's Remains: Les Leiux de Mémoire," *History and Memory* 6 (Spring–Summer 1994): 123–49.

11. On "movement history," see James Green, *Taking History to Heart: The Power of the Past in Building Social Movements* (Amherst: University of Massachusetts Press, 2000), 2–3. On the conflict between official history and vernacular memory, see John Bodnar, *Remaking America: Public Memory, Commemoration, and Patriotism in the Twentieth Century* (Princeton: Princeton University Press, 1992). The framework underlies many of the essays in *Commemorations: The Politics of National Iden-*

*tity*, ed. John Gillis (Princeton: Princeton University Press, 1994). On earlier formulations, see Michel Foucault, *Language, Countermemory, Practice: Selected Essays and Interviews*, ed. Donald F. Bouchard (Ithaca, N.Y.: Cornell University Press, 1977); George Mosse, *The Nationalization of the Masses: Political Symbolism and Mass Movements in Germany from the Napoleonic Wars through the Third Reich* (New York: H. Fertig, 1975), and *Fallen Soldiers: Reshaping the Memory of the World Wars* (New York: Oxford University Press, 1990); Raphael Samuel, ed., *Patriotism: The Making and Unmaking of British National Identity* (London: Routledge, 1989), and Robert Johnston et al., eds., *Making Histories: Studies in History Writing and Politics* (Minneapolis: University of Minnesota Press, 1982).

12. An insightful criticism of the civil religion approach appears in Steven Lukes, "Political Ritual and Social Integration," *Sociology* 9 (May 1975): 289–308; for a lengthier critique of the historiography of American patriotism, see my review essay "Patriotism from the Ground Up," *Reviews in American History* 21 (March 1993): 1–7. Since that essay appeared, both John Bodnar and Raphael Samuel have revised their frameworks to accommodate the study of patriotism as a grassroots sentiment. In *Theatres of Memory* (New York: Verso, 1994), Samuel distinguishes between patriotism as attachment to the nation-state and as popular attachment to a national folk past. Bodnar's recent work emphasizes the national ideals of ordinary Americans, along with their strong feeling that government is not living up to them. Bodnar, "Moral Patriotism and Collective Memory in Whiting, Indiana, 1920–92," in *Bonds of Affection: Americans Define Their Patriotism*, ed. John Bodnar (Princeton: Princeton University Press, 1996), 290–304.

13. In conceptualizing how public historical imagery both reproduces and transforms political relationships, my thought has been influenced by William H. Sewell Jr., "A Theory of Structure: Duality, Agency, and Transformation," *American Journal of Sociology* 98 (July 1992): 1–29. For an exemplary case study examining the conflation of local and national historical imagery, see Alon Confino, "The Nation as a Local Metaphor: Heimat, National Memory, and the German Empire, 1871–1918," *History and Memory* 5 (Spring–Summer 1993): 42–86.

14. James E. Young, *The Texture of Memory: Holocaust Memorials and Meaning* (New Haven: Yale University Press, 1993). For more on the historian's role as a creator of public spaces for dialogue about the past, see John Kuo Wei Tchen, "Creating a Dialogic Museum: The Chinatown History Museum Experiment," in *Museums and Communities: The Politics of Public Culture*, ed. Ivan Karp, Christine Mullen Kreamer, and Steven D. Lavine (Washington, D.C.: Smithsonian Institution Press, 1992), 285–326.

15. "Historic Villages Take a Page from Disney," *Wall Street Journal*, August 22, 1997, 1.

16. My thinking about the potential for commercial historical attractions taking over the educational role of public ones has been greatly influenced by Susan G.

Davis's discussion of how Sea World in San Diego has assumed the civic and educational role that otherwise would have been performed by a local public aquarium. Davis, *Spectacular Nature: Corporate Culture and the Sea World Experience* (Berkeley: University of California Press, 1997). On popular craving for the experience of the past in museums, historic sites, and popular films, see Alison Landsberg, "America, the Holocaust, and the Mass Culture of Memory: Toward a Radical Politics of Empathy," *New German Critique* 71 (Spring–Summer 1997): 63–86. Roy Rosenzweig documents how the popular journalistic convention of the human interest story permeated the presentation of history in *American Heritage* magazine in the 1950s and 1960s. Roy Rosenzweig, "Marketing the Past: *American Heritage* and Popular History in the United States," in *Presenting the Past: Essays on History and the Public*, ed. Susan Porter Benson, Stephen Brier, and Roy Rosenzweig (Philadelphia: Temple University Press, 1986), 21–49. Susan G. Davis demonstrates how the dictates of commercial television broadcasting shaped the commemoration of the Constitution bicentennial in "Set Your Mood to Patriotic: History as Televised Special Event," *Radical History Review* 42 (1988): 122–43. On the Disney version of history, see Richard Francaviglia, "Main Street USA: A Comparison/Contrast of Streetscapes in Disneyland and Walt Disney World," *Journal of Popular Culture* 15 (Summer 1981): 141–56, and Michael Wallace, *Mickey Mouse History and Other Essays on American Memory* (Philadelphia: Temple University Press, 1996), 133–74. On Disney's unsuccessful effort to create a theme park in Virginia in the early 1990s, see "Disney Park World Show 'Painful Side' of U.S. Past," *Sacramento Bee*, November 12, 1993, A1, 24; and "Symposium: Disney and the Historians—Where Do We Go from Here?" *Public Historian* 17 (Fall 1995): 43–89. On the convergence of historical theme parks and the outside world, see Mira Engler, "Drive-Thru History: Theme Towns in Iowa," *Landscape* 32 (1993): 8–18.

17. George Lipsitz, *Time Passages: Collective Memory and American Popular Culture* (Minneapolis: University of Minnesota Press, 1990).

18. In a national survey conducted for Indiana University's Center for the Study of History-Making in America in 1994, history museums were rated the most trusted sources of information about the past, while television and motion pictures were the least trusted. See David Thelen and Roy Rosenzweig, *Presence of the Past: Popular Uses of History in American Life* (New York: Columbia University Press, 1998), 91. On the role of interpretive conventions in guiding audience reception, see Robert Allen, "Reader Oriented Criticism" in *Channels of Discourse: Television and Contemporary Criticism* (Chapel Hill: University of North Carolina Press, 1987), 254–89; see also Celeste Michelle Condit, "The Rhetorical Limits of Polysemy," *Critical Studies in Mass Communication* 6 (June 1989): 103–22.

19. Janice Radway, *Reading the Romance: Women, Patriarchy, and Popular Literature* (Chapel Hill: University of North Carolina Press, 1984). Excellent examples of research on how audience expectations affect historical interpretation appear in two

anthologies published by the Smithsonian Institution Press: Blatti, *Past Meets Present: Essays about Historic Interpretation and Public Audiences*, and Karp et al., *Museums and Communities: The Politics of Public Culture*.

20. As a way of extending its meager resources, increasingly the National Park Service has entered into agreements with local historical agencies and volunteer groups, as Lowell National Historical Park in Massachusetts has done.

21. See my "Dear Ken Burns: Letters to a Filmmaker," *Mosaic: Newsletter of the Center for History-Making in America* 1 (Fall 1991): 1, 8.

22. Among the most useful works connecting memory and place from the perspective of developmental psychology is the anthology *Place Attachment*, ed. Irwin Altman and Setha Low (New York: Plenum, 1992). The emotional power of remembered places is especially articulated in the work of artists and writers, who use this power to create identities for themselves. See, for example, Louise Erdrich, "A Writer's Sense of Place," in *A Sense of Place: Essays in Search of the Midwest*, ed. Michael Martone (Iowa City: University of Iowa Press, 1988), 34–44, and Wallace Stegner, "The Sense of Place," in *Where the Bluebird Sings to the Lemonade Springs: Living and Writing in the West* (New York: Random House, 1992). On social networks and place, see Kathleen Gerson, C. Ann Steuve, and Claude S. Fischer, "Attachments to Place," in *Networks and Places: Social Relations in the Urban Setting*, ed. Fischer et al. (New York: Free Press, 1977), 139–61. On urban renewal in Boston, see Marc Fried, "Grieving for a Lost Home," in *The Urban Condition: People and Policy in the Metropolis*, ed. Leonard J. Duhl (New York: Basic Books, 1963), 151–71.

23. Stegner, "The Sense of Place," 202.

24. The folklorist Henry Glassie proclaims that "History is the essence of the idea of place." Glassie, *Passing the Time in Ballymenone: Culture and History of an Ulster Community* (Philadelphia: University of Pennsylvania Press, 1982), 664. The term "storied place" comes from nature writer Robert Finch, who describes being initially attracted to Cape Cod not by its natural features but by the many stories that had been written about it over the years. See *Writing Natural History: Dialogues with Authors*, ed. Edward Lueders (Salt Lake City: University of Utah Press, 1989), 44. A superb introduction to how contemporary folklorists write about place is Mary Hufford, *One Space, Many Places: Folklife and Land Use in New Jersey's Pineland's National Reserve* (Washington, D.C.: Library of Congress, 1986), and Hufford's anthology *Conserving Culture: A New Discourse on Heritage* (Urbana: University of Illinois Press, 1994). On cultural geography's concern with how the social production of space shapes the subjective experience of place, see John Agnew, "Representing Space: Space, Scale, and Culture in Social Science," in *Place/Culture/Representation*, ed. James Duncan and David Ley (New York: Verso, 1993), 251–71.

25. Glassie, *Passing the Time in Ballymenone*, 608.

26. Attacks on the pioneer past as rootless grew especially prominent in the

decades between the world wars, though this is a critique that stretches back to the nineteenth century and forward to contemporary environmental writers such as Wendell Berry. See Robert Dorman, *The Revolt of the Provinces: Regionalist Movement in America, 1920–1945* (Chapel Hill: University of North Carolina Press, 1993), and Wendell Berry, *The Unsettling of America: Culture and Agriculture* (San Francisco: Sierra Club Books, 1977); on placelessness and modern architecture, see Edward Relph, *Place and Placelessness* (London: Pion, 1976), and James Howard Kunstler, *Geography of Nowhere: Rise and Decline of America's Manmade Landscape* (New York: Simon and Schuster, 1993); on the impact of electronic communications, see Joshua Meyrowitz, *No Sense of Place: Impact of Electronic Media on Social Behavior* (New York: Oxford University Press, 1985).

27. Interestingly, Frederick Jackson Turner pioneered the study of how Americans interacted with particular environments to produce distinctive, place-based local and regional identities, but the historical profession by and large abandoned this study in subsequent years. On Turner's relationship to place consciousness, see Michael Steiner, "From Frontier to Region: Frederick Jackson Turner and the New Western History," *Pacific Historical Review* 64 (November 1995): 479–501.

28. Randy Hester describes community memory sites as "subconscious landscapes of the heart," the places that local residents feel are part of the "sacred structure" of their town. Randy Hester, "Subconscious Landscapes of the Heart," *Places* 2 (1985): 10–22. While the residents of a town or neighborhood are more interested in preserving the places of which they have a personal memory than those of the remote past, historic preservation—in both legislation and practice—emphasizes the remote over the immediate past. In the words of Kevin Lynch, "near continuity is emotionally more important than remote time," Lynch, *What Time Is This Place?* (Cambridge: MIT Press, 1972), 61. David Lowenthal observes that governments value a remote, malleable past more highly than a recent one painfully recalled. Lowenthal "Revisiting Valued Landscapes," in *Valued Environments*, ed. John R. Gold and Jacqueline Burgess (Boston: Allen and Unwin, 1982), 78.

29. Michael Frisch, *A Shared Authority: Essays on the Craft and Meaning of Oral and Public History* (Albany: SUNY Press, 1990).

## 2. Remembering a War

1. The phrase "biography of a monument" is borrowed from James E. Young, "The Biography of a Memorial Icon: Nathan Rapoport's Warsaw Ghetto Monument," *Representations* 26 (Spring 1989): 69–106.

2. Scholars sought to distinguish patriotism—a healthy love of country—from nationalism—a dangerous belief in the superiority of one's country to other countries. See, for example, Carlton J. H. Hayes, *Essays on Nationalism* (New York: Macmillan, 1926). The scholarly critique of nationalism after World War I is ana-

lyzed in Merle Curti, *Roots of American Loyalty* (New York: Columbia University Press, 1946), and Weston Gladding Donehower, "Conflicting Interpretations of American Patriotism in the 1920s" (Ph.D. diss., University of Pennsylvania, 1982). The most famous of the psychological studies of nationalism that emphasized the importance of an enemy out-group for maintaining in-group solidarity is Theodore Adorno et al., *The Authoritarian Personality* (New York: Harper and Row, 1950). For a summary of Adorno and other early psychological literature on nationalism, see Leonard Doob, *Patriotism and Nationalism: Their Psychological Foundations* (New Haven: Yale University Press, 1964).

3. W. Lloyd Warner, *The Living and the Dead* (New Haven: Yale University Press, 1959), 274, 276.

4. See George L. Mosse, *Fallen Soldiers: Reshaping the Memory of the World Wars* (New York: Oxford University Press, 1990); Eric Hobsbawm, "Introduction" and "Mass Producing Traditions," in *The Invention of Tradition*, ed. Hobsbawm and Terence Ranger (New York: Cambridge University Press, 1983), 1–14, 263–307; and Raphael Samuel, "Introduction," in *Patriotism: The Making and Unmaking of British National Identity*, ed. Samuel, vol. 1, *History and Politics* (New York: Routledge, 1989), xviii–lxvii.

5. Richard Wilke and Jack Tager, eds., *Historical Atlas of Massachusetts* (Amherst: University of Massachusetts Press, 1991), 143.

6. Of 264 men from Orange listed as having served in World War I, 54 belonged to Company E. Service Records, World War I, Volume 24, "Orange," Massachusetts Military Records Center, Boston. The nucleus of the 104th Infantry were several western Massachusetts State Guard units that had seen service in Mexico in 1916 and thus were ready to go to France before most other Regular Army units could be formed or trained. James H. Fifield, *The Regiment: A History of the 104th U.S. Infantry, AEF* (Springfield, Mass., 1946), pp. 2–14.

7. The American Federation of Arts, an organization of professional artists, strongly endorsed the creation of symbolic World War memorials to promote idealism and combat what they saw as the materialism and literal-mindedness of Americans. The federation organized a monuments committee within a week after the Armistice to advise local communities, and published guidelines in its journal, *American Magazine of Art*. A list of committee members and the committee's guidelines appears in "War Memorials," *American Magazine of Art* 10 (March 1919): 180–83. Fifteen artists elaborated on the federation's position in a special issue of the *American Magazine of Art*, May 1919. The artists had more success influencing the design of American battle monuments overseas than in towns back home. On monuments overseas, see G. Kurt Piehler, "The War Dead and the Gold Star: American Commemoration of the First World War," in *Commemorations: The Politics of National Identity*, ed. John Gillis (Princeton: Princeton University Press, 1994), 168–85. On American traditions of monumental art before the World War,

see Michele H. Bogart, *Public Sculpture and the Civic Ideal in New York City, 1880–1930* (Chicago: University of Chicago Press, 1989).

8. Orange *Enterprise and Journal*, January 31, 1919, 2; *Enterprise and Journal*, February 28, 1919, 2.

9. Ibid., February 28, 1919, 2. Many of the newspaper citations in this chapter come from a scrapbook kept by Richard Chaisson, who recorded the date, but not always the paper and page number, of the articles he clipped.

10. Recreation organizations pushed the "living memorial" idea nationwide in a series of pamphlets distributed by Community Service, Inc., an offshoot of the Playground and Recreation Association of America. See War Camp Community Service, Bureau of Memorial Buildings, *Community Buildings as War Memorials* (N.p., 1919).

11. The town voted to borrow $30,000, which represented the asking price from the owners of the three parcels that would become the park. The assessed value of the sites was approximately half of that; since the law did not allow for the town to pay more than 25% over assessed value, the town offered $19,500 and took the parcels by eminent domain.

12. *Enterprise and Journal*, November 21, 1919, 2.

13. By 1920 there were 60,000 American Legion members in Massachusetts, the highest number of any state in the United States. William Pencack, *For God and Country: The American Legion, 1919–1941* (Boston: Northeastern University Press, 1989), 67. Among the Legion's prominent members was Howard Warren, manager of Minute Tapioca Company, one of the first post commanders. Of the 94 membership cards that survive from 1923, 67 give the occupation of members; of these, 29% were merchants or professionals, 36% skilled craftsmen, and 33% semiskilled factory workers. This compares with approximately 20%, 24%, and 56% for each occupational category in a sample of the 1920 Orange city directory. Membership cards, American Legion Post 172 Legion Hall, Orange, Mass.; *Orange City Directory 1920* (New Haven: Price and Lee, 1920).

14. "So into the Tank He Went," *Enterprise and Journal*, November 13, 1925.

15. Ibid., November 5, 1926, 4.

16. Between 1919 and 1924, Massachusetts collected a poll tax of five dollars to finance a bonus to Massachusetts World War veterans. Perhaps the passage of the federal bonus bill in 1924 allowed the Legionnaires to use their state bonus for a town memorial; their decision might also have reflected the fact that Legion members were more affluent than the average veteran. On the struggle over the federal bonus bill, see Pencack, *For God and Country*.

17. In addition to the lifesized doughboy for towns, the studio also sold a twelve-inch size for home and office. Most of the sixty towns listed in the brochure as "some of the many communities" that purchased the statue were in the Midwest, but several were in New Jersey, Pennsylvania, New York, and Vermont. *The Spirit of the*

*American Doughboy*, Memorials File, microfilm no. 89-14013, American Legion Library, Indianapolis. According to T. Perry Wesley, editor emeritus of the Spencer, Indiana, *Evening World*, the statue also was erected in Bethel and Canaan, Connecticut. T. Perry Wesley, correspondence with author, January 30, 1995.

18. *Enterprise and Journal*, March 4, 1927, 9.

19. Ibid., November 8 and 15, 1929.

20. Ibid., May 1, 1931, 1.

21. Ibid., August 25, 1932, 1. This was not the first monument to be set up in Memorial Park; in May 1932, the American Legion accepted a spruce tree as a community Christmas tree from the Women's Club. It is significant that Memorial Park was considered veterans' space; they were the ones who accepted the tree on behalf of the town, even though the tree was not explicitly a World War memorial. On the use of natural features such as boulders for war memorials in western Europe, see Mosse, *Fallen Soldiers*.

22. *Enterprise and Journal*, October 13, 1932. The local VFW post was approximately half the size of the American Legion post; many VFW members belonged to the Legion as well. The post was named after Henry Damon and Ralph Spooner, both of whom died at Apremont. The cannon was dedicated by May Spooner, Ralph Spooner's mother.

23. On the GAR's origination of the role of patriotic veteran in the decades after the Civil War see Stuart McConnell, *Glorious Contentment: The Grand Army of the Republic, 1865–1900* (Chapel Hill: University of North Carolina Press, 1992).

24. *Enterprise and Journal*, August 18, 1932, 2.

25. While there is no record of Orange veterans participating in the Bonus March, the Massachusetts American Legion invited Bonus March leader Walter Waters to be the keynote speaker at its 1932 state convention. Pencack, *For God and Country*, 203. The American war veterans' sense of entitlement from civil society seemed to parallel that of British ex-servicemen, as described in Eric J. Leed, *No Man's Land: Combat and Identity in World War I* (New York: Cambridge University Press, 1979), and Stephen R. Ward, "Land Fit for Heroes Lost," in *The War Generation: Veterans of the First World War*, ed. Stephen R. Ward (Port Washington, N.Y.: Kennikat Press, 1975), 10–37. Some evidence suggests that Legion membership grew in importance in the Depression as a source of business connections; after ignoring "occupation" on membership cards through the 1920s, members almost unfailingly filled it out in the 1930s. Paralleling the national pattern, a substantial proportion of members of the Orange American Legion post were merchants or in sales. In a 1938 national survey of Legion members, Pencack found that one-quarter were retail shop owners; in Orange in 1934, the proportion was 26%. Pencack, *For God and Country*, 81; American Legion Post 172 Membership Cards.

26. We know that mass media versions of the war such as "What Price Glory?" (1927) and "The Lost Squadron" (1932) played in the movie theaters of Orange and

the nearby town of Athol, though it is unclear how they shaped the memory of the war.

27. At 250 members, the Universalists were among the largest Protestant denominations in Orange in 1932; others were Swedish Lutherans (252), Congregationalists (200), Methodists (200), and Baptists (172). There were 700 Catholics. *Enterprise and Journal*, February 4, 1932.

28. Ibid., June 1, 1923, 4; November 14, 1924; May 31, 1929.

29. Author's interview with Henry W. Littlefield, Bridgeport, Conn., July 14, 1993.

30. *Enterprise and Journal*, May 29, 1931.

31. "List of Material for Work with Boys and Girls, 1931," National Council for Prevention of War Educational Department papers, Peace Collection, Swarthmore College Library, Swarthmore, Pa., micro reel 41.32. Holiday suggestions also appear in a book by the head of the NCPW education department, Florence Brewer Boeckel, *Between War and Peace: A Handbook for Peace Workers* (New York: Macmillan, 1928). The slogan "the new patriotism is peace" appeared in the Annual Report of the Massachusetts WILPF for 1929.

32. "Disarmament Caravan Reaches Orange," *Enterprise and Journal*, September 4, 1931, 7. See the records of the Massachusetts WILPF in WILPF Papers, U.S. Section—Massachusetts, box 8; also Peace Caravan materials in box 4, WILPF Papers, Peace Collection, Swarthmore College Library.

33. *Enterprise and Journal*, June 1, 1933, 1.

34. J. Michael Moore's interview with Wallace Fiske, West Hartford, Conn., April 4, 1991.

35. I found the Paul Saint-Gaudens (1900–1954) sketch, with Wallace Fiske's mailing address, in the "Peace Monuments and Symbols, 1932– " folder, Peace Collection, Swarthmore College Library. But no record of the design, or correspondence with Fiske, appears in the Paul Saint-Gaudens Papers, Dartmouth College Library, Hanover, N.H.

36. Pollia had made his living as a sculptor of war memorials in the New York City area since the middle twenties. His first commission in western Massachusetts came in the summer of 1928 when the Massachusetts United War Veterans invited him to create a memorial in Greenfield marking the thirtieth anniversary of the Spanish-American War. Biographical references to Pollia (1893–1954) pieced together from Boston Museum of Fine Arts Scrapbooks, 3:56; 10:118; 11:29; 13:122; 17:120; as well as *Who Was Who in American Art*, ed. Peter Hastings Falk (Madison, Conn.: Soundview Press, 1985), 489; Mantle Fielding's *Dictionary of American Painters, Sculptors, and Engravers*, 2d ed., ed. Glen B. Opitz (Poughkeepsie, N.Y.: Appolo Books, 1987), 733; *Who Was Who in America*, vol. 3: *1951–60*, 692.

37. Thanks to Karal Ann Marling for information about "the educator" as a genre of public sculpture.

38. On European war memorials as sites of mourning rather than national glorification, see Jay Winter, *Sites of Memory, Sites of Mourning: The Great War in European Cultural History* (Cambridge University Press, 1995). Winter observes that "Citizenship is affirmed in war memorial art, but it is expressed in terms of a sacrifice which must never be allowed to happen again" (95). An excellent image of Albert Toft's World War memorial in Streatham, dedicated "to our glorious dead" in 1921, appears in Derek Boorman, *At the Going Down of the Sun: British First World War Memorials* (York, Eng.: Ebor Press, 1988). On the funereal aspects of British war memorials, see Thomas Laqueur, "Memory and Naming in the Great War," in Gillis, *Commemorations*, 150–67. While many figurative statues appear in World War I monuments in Great Britain, many more monuments contain allegorical and religious imagery, especially crosses, a feature seldom found in American or French memorials. Besides Boorman's photo book, other sources for images of World War I memorials in Britain are Colin McIntyre, *Monuments of War: How to Read a War Memorial* (London: Robert Hale, 1990), and Alan Borg, *War Memorials: From Antiquity to the Present* (London: Leo Cooper, 1991), which despite its title focuses primarily on the 1919–39 period. Käthe Kollwitz's *Mourning Parents* sculpture in memory of her son Peter who was killed in the war is described in Robert Cowley, "The Mourning Parents," *MHQ: Quarterly Journal of Military History* 3 (1990): 30–39. The most extensive research on World War I memorials in France appears in Antoine Prost, *Les anciens combattants et la société française, 1914–39*, vol. 3 (Paris, 1977), "Mentalités et idéologies," 48–50. Prost's typology of war memorials, ranging from nationalistic to pacifistic, also appears in his chapter "Les monuments aux morts," in *Les lieux de mémoire*, ed. Pierre Nora, vol. 1 (Paris, 1984), "La Republique," pp. 195–225. A comparative treatment of war memorials appears in a special issue of *Guerres Mondiales et Conflits Contemporains*, no. 167 (July 1992). It includes essays in French on Britain, France, Italy, Australia, and New Zealand, as well as an introductory essay in English by K. S. Inglis, "War Memorials: Ten Questions for Historians," 5–21.

39. An account of the debate over whom to include on the plaque appeared in the *Enterprise and Journal*, March 8, 1934. On the gendered memory of war, see the "Introduction" in *Behind the Lines: Gender and the Two World Wars*, ed. Margaret Randolph Higonnet, Jane Jenson, Sonya Michel, and Margaret Collins Weitz (New Haven: Yale University Press, 1987).

40. Pollia, conveniently ignoring his earlier commissions, declared at the dedication that he never liked to see the "machinery of war memorialized in bronze," and never included weapons in his memorials. "World War Monument Dedicated," *Enterprise and Journal*, May 31, 1934, 1.

41. Four weeks before the dedication, on May 2, 1934, the American Legion Americanism Commission meeting in Indianapolis passed a resolution "That we decry and deplore the unwarranted, unpatriotic, and subversive pacifistic activities

of so many individuals and organizations over the country, particularly those following a religious calling" (American Legion Library, Indianapolis). There is no evidence that the national American Legion was aware of the monument. In July 1935, Thomas Owens, national historian of the American Legion, sent a request to state historians for information on and photographs of war memorials. The Massachusetts survey lists monuments in several western Massachusetts towns, including the state memorial at Mount Greylock, but nothing built after 1933. Microfilm 90-14019, American Legion Library, Indianapolis.

42. Fiske had organized the Orange Community Forum to present free lectures on the issues of the day. The Fall 1934 line-up included Professor Ralph S. Harlow of Smith College, who used Nye Committee testimony to talk about the evils of the "munitions racket," and Sidney B. Fay, chair of the Department of History and Government at Harvard University, who told his audience that "the illusion that war pays has been destroyed." *Enterprise and Journal*, December 13, 1934, 5.

43. A summary of the 1939 survey appears in Pencack, *For God and Country*, 44. On the veterans and American foreign policy, see Donald J. Lisio, "The United States: Bread and Butter Politics," in Ward, *The War Generation*, 38–58. For a contemporary argument that Legion members had diverse political opinions not expressed by their national leaders, see Sylvanus Cook, "The Real American Legion," *Nation*, September 7, 1927, 224–25.

44. There was sizable antimilitary sentiment among British and French world war veterans. On the French, see Antoine Prost, *In the Wake of War: Les Anciens Combattants and French Society*, trans. Helen McPhail (Oxford: Berg, 1992). This translation, which condenses Prost's three-volume original, includes more of his material on veterans politics than that on war memorials. Of course, the principal work arguing for the antimilitarism of English World War veterans is Paul Fussell's *The Great War and Modern Memory* (New York: Oxford University Press, 1975). There is little evidence that Orange's World War veterans shared the alienation of the "lost generation" of British writers, or even of American counterparts such as Ernest Hemingway or John Dos Passos. But their focus on their buddies and insistence on a figurative statue rather than the kind of allegorical nationalistic monument prevalent at the turn of the century does suggest the break with earlier idealistic traditions of memorializing war that Fussell argues for.

45. *Enterprise and Journal*, May 31, 1934, 8.

46. Ibid., April 25, 1935. Several monuments to the 104th's role in the battle of Apremont exist in western Massachusetts, including Apremont Square in Springfield and a monument in Westfield.

47. See "Adorns Front Page," *Enterprise and Journal*, August 30, 1934; "Local Monument Gets Wide Recognition," *Enterprise and Journal*, November 12, 1936, 1, 3; "Orange Memorial Is Unique in Absence of War Feeling," unknown newspaper in Chaisson scrapbook, May 28, 1938. It is unclear how widely the Orange monu-

ment was known in peace circles in the 1930s. While a photo and press release about the monument appear in the "Peace Monuments and Symbols, 1932– " file of the Swarthmore College Peace Collection, the monument does not appear in any of the educational materials on "peace symbols" that Zonia Baber prepared for distribution by the WILPF in the late 1930s. See Baber, "Peace Symbols," *Chicago Schools Journal* 18 (March–June 1937): 151–58.

48. "Time to Teach Americanism," *Enterprise and Journal*, May 14, 1936, 2; "In Memory of Those Who Served," *Enterprise and Journal*, May 28, 1936, 2. These editorials appeared in the midst of a newspaper debate over Jehovah's Witnesses' refusal to salute the flag. Editor Roy French attacked the religious sect as unpatriotic; Wallace Fiske wrote in defending the Witnesses (April 30, 1936), prompting an editorial response attacking "those who don't believe anyone should salute the flag if they don't choose to and those who think a religion which preaches such stuff should be tolerated" (*Enterprise and Journal*, May 28, 1936, 2).

49. *Enterprise and Journal*, November 12, 1936, 5. In 1931, Talbot declared, "I could not stand on the same platform with men like John Haynes Holmes, Rabbi Steven Wise, Harry Emerson Fosdick, and others that seek to destroy our religious convictions and true spirit of patriotism" (*Enterprise and Journal*, May 29, 1931).

50. "Orange Internationally Known," ibid., June 3, 1937. A picture of the statue was prominently featured in a proposal sent to the United Nations site selection committee. "Presenting Orange, Massachusetts, as a Site of the Permanent Seat of the United Nations Organization," December 1945, ms. in possession of Richard Chaisson, Athol, Mass. Orange was not the only Massachusetts town that dreamed of hosting the UN; in the wake of a comment from a member of the site selection committee that he favored a "New England town," several other municipalities, including West Boylston (near Worcester), Lexington, and Concord, sent in bids. Richard J. Chaisson, "United Nations Might Have Settled in Orange in 1945," *Worcester Sunday Telegram*, October 25, 1970.

51. The "We Wonder?" cartoon appeared in the *Enterprise and Journal*, November 11, 1937; "Twenty Years After, Preparedness Again," *Enterprise and Journal*, November 17, 1938, 3; "Armistice Day Will Be Observed on Saturday," *Enterprise and Journal*, November 9, 1939, 1; "Another Memorial Day," *Enterprise and Journal*, May 30, 1940, 2.

52. Ibid., August 22, 1946, 1; November 27, 1947. Of course, VJ Day never became a federal holiday, and became a state holiday only in Rhode Island, which in 1980s considered abolishing it for fear that it discouraged Japanese investment in the state. G. Kurt Piehler, *Remembering War the American Way* (Washington, D.C.: Smithsonian Institution Press, 1995). At the national level, there existed an American Commission for Living War Memorials, but it's unclear how active it was in Massachusetts. In 1944, the *Saturday Evening Post* featured a letter from a World War II soldier attacking World War I memorials, stating that the money that might

be used to create World War II memorials should instead "go toward slum clearance, child clinics, or any one of a thousand useful projects." "Letter of the Week," *Saturday Evening Post*, October 7, 1944, 48.

53. *Enterprise and Journal*, November 11, 1948; "Cyril Brubaker Stresses Peace in Veterans Day Address," *Enterprise and Journal*, November 15, 1956.

54. "Memorial Committee Shoots for $300 for Flagpole," ibid., October 28, 1965, 6; "Flagpole to be Dedicated," ibid., May 26, 1966, 1; That same year, the high-school students produced their own Memorial Day assembly, reading World War I–era poems by Carl Sandburg, Randall Jarrell, and Siegfried Sassoon, and singing "Where Have All the Flowers Gone?" Orange's elected officials attacked the holiday program as "inappropriate" and "lacking patriotism." "Memorial Day Program Presented at Mahar," ibid., June 9, 1966, 3.

55. "Peace Vigil Permit Denied," Greenfield *Recorder*, May 27, 1971; "Peace Vigil at Orange Monday OK'd," Worcester *Telegram*, May 29, 1971; "Court Ruling Clears Orange Peace Vigil," Worcester *Gazette*, May 29, 1971; "Peace Vigil is Held in Orange," Worcester *Telegram*, June 1, 1971; "Hundreds Turn Out for Ceremonies," *Enterprise and Journal*, June 2, 1971, 1, 9; "Orange Honors Its Own War Dead in Own Way," unknown newspaper in the Chaisson scrapbook, June 2, 1971.

56. The quotation is from "War Has No Winners," *Orange Oracle*, June 1984, 4.

57. "Essay Contest at Mahar," ibid., May 1984, 4; "Peace in 1984," ibid., June 1984, 3. Pacifist vigils in Orange during the Gulf War are described in "Weekly Vigils Begin in Orange," Worcester *Telegram & Gazette*, January 22, 1991; "100 Walk Out on Classes in Protest of War," Springfield *Union-News*, January 17, 1991.

58. In 1984, the Rural Peace Coalition and the Pioneer Junior Women's Club proposed adding a Memorial Day stop at the World War I statue in honor of its fiftieth anniversary, but confessed they were "not sure" how the proposal would be accepted by the American Legion. Letter from Mary-Ann DeVita Palmieri to Joanna Fisher, March 15, 1984, in Richard Chaisson collection. As it turned out, the parade was canceled that year on account of rain.

59. In 1998, a version of the World War I honor roll became part of a redesigned Memorial Park that included new plaques for those who served in World War II, Korea, and Vietnam.

60. The tax bill cartoon appeared in the *Enterprise and Journal*, June 3, 1937, 1; the snow photo appeared in an unknown newspaper in the Chaisson scrapbook, March 20, 1956.

61. Kenneth Richards, *Memories of a Small Town Yankee* (Athol: Millers River Publishing Company, 1985), 39.

62. Author's interview with Robert P. Collen, Orange, Mass., December 15, 1994. In 1951, Collen wrote a poem about Pollia's monument. "Robert Collen of Orange Wins $100 Tufts College Poetry Prize," unidentified newspaper in the Chaisson scrapbook, May 8, 1951.

63. Henry Littlefield recalled the statue as that of a returning soldier comforting the son of one of the men killed in combat, and said that it symbolized how the members of the community cared for one another. Littlefield interview, Bridgeport, Conn., July 14, 1993. The statistic on Orange's per capita income relative to other Massachusetts towns is from 1989, and appears in *Massachusetts Municipal Profiles, 1993–94*, ed. Edith R. Horner (Palo Alto, Calif.: Information Publications, 1993).

64. On the clenched fist as a common image in the Great Depression, especially its advertising, see Roland Marchand, *Advertising the American Dream: Making Way for Modernity, 1920–1940* (Berkeley: University of California Press, 1985), 324–32.

65. "Monument Proposed for Orange Draws Protest," Greenfield *Recorder*, September 15, 1984.

66. Brochure, *Save Our Statue* (1996); Orange, Massachusetts, essay contest described in "What Does It Mean to Them? Children Tell Peace Statue's Story," *Greenfield Recorder*, March 6, 1996, 5. The committee's original plan to move the statue from the center of the park to one side, to allow more space for public events, encountered stiff resistance from veterans' organizations among other groups. I heard a debate over moving the statue at a public meeting held at the Orange Redevelopment Authority, February 11, 1997. Committee members had invited me to their meeting to ask, as a historian who has studied the history of the statue, whether or not I thought it should be moved.

67. On the development of national rituals in the half-century after the Civil War, see Cecilia Elizabeth O'Leary, *To Die For: The Paradox of American Patriotism* (Princeton: Princeton University Press, 1999).

68. *U.S. Statues at Large* 52 (1938): 351.

69. James E. Young, *Texture of Memory: Holocaust Memorials and Meaning* (New Haven: Yale University Press, 1993), xi.

70. On the importance of patriotic symbols as mediating between local and national, vernacular and official interests, see John Bodnar, *Remaking America: Public Memory, Commemoration, and Patriotism in the Twentieth Century* (Princeton: Princeton University Press, 1992).

71. On the essential sameness of local Civil War soldier monuments as embodiments of national memory, see Kirk Savage, *Standing Soldiers, Kneeling Slaves: Race, Art, and Monument in Nineteenth-Century America* (Princeton: Princeton University Press, 1997). On the factors making for uniformity versus diversity in France, see Antoine Prost, "Mémoires locales et mémoires nationales: Les monuments de 1914–18 en France," *Guerres Mondiales et Conflits Contemporains*, no 167 (July 1992): 41–50; Daniel Sherman, "Art, Commerce, and the Production of Memory in France after World War I," in Gillis, *Commemorations*, 186–211; and David G. Troyansky, "Monumental Politics: National History and Local Memory in French Monuments aux Morts in the Department of the Aisne since 1870," *French Historical Studies* 15 (Spring 1987): 121–41. For an example of how local circumstances

shaped monument making in England, see K. S. Inglis, "The Homecoming: The War Memorial Movement in Cambridge, England," *Journal of Contemporary History* 27 (October 1992): 583–605.

72. Robert Musil, "Monuments," in *Posthumous Papers of a Living Author,* trans. Peter Wortsman (Hygiene, Colo.: Eridanos Press, 1987), 61–64. Musil's essay was originally published in 1936.

73. As part of the effort to publicize the statue to tourists, in April 1999 State Senator Stephen Brewer introduced legislation designating the Orange memorial "Massachusetts' Official Peace Statue." "War Statue Could Be Paean to Peace," *Springfield Sunday Republican,* Franklin County Edition, April 4, 1999, A9.

74. See Maria Sturken, "The Wall, the Screen, and the Image: The Vietnam Veterans Memorial," *Representations* 35 (Summer 1991): 118–42. For a critique of both the Goodacre and the Hart statues, see Christopher Knight, "Politics Mars Remembrance," *Sacramento Bee,* November 7, 1993, Forum section, 1, 6. Knight's critique originally appeared in the *Los Angeles Times* "Calendar" section.

75. A survey of approximately three hundred Vietnam War memorials in 1988 showed that figurative statuary, especially black and white soldiers in a "buddies" pose, was common, though representations of a black assisting a white soldier, as in memorials in Wilmington, Delaware, and Phoenix, Arizona, seem more common than depictions of a white soldier helping a black one. Among the nonfigurative memorials of the 1980s, many combined commemoration of World War II, Korea, and Vietnam, suggesting not only attempts to associate Vietnam and Korea with the more popular earlier war but also perhaps how the Vietnam veterans' push for recognition stimulated World War II veterans' belated efforts to memorialize themselves. Jerry L. Strait and Sandra S. Strait, *Vietnam War Memorials: An Illustrated Reference to Veterans Tributes throughout the United States* (Jefferson, N.C.: McFarland, 1988).

76. See, for example, the foreword to Charles W. Sweeney with James A. and Marion K. Antonucci, *Wars' End: An Eyewitness Account of America's Last Atomic Mission* (New York: Avon Books, 1997). Sweeney was the commander of the plane that dropped the atomic bomb on Nagasaki. Up until 1994, Sweeney said, "speaking out about our mission never struck me as an urgency. I did not doubt for a moment that the historical facts spoke for themselves" (x). But upon hearing of the Smithsonian's plans for the exhibition of the *Enola Gay,* he felt "outraged and betrayed" at the curators' attempt to "change the history of the war in the Pacific" (xi). Sweeney wrote his book because "soon those of us who fought the war will no longer be here to set the record straight" (xii).

77. On the equation of the protection of America with that of hometown and family during World War II, see Robert Westbrook, "I Want a Girl, Just Like the Girl That Married Harry James: American Women and the Problem of Political Obligation in World War II," *American Quarterly* 42 (December 1990): 587–614, and Westbrook, "Fighting for the American Family: Private Interests and Political

Obligation in World War II," in *The Power of Culture: Critical Essays in American History*, ed. Richard W. Fox and T. J. Jackson Lears (Chicago: University of Chicago Press, 1993), 194–221.

## 3. Celebrating the City

1. The view of ritual as functioning to integrate society and relieve social tensions is rooted in the tradition of British social anthropologists such as A. R. Radcliffe-Brown; that of ritual as a collective representation is rooted in the traditional of French anthropologists such as Emile Durkheim. These schools are neatly summarized in Sherry Ortner, "Theory in Anthropology since the 1960s," *Comparative Studies in Society and History* 26 (January 1984): 126–66. Their concepts have been applied to America in the works of scholars interested in "civil religion" such as Robert Bellah and W. Lloyd Warner; the limitations of these approaches are succinctly noted in Steven Lukes, "Political Ritual and Social Integration," *Sociology* 9 (May 1975): 289–308. On ritual as communication, see Sally Faulk Moore and Barbara Myerhoff, "Introduction," in *Secular Ritual*, ed. Moore and Myerhoff (Amsterdam: Van Gorcum, 1977), and Clifford Geertz, *The Interpretation of Cultures* (New York: Basic Books, 1973); the limitations of Geertz's assumption that culture as a "text" contains more consonance than dissonance are discussed in Ronald G. Walters, "Signs of the Times: Clifford Geertz and Historians," *Social Research* 47 (Autumn 1980): 537–56, and Aletta Biersack, "Local Knowledge, Local History: Geertz and Beyond," in *The New Cultural History*, ed. Lynn Hunt (Berkeley: University of California Press, 1989), 72–96. On hegemony and the idea of a public culture, see T. J. Jackson Lears, "The Concept of Cultural Hegemony: Problems and Possibilities," *American Historical Review* 90 (June 1985): 567–93, and Thomas Bender, "Wholes and Parts: The Need for Synthesis in American History," *Journal of American History* 73 (June 1986): 120–36.

2. On Christmas revelry in the colonial and antebellum city as expressions of suppressed early modern English rituals, see Stephen Nissenbaum, *The Battle for Christmas* (New York: Knopf, 1996), and Susan G. Davis, *Parades and Power: Street Theatre in Nineteenth-Century Philadelphia* (Philadelphia: Temple University Press, 1986). On the German holiday custom of "belsnickeling," see Davis, *Parades and Power*, 104–5. On "Pinkster," "Election Day," and the African content of African American holiday customs, see Shane White, "It Was a Proud Day: African-Americans, Festivals, and Parades in the North, 1741–1834," *Journal of American History* 81 (June 1994): 13–50. On the increasingly militant nationalism of Irish Catholics on St. Patrick's Day, see Kenneth Moss, "St. Patrick's Day Celebrations and the Formation of Irish-American Identity, 1845–1875," *Journal of Social History* 29 (Fall 1995): 125–48, and Timothy J. Meagher, "Why Should We Care for a Little Trouble or a Walk through the Mud? St. Patrick's Day and Columbus Day Pa-

rades in Worcester, Massachusetts, 1845–1915," *New England Quarterly* 58 (March 1985): 5–26. On German Americans' penchant for colorful street display, see Kathleen Neils Conzen, "Ethnicity as Festive Culture: Nineteenth-Century German-America on Parade," in *The Invention of Ethnicity*, ed. W. Sollars (New York: Oxford University Press, 1989), 44–76.

3. On "rough" and "respectable" parade styles, see Davis, *Parades and Power*, 159–66. On popular protest during the Revolution and after, see Beverly Orlove Held, "To Instruct and Improve . . . To Entertain and Please: American Civic Protests and Pageants, 1765–1784" (Ph.D. diss., University of Michigan, 1987); Paul Gilje, *The Road to Mobocracy: Popular Disorder in New York City, 1763–1834* (Chapel Hill: University of North Carolina Press, 1987); Thomas Slaughter, "The Crowd in Eighteenth-Century America: Reflections and New Directions," *Pennsylvania Magazine of History and Biography* 115 (January 1991): 3–34; Barbara Clark Smith, "Food Rioters in the American Revolution," *William and Mary Quarterly* 51 (January 1994): 3–38. More on antebellum Philadelphia's working-class political and nativist processions appears in Bruce Laurie, *Working People of Philadelphia, 1800–1850* (Philadelphia: Temple University Press, 1980), and David Montgomery, "The Shuttle and the Cross: Weavers and Artisans in the Kensington Riots of 1844," *Journal of Social History* 5 (1972): 411–46. The above works largely root American forms of political demonstration in those of England, as described in E. P. Thompson, "Moral Economy of the English Crowd in the Eighteenth Century," *Past and Present* 50 (1971): 76–136.

4. On the Grand Federal Procession of 1788, burlesque militia processions, and other "class dramas," see Davis, *Parades and Power*, 113–53. David Waldstreicher argues that during the American Revolution newspapers played a crucial role in papering over local class differences with images and rhetoric of American nationalism, depicting the urban crowd as always giving voluble and visible assent to the actions of their elite leaders. Waldstreicher, "Rites of Rebellion, Rites of Assent: Celebrations, Print Culture, and the Origins of American Nationalism," *Journal of American History* 82 (June 1995): 37–61. According to Len Travers, July Fourth in the early years of the republic witnessed considerable competition between Federalist and Republican elites seeking to define the day's political meaning through ceremony, as well as the growing separation of those elites from the urban working class which celebrated the day as a holiday. Len Travers, *Celebrating the Fourth: Independence Day and the Rites of Nationalism in the Early Republic* (Amherst: University of Massachusetts Press, 1997).

5. Sean Wilentz described artisanal festivals in New York City in the early nineteenth century changing "from rituals of mutuality to declarations of class." Sean Wilentz, "Artisan Republican Festivals and the Rise of Class Conflict in New York City, 1788–1837," in *Working-Class America: Essays on Labor, Community, and American Society*, ed. Michael H. Frisch and Daniel J. Walkowitz (Urbana: Univer-

sity of Illinois Press, 1983), 37–77. On women's largely unexamined role in civic celebrations, see Mary Ryan, "The American Parade: Representations of Nineteenth Century Social Order," in *The New Cultural History*, ed. Lynn Hunt (Berkeley: University of California Press, 1989), 131–53. Ryan's study of civic celebrations in New York City, New Orleans, and San Francisco in the mid-nineteenth century confirms the importance of these events, and the voluntary organizations formed to participate in them, for the consolidation of particular ethnic, class, and religious identities in the city, as well as the absence of any iconography designed to symbolize the city as a whole. Mary P. Ryan, *Civic Wars: Democracy and Public Life in the American City during the Nineteenth Century* (Berkeley: University of California Press, 1997).

6. Among evidence that the elite were abandoning downtown civic celebrations by the late nineteenth century were pleas that they stay in town for the occasion, such as that of Julia Ward Howe, "How the Fourth of July Should Be Celebrated," *Forum* 15 (July 1893): 567–74. Mary Ryan also notes this phenomenon in *Civic Wars*.

7. *North American Review* 84 (April 1857): 353.

8. On downtown cultural institutions as civic symbols, see Helen Horowitz, *Culture and the City: Cultural Philanthropy in Chicago from the 1880s to 1917* (Lexington: University of Kentucky Press, 1976). On municipal sponsorship of holiday amusements, see Frank Couvares, "The Triumph of Commerce: Class Culture and Mass Culture in Pittsburgh," in Frisch and Walkowitz, *Working Class America*, 123–52.

9. Barr Feree, "Elements of a Successful Parade," *Century* 60 (July 1990): 459. On symbolic representations of the civic ideal in public sculpture, see Michele H. Bogart, *Public Sculpture and the Civic Ideal in New York City, 1890–1930* (Chicago: University of Chicago Press, 1989).

10. E. A. Ross, "The Mob Mind," *Popular Science Monthly* 51 (July 1897): 390–98. Ross was among the many American sociologists of the period influenced by the work of the French writer Gustav Le Bon, who sought to develop theories of crowd behavior as a way to delegitimize mass proletarian action. See Susanna Barrows, *Distorting Mirrors: Visions of the Crowd in Late Nineteenth-Century France* (New Haven, Conn.: Yale University Press, 1981), and Gregory W. Bush, *Lord of Attention: Gerald Stanley Lee and the Crowd Metaphor in Industrializing America* (Amherst: University of Massachusetts Press, 1991).

11. William Orr, "An American Holiday," *Atlantic Monthly* 103 (June 1909): 788.

12. On the growth of Labor Day, see Michael Kazin and Steven J. Ross, "America's Labor Day: The Dilemma of a Workers' Celebration," *Journal of American History* 78 (March 1992): 1294–1323.

13. The early modern city was replete with elaborate forms of public ritual,

including royal, religious, military, and craft processions as well as carnivals, commercial displays, and outdoor drama. Indeed the origins of many cities lay in their role as centers for religious and political ritual as well as economic exchange; Richard Trexler notes that in the early modern city the cleric, noble, and merchant worked hand in hand in the "civic cultivation of holiness." Richard C. Trexler, *Public Life in Renaissance Florence* (New York: Academic Press, 1980), 1. Among many other analyses of early modern public ritual and politics are Edward Muir, *Civic Ritual in Renaissance Venice* (Princeton: Princeton University Press, 1981); David Bergeron, *English Civic Pageantry, 1558–1642* (Columbia: University of South Carolina Press, 1971); and the essays in *Rites of Power: Symbolism, Ritual, and Politics since the Middle Ages*, ed. Sean Wilentz (Philadelphia: University of Pennsylvania Press, 1985).

14. In a second version of the Philadelphia pageant, staged in 1912, the consolidated city was personified by the wife of the reform mayor Rudolph Blankenburg, whose administration, not coincidentally, was in constant battle with the ward-based city council. I discuss the Philadelphia historical pageants more fully in "Public Ritual and Cultural Hierarchy: Philadelphia's Civic Celebrations at the Turn of the Twentieth Century," *Pennsylvania Magazine of History and Biography* 107 (July 1983): 421–48.

15. St. Louis labor leaders dismissed the pageant's representation of social harmony, instead invoking the image of the protest march by suggesting that a procession of 10,000 unemployed carrying banners condemning "the beastly stupidity of an industrial system which starves the workers in the midst of fabulous wealth" would be more appropriate. Otto Paul, "Life as It Is," *St. Louis Labor*, March 14, 1914, 8. I discuss the St. Louis pageant and masque of 1914 more fully in *American Historical Pageantry: The Uses of Tradition in the Early Twentieth Century* (Chapel Hill: University of North Carolina Press, 1990), 157–99.

16. On audience reactions to Oberholtzer's pageant, see Glassberg, "Public Ritual and Cultural Hierarchy," 436–42; on the St. Louis pageant crowd, see Glassberg, *American Historical Pageantry*, 191–94.

17. On the evolution of Mardi Gras into a "civic festival" in the late nineteenth century, see Reid Mitchell, *All on a Mardi Gras Day: Episodes in the History of New Orleans Carnival* (Cambridge: Harvard University Press, 1995) and Samuel Kinser, *Carnival, American Style: Mardi Gras at New Orleans and Mobile* (Chicago: University of Chicago Press, 1990), 75–118; on Philadelphia's Mummers, see Charles E. Welsh, *O' Dem Golden Slippers* (New York: Thomas Nelson, 1970); on St. Louis, *The Veiled Prophets Golden Jubilee: A Short History of St. Louis' Annual Civic Carnival, 1878–1928* (St. Louis: n.p., 1928); on Louisville, *Souvenir Program: Louisville Fall Celebration* (Louisville: George G. Fetter Printing, 1889); on the New York Hudson-Fulton celebration see Edward Hagaman Hall, ed., *Hudson-Fulton Celebration, 1909* (Albany, N.Y.: J. B. Lyon, 1910).

18. Ray Stannard Baker, "A Corner in Labor: What Is Happening in San Fran-

cisco, Where Unionism Holds Undisputed Sway," *McClure's Magazine* 22 (February 1904): 366–78. A copy of Phelan's address, "The New San Francisco," given at the opening of the Mechanic's Institute Fair on September 1, 1896, is in carton 2, James D. Phelan Papers, Bancroft Library, University of California, Berkeley. Though Phelan had campaigned with Patrick McCarthy for charter reform in 1899, ten years later when he considered the prospect of McCarthy becoming mayor, he remarked, "We will try to avert the calamity." Phelan to Alexander Hawes, September 27, 1909, box 2, James D. Phelan Papers. My synopsis of San Francisco political history is based on William Issel and Robert Cherny, *San Francisco, 1865–1932: Politics, Power, and Urban Development* (Berkeley: University of California Press, 1986); Issel, "Business Power and Political Culture in San Francisco, 1900–1940," *Journal of Urban History* 16 (November 1989): 52–77; Gray A. Brechin, "San Francisco: The City Beautiful," in *Visionary San Francisco,* ed. Paolo Polledri (San Francisco: Museum of Modern Art, 1990), 40–61; Terrence McDonald, *The Parameters of Urban Fiscal Policy: Socioeconomic Change and Political Culture in San Francisco, 1860–1906* (Berkeley: University of California Press, 1986); Michael Kazin, *Barons of Labor: The San Francisco Building Trades and Union Power in the Progressive Era* (Urbana: University of Illinois Press, 1987); and Jules Tygiel, "Where Unionism Holds Undisputed Sway: A Reappraisal of San Francisco's Union Labor Party," *California History* 62 (Fall 1983): 196–215.

19. A list of prominent figures behind the festival appears in "Great Fete to Come Yearly," San Francisco *Call,* October 25, 1909, 1. The city directory reveals that every member of the Portolá executive committee was either a merchant or in real estate. Peixotto quoted in "Joseph Rolph, Jr. is Host at Luncheon," San Francisco *Chronicle,* October 24, 1909, p. 29. While the papers of the Portolá Festival Committee apparently have not survived, the personal papers of several festival organizers are at the California Historical Society, as well as those of the San Francisco Merchants Association and its successor, the San Francisco Chamber of Commerce.

20. A full description of Portolá Week activities appears in *Portolá Festival: Official Souvenir Program, October 19 to 23, 1909* (San Francisco, 1909); also see newspaper descriptions in the *Call, Chronicle,* and *San Francisco Examiner* for that week. On the floats, see "Carnival Closes in Riot of Light," *Call,* September 19, 1909, 34; Arthur H. Dutton, "Creating the Marvelous Portolá Floats," *Call,* October 3, 1909, 3; and "Portolá Decorations to Be on Very Elaborate Scale," *Grizzly Bear* 5 (October 1909): 2.

21. Philip T. Clay, "The Portolá Festival," *Out West* 31 (July 1909): 665. One newspaper commented that "Don Nicholas' blood is as eager for festivity as it was in the days when he was a lusty young hero of the fiestas of the mission settlements." "City Glows in Happy Spirit: San Francisco Ready to Enter Festal Week with Care Thrown to the Winds," *Call,* October 16, 1909, 1. The contrast between displays of

Spanish colors in 1898 and 1909 noted in "Don Gaspar Hailed by Merry Throngs," *Call*, October 20, 1909. Festival Queen Virgilia Bogue's novel described in "Portolá Queen near Dead Line in Caloric Tale," *Call*, August 10, 1909, 3. "Old Spanish" imagery was prevalent throughout the Southwest in civic celebrations at the turn of the century. The organizers of San Francisco's Portolá Festival had the example of "La Fiesta de Los Angeles," sponsored by the Los Angeles Merchants Association between 1894 and 1898. See Isabel C. Wielus, "Las Fiestas de Los Angeles: A Survey of the Yearly Celebrations, 1894–1898" (M.A. thesis, UCLA, 1946), and *Sixty Years in Southern California, 1853–1913: Containing the Reminiscences of Harris Newmark*, ed. Maurice H. Newmark and Marco R. Newmark, 3d ed. (Boston: Houghton Mifflin, 1930), 605–7. See also Leonard Pitt, *The Decline of the Californios: A Social History of the Spanish-Speaking Californians, 1846–1890* (Berkeley: University of California Press, 1966), 283–90; and Ronald Grimes's fascinating study of the fiesta in Santa Fe, which started in 1911, *Symbol and Conquest: Public Ritual and Drama in Santa Fe, New Mexico* (Ithaca: Cornell University Press, 1976).

22. See Charles Gayles to James D. Phelan, September 21, 1909, box 97, folder 5, James D. Phelan Papers. Its representation of charismatic female sexual power is similar to burlesque posters of the period described in Robert C. Allen, *Horrible Prettiness: Burlesque and American Culture* (Chapel Hill: University of North Carolina Press, 1991).

23. The line-up of the civic and industrial parade appears in "The Great Civic Parade in Detail," *Chronicle*, October 22, 1909, 7, 9. According to one estimate, at least 5,000 of the 20,000 marchers came from various "parlors" of the Native Sons and Daughters of the Golden West. "Portolá Week Great Success for NDGW and NSGW," *Grizzly Bear* 6 (December 1909): 7. On the public representation of Chinese residents in San Francisco, see Catherine Cocks, "Other People's History: Slumming and the Shaping of the American Metropolis, 1870–1915," Organization of American Historians annual meeting, San Francisco, April 1997.

24. "Bread and the Circus," *San Francisco Star*, October 9, 1909, 1. The pamphlet proclaiming that all San Francisco supported the festival was enclosed in a letter from Louis Sloss to James D. Phelan, July 24, 1909, box 102, Phelan Papers. During the fall of 1909 the city's labor newspapers, such as the *Star*, *Labor Clarion*, *Organized Labor*, and the *Coast Seamen's Journal*, devoted much more coverage to the city's Labor Day ceremonies and the commemoration of Henry George's birthday (September 2, 1909), than to the Portolá Festival. The Labor Council boasted that its "Portolá Carnival and Industrial Exposition" was "a sister festival to the city's celebration," and had the approval of the city's "principal business houses and manufacturers." The *Clarion* indicated that manufacturers rented exhibit space, but the only two mentioned by name were quite small, and not located downtown. The Labor Carnival was professionally managed, importing many of its floats and sideshows from the 1909 Seattle Alaska-Yukon-Pacific Exposition, and it appears that

despite tickets sold in advance through the Labor Council's affiliated unions, the carnival failed to raise significant amounts of money above expenses. See "Labor's Portolá Carnival," San Francisco *Labor Clarion*, September 3, 1909, 22; San Francisco *Coast Seamen's Journal* 23 (September 29, 1909): 7; *Call*, October 22, 1909, 11; "Carnival for Labor Temple," *Labor Clarion*, October 24, 1909, 11. Financial information appears in *Labor Clarion*, December 31, 1909, 15; April 15, 1910, 1; May 27, 1910, 13.

25. Quote on the Portolá Festival as evidence of the "community undivided" by real estate man A. S. Baldwin in "Carnival Is City's Crowning Success," *Chronicle*, October 24, 1909, 29. Editorials attacking McCarthy during the festival appeared in "Crocker Will Be Mayor of San Francisco," *Chronicle*, October 19, 1909, 6, and "Let San Franciscans Pull Together Public Welfare Demands that We Carry the Portolá Spirit into the Coming Election," *Chronicle*, October 26, 1909, 6.

26. Quote about the "little brown men" from "The Portolá Parade," *Chronicle*, October 20, 1909, 10. Evidence of underlying hostility toward Asians in "Chinese Float On Fire," *Chronicle*, October 24, 1909, 30. The Japanese population of San Francisco grew nearly eightfold between 1800 and 1910, but it was still only 1% of the city's total population. Meanwhile the percentage of first- and second-generation Chinese immigrants in San Francisco plummeted from 9% of the population in 1890 to less than 3% in 1910. In 1910, the U.S. census counted slightly over 2,800 first- and second-generation Mexican Americans, less than 1% of the city's population, while African Americans constituted less than half of one percent of San Francisco's population that year. *Thirteenth Census of the U.S., 1910*, vol. 2, *Population* (Washington, D.C.: U.S. Government Printing Office, 1913), 162, 166, 174. Local African Americans possibly marched with military or fraternal organizations during Portolá Week, though none of the three African American masonic lodges in San Francisco at the time were listed among the organizations that participated in the civic and industrial procession. Douglas Henry Daniels, *Pioneer Urbanites: A Social and Cultural History of Black San Francisco* (Philadelphia: Temple University Press, 1980), 135.

27. "Parade Crowd Good-Natured: Police Say Spectators Were All Easily Handled and Ready to Obey," *Chronicle*, October 2, 1909, 4. Accounts of Johnson's stay in San Francisco appear in Jack Johnson, *In the Ring and Out* [1927], ed. Gilbert Odd (London: Proteus, 1977), 152, and Randy Roberts, *Papa Jack: Jack Johnson and the Era of White Hopes* (New York: Free Press, 1983), 80, 86.

28. "San Francisco Will Be the City of Carnivals and Large Conventions," *Call*, October 25, 1909, 1. A plan for a Convention League first appeared in Minutes of Board of Directors, San Francisco Merchants Association, July 2, 1909, MS 871, box 6, folder 1, California Historical Society, San Francisco. The Merchants Association launched its Convention League in 1910, and the league secured 23 conventions for the city in 1911. See Issel and Cherney, *San Francisco*, 160. On the festival

as a stimulus to trade, see "City Tired But Happy Counts $5,000,000 in Profits," *Examiner*, October 25, 1909, 1, and "Fiesta Cost Ten Cents a Person," *Call*, October 26, 1909, 1. On November 12, 1909, festival committee member Milton Esberg persuaded the Merchants Association to contribute an additional $1,000 to help erase a deficit of $10,000. Minutes of Board of Directors, San Francisco Merchants Association, MS 871, box 6, folder 1, California Historical Society, San Francisco. See also "Portolá Festival Committee in Need of Ten Thousand Dollars," *Call*, November 19, 1909, 4, and a letter comparing 1909 and 1913 Portolá festival deficits from J. Frank Moroney to James D. Phelan, January 16, 1914, box 97, Phelan Papers.

29. Blaine Phillips, "Harlequin Rules in Don Gaspar's Stead," *Chronicle*, July 24, 1909, 27.

30. Al C. Joy, "Laughing Multitude Frolics in Streets Until Grey Dawn," *Examiner*, October 24, 1909, 1.

31. Newspapers announced the festival with an image of a medieval English–style herald proclaiming Portolá's "order" that the city "let the spirit of Mirth and Folly have free reign." "Gaspar de Portolá Proclaims Coming with Mirth and Folly," *Call*, January 22, 1909, 14. See also "Monarchs of Carnival Launch Reign of Mirth," *Call*, October 20, 1909, 1.

32. Frederick B. Wood, "One Million People See Great Pageant," ibid., October 22, 1909, 4; the "mountain torrents" in "Stupendous Tableau Presents Vision of the Ultimate Joy," ibid., October 24, 1909, 18; and the "storm of pleasure" in "Success of Immense Festival Dumfounds [*sic*] the World and City," *Chronicle*, October 21, 1909, 1. The *Examiner* headlines proclaimed "Mile after Mile Flows on in Dazzling Stream," and "Skies Smile as Living Stream Pours into Carnival City," October 22, 1909, 2, 7; and "Fiesta Fervor Rises to Flood Point as End Nears," October 23, 1909, 2.

33. "City Throbs in Expectation of Tonight's Crashing Finale," *Examiner*, October 23, 1909, 7; "Stupendous Tableau Presents Vision of the Ultimate Joy," *Call*, October 24, 1909, 18.

34. "Women Use Hatpins When in Big Crowd," *Call*, October 24, 1909, 18; Harry Davids, "Epochal Periods of Life Past in Pictured Allegory of Light," ibid., October 24, 1909, 19.

35. William F. Williamson, "The Portolá Festival and the Rebuilding of San Francisco," *Travel Magazine* 15 (October 1909): 15–18, "San Francisco's Great Portolá Festival," *Grizzly Bear* 15 (September 1909): 6, 9; "Show to Raise Funds for Portolá Fete," *Call*, October 7, 1909, 18. Among the works exploring carnival imagery as social criticism are Natalie Zemon Davis, "The Reasons of Misrule,"in *Society and Culture in Early Modern France* (Stanford, Calif.: Stanford University Press, 1975), 97–123, and Davis, *Parades and Power*.

36. Charles Remington, "San Francisco City of Gaiety Where Carnivals Find a

Home," *Chronicle*, October 22, 1909, 4; Edward H. Hamilton, "Well, Wasn't it Amazing? And a First Effort, Too," *Examiner*, October 24, 1909, 64; "The Portolá Atmosphere," *Chronicle*, October 21, 1909, 6; Jesse Cook (San Francisco Police Chief), "Big Crowd Not Unruly," *Call*, October 25, 1909, 2; "Handling the Portolá Crowds," *Call*, October 23, 1909, 14; Santa Fe Railroad brochure promoting the Portolá Festival in "Miscellaneous Items, Portolá Festival," San Francisco Archives, San Francisco Public Library; "Epochal Periods of Life Past in Pictured Allegory of Light," *Call*, October 24, 1909, 19.

37. Moses Rischin, "Sunny Jim Rolph: The First Mayor of All the People," *California Historical Quarterly* 53 (Summer 1974): 165–72. Herman Goldbeck, "The Political Career of James Rolph, Jr.: A Preliminary Study" (M.A. thesis, University of California, Berkeley, 1936). Also see extensive correspondence between Rolph and Phelan, 1909–30, in box 92, Phelan Papers.

38. "Orientals Provide Bright Pageantry Features," *Chronicle*, October 25, 1913, 4; "The Portolá Parades," *Chronicle*, October 25, 1913, 6 (another source of information on the 1913 festival is the papers of "Balboa" Ralph D. Phelps, in the Bancroft Library, University of California, Berkeley); C. V. Horne, "Throngs Cheer Mighty Pageant," *Chronicle*, October 25, 1913, 1. Another author describing the crowd in 1913 noted, "It was a San Francisco crowd. And of all the crowds of all the cities in the world, none knows better the business of being a crowd." J. Lawrence O'Toole, "Crowd Makes the Biggest Spectacle: Memory of It Will Outlive Parade," *Examiner*, October 25, 1913, 3.

39. The deficit of the 1913 fete was $11,000. J. Frank Moroney to James D. Phelan, January 16, 1914, box 97, Phelan Papers. As in 1909, the Board of Supervisors in 1913 apparently did not appropriate money for the festival. It even refused Mayor Rolph's request for $250 for bunting for City Hall, though it did approve the erection of new flagpoles in Union Square. "Mayor Hot at Supervisors," *Daily News*, October 21, 1913, 1; Clerk of the Board of Supervisors, *Journal of the Proceedings, Board of Supervisors, City and County of San Francisco* 8 (1913): 1006. On the various unsuccessful efforts to revive the Portolá festival, see *Chronicle*, July 7, 1922, 3, 18; July 14, 1922, 13, 20; July 18, 1922, 1; July 19, 1922, 13, 22; July 22, 1922, 4; September 20, 1922, 22; October 6, 1922, 3, 9; *Call*, March 30, 1928, 17; *Examiner*, May 11, 1928, 21; May 12, 1928, 28; *Chronicle*, May 11, 1928, 1–2; May 15, 1928, 6; May 18, 1928, 6; October 23, 1929, 19; March 23, 1931, 2; March 23, 1936, 15.

40. On the 1948 festival, see *Portolá Festival: Official Souvenir Program, October 2–November 7, 1948*, Bancroft Library, University of California, Berkeley. On the incongruity of an invented Spanish past and real Mexicans in the present, and wealthy Californians of Spanish descent "representing" Chicanos in civic celebrations of the mid-twentieth century, see Pitt, *Decline of the Californios*, 290–96. Also see Carey McWilliams, *North of Mexico*, and an exchange in the *Santa Barbara News Press* during the Santa Barbara Fiesta in 1969, both reprinted in *Minorities in Califor-*

*nia History*, ed. George E. Frakes and Curtis B. Solberg (New York: Random House, 1971), 145–53.

41. While the symbolism of the urban crowd as a microcosm of national unity was an important element of World War I rallies in America, it was never as strong as in Europe, where it developed further in the interwar years in support of fascist politics. On the role of crowd imagery in World War I rallies, see my *American Historical Pageantry*, 216–27. On crowd symbolism and nationalism in America during the 1930s, see Warren Susman, "The People's Fair: Cultural Contradictions of a Consumer Society," in *Culture as History: The Transformation of American Society in the Twentieth Century* (New York: Pantheon, 1984), 211–29. On the connection between crowd symbolism and nationalism in Europe, see Eric Hobsbawm, "Mass Producing Traditions: Europe, 1870–1914," in *The Invention of Tradition*, ed. Eric Hobsbawm and Terence Ranger (New York: Cambridge University Press, 1983), 263–307, and George Mosse, *The Nationalization of the Masses: Political Symbolism and Mass Movements in Germany from the Napoleonic Wars through the Third Reich* (New York: H. Fertig, 1975). On the rise of festival marketplaces in American cities since the 1970s, see M. Christine Boyer, "Cities for Sale: Merchandising History at South Street Seaport," in *Variations on a Theme Park: The New American City and the End of Public Space*, ed. Michael Sorkin (New York: Hill and Wang, 1992), 181–204. The connection between urban festivity and consumption can be traced back to the public celebrations created by department stores at the turn of the century, such as Thanksgiving Day parades. William R. Leach, "Transformations in a Culture of Consumption: Women and Department Stores, 1890–1913," *Journal of American History* 71 (September 1984): 319–42.

42. On professional sports arenas as private enterprises considered as public spaces, see Steven A. Riess, "Spectator Sport and Semi-Public Space," in *City Games: The Evolution of American Urban Society and the Rise of Sports* (Urbana: University of Illinois Press, 1989), 203–28. On the possible connections between sport, popular entertainment, and politics, see John J. MacAloon, "Sociation and Sociability in Political Celebrations," in *Celebration: Studies in Festivity and Ritual*, ed. Victor Turner (Washington, D.C.: Smithsonian Institution Press, 1982), 255–71.

## 4. Watching *The Civil War*

1. I will be discussing *The Civil War* as a single eleven-hour film designed to be shown in segments on television over the course of a week. That is the way the viewers who wrote to Burns first experienced it, rather than as a series of nine separate episodes, the way it was packaged on videocassette. With widespread sales of videocassettes for home and classroom use, the experience of viewing the film from beginning to end over a single week is probably less common than that of watching favorite episodes.

2. On the separation between highbrow and lowbrow, see Lawrence W. Levine, *Highbrow and Lowbrow: The Emergence of Cultural Hierarchy in America* (Cambridge: Harvard University Press, 1988). On the early folklorists' quest for traditions untainted by modern commercial popular culture, see the essays in *Folk Roots, New Roots: Folklore in American Life*, ed. Jane S. Becker and Barbara Franco (Lexington, Mass.: Museum of Our National Heritage, 1988) and David Whisnant, *All That Is Native and Fine: The Politics of Culture in an American Region* (Chapel Hill: University of North Carolina Press, 1983); and Joan Shelley Rubin, *Constance Rourke and American Culture* (Chapel Hill: University of North Carolina Press, 1980). The heirs of this approach can be found in community oral history projects' efforts to uncover an authentic people's history apart from commercial mass culture; for examples, see Linda Shopes, "Oral History and Community Involvement: The Baltimore Neighborhood Heritage Project," and James R. Green, "Engaging in People's History: The Massachusetts History Workshop," both in *Presenting the Past: Essays on History and the Public*, ed. Susan Porter Benson, Stephen Brier, and Roy Rosenzweig (Philadelphia: Temple University Press, 1986), 249–63, 339–59. Among the best examples of American studies scholars using popular culture as evidence of an "American" historical consciousness are Henry Nash Smith, *Virgin Land: The American West as Symbol and Myth* (Cambridge: Harvard University Press, 1950); David Grimsted, *Melodrama Unveiled: American Theatre and Culture, 1800–1850* (Chicago: University of Chicago Press, 1968); and John Cawelti, *Adventure, Mystery, and Romance* (Chicago, 1976).

3. Robert Sklar, "Historical Films: Scofflaws and the Historian-Cop," *Reviews in American History* 25 (June 1997): 346–50. Sklar is reviewing Robert Brent Toplin, *History by Hollywood: The Use and Abuse of the American Past* (Urbana: University of Illinois Press, 1996), one of the better volumes that attempt a close analysis of the production of historical films, the themes filmmakers try to express, the values of their times the film embodies, and the use of reviews to get at audience response. See also *American History/American Film: Interpreting the Hollywood Image*, ed. John E. O'Connor and Martin A. Jackson (New York: Frederick Ungar, 1979).

4. For a concise summary of audience response theory, see Robert C. Allen, "Reader-Oriented Criticism and Television," in *Channels of Discourse: Television and Contemporary Criticism*, ed. Robert C. Allen (Chapel Hill: University of North Carolina Press, 1987), 72–112. See also Stuart Hall, "Notes on Deconstructing the Popular," in *People's History and Socialist Theory*, ed. Raphael Samuel (London: Routledge, 1981), 227–40. Among recent works that use this body of theory to understand audiences for popular culture in the American past are Michael Denning, *Mechanic Accents: Dime Novels and Working-Class Culture in America* (New York: Verso, 1987) and George Lipsitz, *Time Passages: Collective Memory and American Popular Culture* (Minneapolis: University of Minnesota Press, 1990).

5. In an interview in 1994, Burns stated that he sees himself as the audience's representative, able to present what "an interested but ignorant member of the

audience, an eighth grader perhaps, might need to know to keep them in their chair." David Thelen, "The Movie Maker as Historian: Conversations With Ken Burns," *Journal of American History* 81 (December 1994): 1043.

6. Burns states this in many interviews, including "Four O'Clock in the Morning Courage," in *Ken Burns's Civil War: Historians Respond*, ed. Robert Brent Toplin (New York: Oxford University Press, 1996), 157.

7. *Telling the Story: The Media, the Public, and American History*, ed. Sean Dolan (Boston: New England Foundation for the Humanities, 1994), 61.

8. Thelen, "The Movie Maker as Historian," 1036–37.

9. Ibid., 1040.

10. Bernard Weisberger, "The Great Arrogance of the Present Is to Forget the Intelligence of the Past," *American Heritage* (September–October 1990): 99.

11. Burns used this formulation consistently, including in the standard letter he sent out in response to those who wrote him about the series. I have a sample letter dated March 11, 1991.

12. Burns stated that Foote knew how to speak succinctly and simply say "what happened here" in a way that academics on camera could not. Thomas Cripps, "Historical Truth: An Interview With Ken Burns," *American Historical Review* 100 (June 1995): 761. The interview took place on November 17, 1994.

13. Burns discussed these aspirations in a variety of venues, including an interview with Gary Edgerton on February 11, 1993. See Edgerton, "Ken Burns America: Style, Authorship, and Cultural Memory," *Journal of Popular Film and Television* 21 (Summer 1993): 50–62. Foote's aspirations are discussed in William C. Carter, "Seeking the Truth in Narrative: An Interview With Shelby Foote," *Georgia Review* 46 (Spring 1987): 145–72. Carter's interview with Foote took place before Burns's film was released but after his collaboration with Burns had begun.

14. Steve Coe, "CBS, PBS Factors in Surprising Prime Time Start," *Broadcasting*, October 1, 1990, 27–28. Also "PBS Turns Swords into Shares," ibid., 38.

15. Sales data for the book from "After the Civil War: No Peace," *Washington Post*, September 22, 1991, G1, G5; for video, from Joshua Levine, "Smarter Boob Tube," *Forbes*, September 16, 1991, 159.

16. See, for example, Richard Zoglin, "Terrible Remedy," *Time*, September 24, 1990, 73; John Leonard, "The Great Divide," *New York Magazine*, September 24, 1990, 110–11; Lewis Lord, "Civil War, Unvarnished," *US News and World Report*, September 24, 1990, 74–75. "Reliving the War between Brothers," *New York Times*, September 16, 1990, 1, 43.

17. Catherine Clinton, in Toplin, *Ken Burns's Civil War*, 67; the book contains several lengthy critiques of Burns's film. Among shorter critical reviews are Ellen DuBois, *American Historical Review* 96 (October 1991): 1140; Jean Attie, *Radical History Review* 52 (Winter 1992): 95–104.

18. "Revisiting the Civil War," *Newsweek*, October 8, 1990, 62.

19. Forum held at Hampshire College, Amherst, Mass., January 15, 1991.

20. The title of the conference was "Telling the Story: The Media, The Public, and American History." It was funded by a grant from the New England Foundation for the Humanities, which published the proceedings the following year (see above, note 7).

21. Eric Foner, "Ken Burns and the Romance of Reunion," in Toplin, *Ken Burns's Civil War*, 118. David W. Blight, "What Will Peace among the Whites Bring? Reunion and Race in the Struggle over the Memory of the Civil War in American Culture," *Massachusetts Review* 34 (Autumn 1993): 393–410. See also Blight, "Homer with a Camera, Our *Iliad* without the Aftermath: Ken Burns's Dialogue with Historians," *Reviews in American History* 25 (June 1997): 351–59.

22. Dolan, *Telling the Story*, 70.

23. Thelen, "The Movie Maker as Historian," 1032.

24. Cripps, "Historical Truth: An Interview with Ken Burns," 749.

25. Thelen, "The Movie Maker as Historian," 1045.

26. Though the "debate" with historians has extended over a number of years—the most recent essay by Burns citing letters appeared in 1996—Burns uses the same letters as evidence as he did in 1991. They originally appeared in "War Correspondents Prove the Pen Really is Mightier Than the Sword," *TV Guide*, July 13, 1991, 2–4.

27. Dolan, *Telling the Story*, 48.

28. As of March 1991, Burns had received over eleven hundred letters. Some had been sent directly to him (national media often mentioned that he lived in Walpole, N.H.); other letters had been sent to local public television stations and forwarded. Based on the skewed geographical distribution of the letters in Burns possession, it appears that not all television stations forwarded the letters they received. So the sample population is not all those who wrote letters, but rather those who wrote letters that Burns received.

29. Nor do we know the age of the letter writers. Perhaps it might have been possible to approximate the race and class backgrounds of the letter writers—as a market researcher might—by compiling statistics on the demographic characteristics of return address zip codes (and Time-Life Books, which supplied Burns with office help in arranging and answering his mail during spring 1991 in return for those addresses, might have this breakdown). For Burns's statement that 30% of his letters were from blacks, see Dolan, *Telling the Story*, 48.

30. PBS Research, *National Audience Report for Summer Quarter, 1990*, quoted in Dirk W. Eitzen, "Bringing the Past to Life: Reception and Rhetoric of Historical Documentaries" (Ph.D. diss., University of Iowa, 1994), chap. 2.

31. On the average, 62% of Americans in 1990 lived in the state in which they were born. U.S. Census, "Selected Place of Birth and Migration Statistics, 1990," CPH-L-121.

32. On Sunday, September 16, 1990, the proportion of homes using television

was 61.9%; on the first night of *The Civil War* it was 65.7%, and researchers estimated that the additional 4% was due to Burns's film. Coe, "CBS, PBS Factors in
Surprising Prime Time Start," 27–28.

33. A woman from California thanked Burns for making history "as real to us as
current events"—but in a sense Burns made history more real. Consider the contrast between the human suffering depicted in the Civil War photographs and the
abstract, bomb's-eye-view images Americans later saw in television coverage of the
Gulf War. Of course this contrast was unavailable to viewers of Burns's film in
September 1990, but it was available to those watching the film in March 1991,
when many public television stations reran the series as part of pledge drives. It
would be interesting to compare letters received in fall 1990 with those being
received in spring 1991, to see if the Gulf War coverage altered letter writers' views
of the Civil War images.

34. Robert Brent Toplin notes that Burns's film reflected the political events of
his youth. Toplin, 25.

35. Dirk Eitzen suggests that fewer reviewers commented on the educational
value of the series than on its emotional content because they expected the series to
be educational, but not to move them to tears. Eitzen, "Bringing the Past to Life,"
chap. 2.

36. On the conventions of Civil War photography, including the staging of
camp scenes for the camera and the possible posing of living soldiers as battlefield
corpses, see Alan Trachtenberg, *Reading American Photographs: Images as History,
Matthew Brady to Walker Evans* (New York: Hill and Wang, 1989), 71–118.

37. "Ken Burns and Historical Narrative on Television," part of *Television: The
Creative Process*, Museum of Television and Radio University Satellite Seminar Series, broadcast November 19, 1996.

38. This was a wise strategy, because in published interviews, Foote spewed a
succession of remarks that surely would have embarrassed Burns. Foote eulogized
the Confederacy as a "noble experiment" and quoted approvingly Thomas Carlyle's
comment that the Civil War was an argument between peoples one of which believed in hiring their servants for life and the other in hiring them by the week.
Carter, "Seeking the Truth in Narrative," 166.

39. Of the 12% of all letters that mentioned historians, 90% mentioned Foote
and 31% mentioned Fields. Of course Foote's familiarity to the audience was the
result of his greater exposure. Simply counting words, Foote spoke 6,700, Field
1,060, the other historians combined 1,530, and David McCullough, the unseen
narrator, 36,000. Judith A. Lancioni, "Rhetorical Analysis and Historical Documentary: A Case Study of The Civil War" (Ph.D. dissertation, Temple University, 1994).

40. Eric Foner, "Ken Burns and the Romance of Reunion," in *Ken Burns's Civil
War: Historians Respond*, 110–11.

41. Douglas A. Cohn, "Critic Says TV Series Opened Old Wounds with Old

Lies," *Chattanooga News–Free Press*, October 7, 1990, section C, 9. Sons of Confederate Veterans response reported in New Orleans *Times-Picayune*, September 21, 1990, and quoted in Eitzen, "Bringing the Past to Life," chap. 2.

42. Tony Horwitz, *Confederates in the Attic: Dispatches from the Unfinished Civil War* (New York: Pantheon Books, 1998).

43. Robert Brent Toplin argues that in contrast to more sectionally partisan films on the Civil War such as *Birth of a Nation, Gone With the Wind,* or even *Roots,* Burns made a concerted effort to "sell" his film to a national audience. Toplin, "The Civil War was an Interpretation of History," 31. In one of the few studies asking why Burns's film was so popular, Gary Edgerton concludes that Burns's romantic nationalism based on a liberal pluralist consensus helped to make the series popular; that the film both explicitly and implicitly echoed metaphors of America as quilt or rainbow. Edgerton, "Ken Burns's America: Style, Authorship, and Cultural Memory," *Journal of Popular Film and Television* 21 (Summer 1993): 50–62. Elsewhere, Edgerton argues that this nationalism is precisely what many academics are least comfortable with in the film and in Burns's approach. Edgerton, "Ken Burns's Rebirth of a Nation: Television, Narrative, and Popular History," *Film and History* 22 (December 1992): 119–33.

44. Interestingly, the proportion of southern men and women mentioning Civil War ancestors (29%) was equal, while northerners not only were less likely to mention ancestors (22% overall), but displayed somewhat of a gender gap as well (24% women, only 18% men).

45. The literary critic Alison Landsberg, writing about the Holocaust Museum in Washington, has described the craving for "the experiential as a form of knowledge—to experience history in a personal, bodily way—to make 'history' into a 'personal memory.'" Lansberg, "America, the Holocaust, and the Mass Culture of Memory: Toward a Radical Politics of Empathy," *New German Critique* 71 (1997): 74.

## 5. Place and Placelessness in American History

1. See Dan Flores, "Place: An Argument for Bioregional History," *Environmental History Review* 18 (Winter 1994): 1–18, and Stephen Frenkel, "Old Theories in New Places? Environmental Determinism and Bioregionalism," *Professional Geographer* 46 (August 1994): 289–95.

2. Yi-Fu Tuan, "Thought and Landscape: The Eye and the Mind's Eye," in *The Interpretation of Ordinary Landscapes,* ed. D. Meinig (New York: Oxford University Press, 1978), 89–102. For an overview of research on environmental perception in cognitive psychology, see Tuan, *Space and Place: The Perspective of Experience* (Minneapolis: University of Minnesota Press, 1977), and Kenneth Craik, "Psychological Reflections on Landscape," in *Landscape, Meaning, and Values,* ed. Edmund Pening-

Rowsell and D. Lowenthal (Boston: Allen & Unwin, 1986), 48–54. There also exists a literature on environmental perception in evolutionary biology that argues that humans have an innate preference for savannas and other landscapes that promoted survival in the early years of the species, as well as traces of the "territorial" instinct found in animals. Even if this is true, it is so heavily modified by culture as to render it irrelevant to the discussion here.

3. Lois Chawla, "Childhood Place Attachments," in *Place Attachment*, ed. Irwin Altman and Setha Low (New York: Plenum, 1992), 63–86; Claire Cooper Marcus, "Environmental Memories," ibid., 87–112.

4. Marcus argues that in America, with its population migration, continuities and home memories are rooted in things—movable, storable, shippable—rather than in the fabric of the house itself. Marcus, "Environmental Memories," 100.

5. Chawla, "Childhood Place Attachments," 82; Marcus, "Environmental Memories," 103.

6. On social networks and attitudes toward place, see Kathleen Gerson, C. Ann Steuve, and Claude S. Fischer, "Attachments to Place," in Fischer et al., *Networks and Places: Social Relations in the Urban Setting* (New York: Free Press, 1977), 139–61; and David Hummon, "Community Attachment: Local Sentiment and Sense of Place," in Altman and Low, *Place Attachment*, 253–78.

7. Marc Fried, "Grieving for a Lost Home," in *The Urban Condition: People and Policy in the Metropolis*, ed. Leonard J. Duhl (New York: Basic Books, 1963), 151–71.

8. Recent research on memory emphasizes its social nature as individuals construct a "collective" memory of a place through conversations with others. Maurice Halbwachs, *The Collective Memory* (1951; reprint, New York: Harper and Row, 1980). See also David Middleton and Derek Edwards, "Introduction," in *Collective Remembering*, ed. Middleton and Edwards (Newbury Park, Calif.: Sage, 1990), 1–22.

9. See Marcus, "Environmental Memories," 90.

10. Robert B. Riley states that "the greater power of place lies not in inhabiting it but remembering it." Riley, "Attachment to the Ordinary Landscape," in Altman and Low, *Place Attachment*, 20.

11. Toni Morison, "The Site of Memory," in *Out There: Marginalization and Contemporary Cultures*, ed. Russell Ferguson, Martha Gever, Trinh T. Minh-Ha, and Cornel West (Cambridge: MIT Press, 1990), 299–305.

12. Louise Erdrich, "A Writer's Sense of Place," in *A Place of Sense: Essays in Search of the Midwest*, ed. Michael Martone (Iowa City: University of Iowa Press, 1988), 34–44.

13. William Cronon, "A Place for Stories: Nature, History, and Narrative," *Journal of American History* 78 (March 1992): 1347–76.

14. The most extensive effort to synthesize the environmental vision of European and American artists and writers over the past four centuries is Simon Schama,

*Landscape and Memory* (New York: Knopf, 1995). On American landscape painters of the nineteenth century, see Barbara Novack, *Nature and Culture: American Landscape and Painting, 1825–1875* (New York: Oxford University Press, 1980), and Angela Miller, *Empire of the Eye: Landscape Representation and American Cultural Politics, 1825–1875* (Ithaca: Cornell University Press, 1993). The landscape photographs of Ansel Adams are well known; among David Plowden's recent volumes of photographs is *Small Town America* (New York: Harry N. Abrams, 1994).

15. Nature writer Robert Finch described being initially attracted to Cape Cod not by its natural features but by its status as a "storied place." *Writing Natural History: Dialogues with Authors*, ed. Edward Lueders (Salt Lake City: University of Utah Press, 1989), 44.

16. Wallace Stegner, "The Sense of Place," in *Where the Bluebird Sings to the Lemonade Springs: Living and Writing in the West* (New York: Random House, 1992), 202.

17. Kevin Lynch, *The Image of the City* (Cambridge: MIT Press, 1960), 4.

18. Mary Hufford, *One Space, Many Places: Folklife and Land Use in New Jersey's Pinelands National Reserve* (Washington, D.C.: Library of Congress, 1986), 49. One recent collection of essays demonstrating folklore approaches to place stories is Barbara Allen and Thomas J. Schlereth, eds., *Sense of Place: American Regional Cultures* (Lexington: University Press of Kentucky, 1990).

19. Tim Cochrane, "Place, People, and Folklore: An Isle Royale Case Study," *Western Folklore* 46 (January 1987): 4. Another superb case study by a folklorist of how economic pressures to represent a place to outsiders shape local place consciousness is James F. Abrams, "Lost Frames of Reference: Sightings of History and Memory in Pennsylvania's Documentary Landscape," in *Conserving Culture: A New Discourse on Heritage*, ed. Mary Hufford (Urbana: University of Illinois Press, 1994), 24–38.

20. Denis Cosgrove and Mona Domosh, "Author and Authority: Writing the New Cultural Geography," in *Place/Culture/Representation*, ed. James Duncan and David Ley (New York: Verso, 1993), 25. Cosgrove and Domosh are summarizing a position stated in N. and J. Duncan, "(Re)reading the Landscape," *Environment and Planning D: Society and Space* 6 (June 1988): 117–26.

21. Michael Keith and Steve Pile, "Introduction: The Politics of Place," in *Place and the Politics of Identity*, ed. Keith and Pile (New York: Routledge, 1993), 1–21.

22. Ed Soja, *Postmodern Geographies: The Reassertion of Space in Critical Society Theory* (New York: Verso, 1989), 6.

23. Of course, different groups in society will perceive traditional and postmodern spatial arrangements as more or less intelligible, depending on what they are accustomed to; the landscape of greater Los Angeles will make more sense to a young person who grew up there than to an elderly transplant from Boston or New York. See Doreen Massey, "Politics and Space/Time," in Keith and Pile, *Place and*

*the Politics of Identity*, 141–61. On Los Angeles, see Soja, *Postmodern Geographies*, 200.

24. E. Relph, *Place and Placelessness* (London: Pion, 1976), 58. On the mass media's changing the sense of place, now that access to place and access to communication are no longer identical, see Joshua Meyrowitz, *No Sense of Place: The Impact of Electronic Media on Social Behavior* (New York: Oxford, 1985).

25. *Variations on a Theme Park: The New American City and the End of Public Space*, is the title of a recent anthology, ed. Michael Sorkin (New York: Noonday Press, 1992), that analyzes shopping malls, gentrification, urban historical markets such as South Street Seaport, and of course, Los Angeles and Disneyland.

26. Critics attack postmodern architecture, celebrated by Robert Venturi and Denise Scott-Brown in *Learning from Las Vegas* (Cambridge: MIT Press, 1972), as a false populism. Dolores Hayden, "The American Sense of Place and the Politics of Space," in *American Architecture: Innovation and Tradition*, ed. David G. DeLong, Helen Searing, and Robert A. M. Stern (New York: Rizzoli, 1986), 184–87; David Ley, "Modernism, Postmodernism, and the Struggle for Place," in *The Power of Place: Bringing Together Geographical and Sociological Imaginations*, ed. John A. Agnew and James S. Duncan (Boston: Unwin Hyman, 1989), 44–65.

27. On intellectuals' concern with loss of diversity in the late nineteenth century, see J. Nicholas Entrikin, "Place, Region, Modernity," in Agnew and Duncan, *The Power of Place*, 30–43; on regionalists of the 1920s and 1930s, see Robert Dorman, *Revolt of the Provinces: The Regionalist Movement in America, 1920–1945* (Chapel Hill: University of North Carolina Press, 1993).

John Agnew sees sociologists' methodologies not only describing but contributing to the devaluation of place by assuming that real social science investigates large social processes and deals in abstraction and theory, not in explicating local context and culture; "Representing Space: Space, Scale, and Culture in Social Science," in Duncan and Ley, *Place/Culture/Representation*, 251–71.

28. For an overview of contemporary environmentalist thought, see Kirkpatrick Sale, *Dwellers in the Land: The Bioregional Vision* (San Francisco: Sierra Club Books, 1985); for a classic statement, see Gary Snyder, "The Place, The Region, and the Commons," in *The Practice of the Wild* (San Francisco: North Point Press, 1990).

29. Attacks on the pioneer past as dysfunctional are summarized in Dorman, *The Revolt of the Provinces*; a powerful contemporary critique of American history as one of "cut and run" appears in Wendell Berry, *The Unsettling of America: Culture and Agriculture* (San Francisco: Sierra Club Books, 1977).

30. Alexis de Tocqueville, "Why the Americans are often so restless in the midst of their prosperity," *Democracy in America*, ed. J. P. Mayer, vol. 2 (Garden City, N.Y.: Doubleday, 1969), 536. Charles Eliot Norton, "The Lack of Old Homes in America," *Scribner's Magazine* 5 (1889): 636–40; Fei Xiaotong, "The Shallowness of Cultural Tradition," in *Land without Ghosts: Chinese Impressions of America from the*

*Mid-Nineteenth Century to the Present,* trans. and ed. R. David Arkush and Leo O. Lee (Berkeley: University of California Press, 1989), 181.

31. Michael Wallace, "Politics of Public History," in *Past Meets Present,* ed. Jo Blatti (Washington, D.C.: Smithsonian Institution Press, 1987), 38; Relph, *Place and Placelessness,* 143. There have been myriad sociological works in the past two decades attacking the lack of commitment to community in American history and echoing Tocqueville's critique of individualism, from Vance Packard's *A Nation of Strangers* (New York: David MacKay, 1972) to Robert Bellah et al., *Habits of the Heart: Individualism and Commitment in American Life* (Berkeley: University of California Press, 1985).

32. Sue Ann Lee, "The Value of Local Area," in *Valued Environments,* ed. John R. Gold and Jacqueline Burgess (Boston: Allen and Unwin, 1982), 163.

33. Geographer Doreen Massey terms this relationship "power geometry." Massey, "Power-Geometry and a Progressive Sense of Place," in *Mapping the Futures: Local Cultures, Global Change,* ed. Jim Bird, Barry Curtis, Tim Putnam, George Robertson, and Lisa Tickner (New York: Routledge, 1993), 59–69.

34. Henry Glassie, *Passing the Time in Ballymenone: Culture and History of an Ulster Community* (Philadelphia: University of Pennsylvania Press, 1982), 608.

35. James Howard Kunstler, *Geography of Nowhere: Rise and Decline of America's Manmade Landscape* (New York: Simon and Schuster, 1993). Scott Russell Sanders, *Staying Put: Making a Home in a Restless World* (Boston: Beacon Press, 1993). Sale, *Dwellers in the Land.* Snyder, *Practice the Wild.*

36. Tony Hiss, *The Experience of Place* (New York, Knopf, 1990). On how social characteristics result in different experiences of the environment, see Massey, "Power-Geometry and a Progressive Sense of Place." In the words of geographer John Agnew, "the local social worlds of place (locale) cannot be understood apart from the objective macro-order of location and the subjective territorial identity of sense of place." Agnew, "Representing Space," 263.

37. A thoughtful discussion of the scale question appears in Mike Featherstone, "Global and Local Cultures," in Bird, et al., eds. *Mapping the Futures,* 169–87.

38. "Multiple streams of collective memories must be brought into some common framework to allow coordinated social action." Kevin Lynch, *What Time Is This Place?* (Cambridge: MIT Press, 1972), 126.

39. David Lowenthal, "Revisiting Valued Landscapes," in Gold and Burgess, *Valued Environments,* 79.

40. Patricia Nelson Limerick offers a superb illustration of this point in her analysis of Asian perceptions of the western landscape, which unlike Anglos, they encountered moving from west to east. Patricia Nelson Limerick, "Disorientation and Reorientation: The American Landscape Discovered from the West," *Journal of American History* 79 (December 1992): 1021–49.

41. Glassie, *Passing the Time in Ballymenone,* 664.

42. Donald Meinig, "Symbolic Landscapes: Some Idealizations of American Communities," in *The Interpretation of Ordinary Landscapes* (New York: Oxford University Press, 1979), 164–92. See also Hummon, "Community Attachment," 259. For English perception of what constitutes traditional landscape, especially the invention of "English landscape" in the eighteenth century by way of landscape painting and gardening practices, see Brian Goodey, "Spotting, Squatting, Sitting, or Setting: Some Public Images of Landscapes," in Pening-Rowsell and Lowenthal, *Landscape Meaning and Values*, 82–101. On maps, see J. B. Hartley, "Maps, Knowledge, and Power," in *The Iconography of Landscape: Essays on the Symbolic Representation, Design, and Use of Past Environments*, ed. Denis Cosgrove (New York: Cambridge University Press, 1988), 277–312.

43. Two excellent examples of this kind of historical study are John F. Sears, *Sacred Places: American Tourist Attractions in the Nineteenth Century* (New York: Oxford University Press, 1989), and Edward T. Linenthal, *Sacred Ground: Americans and Their Battlefields* (Urbana: University of Illinois Press, 1991).

## 6. Rethinking New England Town Character

1. Christopher Kenneally, "The Man Who Made the Civil War," *USAir*, July 1991, 34.

2. Commonwealth of Massachusetts Special Commission on Growth and Change, *Final Report*, January 23, 1990.

3. Philip B. Herr, *Saving Place: A Guide and Report Card for Protecting Community Character* (Boston: National Trust for Historic Preservation, 1991).

4. Joseph Wood, *The New England Village* (Baltimore: Johns Hopkins University Press, 1997). See also Martyn J. Bowden, "The Invention of American Tradition," *Journal of Historical Geography* 18 (January 1992): 3–26.

5. Stephen Nissenbaum, "New England as Region and Nation," in *All Over the Map: Rethinking American Regions* (Baltimore: Johns Hopkins University Press, 1996), 38–61. On the idealization of New England town as cultural template, see also D. W. Meinig, "Symbolic Landscapes: Some Idealizations of American Communities," in *Interpretation of Ordinary Landscapes*, ed. Meinig (New York: Oxford University Press, 1979), 164–92.

6. For more on idyllic representations of colonial New England by artists and writers at the turn of the century, see the essays and illustrations in William H. Truettner and Roger B. Stein, eds., *Picturing Old New England: Image and Memory* (New Haven: Yale University Press, 1999) (catalogue of an exhibition at the Smithsonian's National Museum of American Art, 1999).

7. William Butler, "Another City upon a Hill: Litchfield, Connecticut, and the Colonial Revival," in *The Colonial Revival in America*, ed. Alan Axelrod (New York: Norton, 1985), 15–51.

8. The best account of Deerfield's transformation is David Christopher Bryan, "The Past Is a Place to Visit: Reinventing the Colonial in Deerfield, Massachusetts" (Honors thesis, Amherst College, 1989). On the role of women in Deerfield's revitalization as a colonial village, see Marla Miller and Anne Digan Lanning, "Common Parlors: Women and the Creation of Community Identity in Deerfield, Massachusetts, 1870–1920," *Gender and History* 6 (November 1994): 435–55.

9. Lewis Mumford, "The Fourth Migration," *Survey* 54 (May 1, 1925): 130–33. Benton MacKaye, *The New Exploration* (New York: Harcourt, Brace, 1928). Robert Yaro and Randall Arendt, "Rural Landscape Planning in the Connecticut River Valley of Massachusetts," *APT Bulletin* 21 (1989): 13–20.

10. This complaint also surfaced in a local newspaper article while I was there. See Richie Davis, "Northfield's Forgotten Half Lies Over the River," *Greenfield Recorder*, January 20, 1992, 1.

11. The site is now occupied by a small retirement complex named Squaheag Village. Richie Davis, "History of a House: Releasing the Spirits," ibid., January 9, 1992, 17.

12. Transcript of public meeting to discuss revision of Northfield Master Plan, January 30, 1992, in the author's possession.

13. Transcript of public forum in Wilbraham sponsored by the Wilbraham Planning Board, November 13, 1991, in the author's possession.

14. Transcript of first public forum in the McKnight Historic District, sponsored by the McKnight Neighborhood Council, November 14, 1991, in the author's possession.

15. Ibid.

16. Transcript of second public forum in the McKnight Historic District, sponsored by the McKnight Neighborhood Council, December 16, 1991, in the author's possession.

17. Another study observing the prevalence of "frontier" language among urban residents is Neil Smith, "New City, New Frontier: The Lower East Side as Wild, Wild West," in *Variations on a Theme Park: The New American City and the End of Public Space*, ed. Michael Sorkin (New York: Noonday Press, 1992), 61–93.

18. Transcript of first public forum in the McKnight Historic District.

19. Transcript of second public forum in the McKnight Historic District.

20. Another study observing that urban middle-class residents often define their place in terms of not being in the suburbs is Caroline Mills, "Myths and Meanings of Gentrification," in *Place/Culture/Representation*, ed. James Duncan and David Ley (London: Verso, 1993), 149–70.

21. A succinct critique of traditional geography by geographers aligned with critical cultural studies appears in James Duncan and David Ley, "Introduction: Representing the Place of Culture," in Duncan and Ley, *Place/Culture/Representation*, 1–21.

22. Randy Hester, "Subconscious Landscapes of the Heart," *Places* 2 (1985): 10–22.

23. In the words of Kevin Lynch, "Near continuity is emotionally more important than remote time." Lynch, *What Time Is This Place?* (Cambridge: MIT Press, 1972), 61. David Lowenthal observes that governments value a remote and malleable past over a recent one painfully recalled. Lowenthal, "Revisiting Valued Landscapes," in *Valued Environments*, ed. John R. Gold and Jacqueline Burgess (Boston: Allen and Unwin, 1982), 78. See also Lowenthal, *The Past Is a Foreign Country* (New York: Cambridge University Press, 1985).

24. See Sidney Brower, "Residents and Outsiders' Perceptions of the Environment," in *Housing, Culture, and Design* (Philadelphia: University of Pennsylvania Press, 1989), 189–202. For a case study of historic preservation directed at tourists, see Martha Norkunas, *The Politics of Public Memory: Tourism, History, and Ethnicity in Monterey, California* (Albany: SUNY Press, 1993).

25. Transcript of second public forum in the McKnight Historic District.

26. The Orange Line project, which ran from approximately 1983 to 1990, is described in Myrna Breitbart, Will Holton, et al., *Creating a Sense of Place in Urban Communities* (Cambridge, Mass.: Urban Arts, Inc., 1992). For additional examples of public art developed to represent neighborhood histories rather than grand civic themes, see Lucy Lippard, *The Lure of the Local: Senses of Place in a Multicentered Society* (New York: New Press, 1997).

27. The exhibition ran from October 1992 through March 1994. See the catalogue: The Bostonian Society, *The Last Tenement: Confronting Community and Urban Renewal in Boston's West End*, ed. Sean M. Fisher and Carolyn Hughes (Boston: Bostonian Society, 1992).

28. Dolores Hayden, "The American Sense of Place and the Politics of Space," in *American Architecture: Innovation and Tradition*, ed. David G. DeLong, Helen Searing, and Robert A. M. Stern (New York: Rizzoli, 1986), 191. Hayden describes her "Power of Place" projects in Los Angeles in *The Power of Place: Urban Landscapes as Public History* (Cambridge: MIT Press, 1995); a short summary appears in Jane Brown Gillette, "The Power of Place," *Historic Preservation* 42 (July–August 1990): 44–49, 70–71.

29. See Doreen Massey, "Power-Geometry and a Progressive Sense of Place," in *Mapping the Futures: Local Cultures, Global Change*, ed. Jon Bird, Barry Curtis, Tim Putnam, George Robertson, and Lisa Tickner (New York: Routledge, 1993), 59–69.

## 7. Making Places in California

1. Based on a sample of the 1980 census, 68% of Massachusetts residents were born in Massachusetts while only 30% of California residents were born in California. U.S. Census, 1980. For 1990, the percentage of residents born in state is 69%

for Massachusetts and 46% for California (which is higher than New Hampshire's 44%). U.S. Census, "Selected Place of Birth and Migration Statistics, 1990," CPH-L-121.

2. In the 1930s, even as tens of thousands of easterners moved to California to start over, westerners such as Bernard DeVoto took comfort in the strong sense of place and history evident in New England. Bernard DeVoto, "New England: There She Stands," *Harpers*, March 1932, 405–15.

3. Joan Didion, "The Golden Land," *New York Review of Books*, October 21, 1993, 91.

4. Old Sturbridge Village opened to the public in 1946; Pioneer Village in Bakersfield in 1950; and Disneyland in 1955.

5. "Anglo" is a problematic term, in that it lumps together people of English, Welsh, Irish, German, Jewish, Italian, and many other distinctive European ethnic identities. Part of the story is the extent to which these ethnic groups came to identify themselves with a "white" pioneer heritage by the 1930s. And clearly the rest of the story is how Native Americans, Californios, African Americans, and immigrants from Asia and Mexico developed and maintained memory sites within their communities, and ultimately, in the second half of the twentieth century, pressed the state for public recognition of them. A model study that explores questions of ethnic identity and place for Native Americans and Californios in southern California is Lisbeth Haas, *Conquests and Historical Identities in California, 1769–1936* (Berkeley: University of California Press, 1995).

6. Chaw'se, near Jackson in Amador County, became a California State Park in 1968. It is still used for ceremonies by Native American groups in the region. *Chaw'se, Indian Grinding Rock State Historical Park*, brochure, California Department of Parks and Recreation, Sacramento, 1994.

7. Elliot West, *The Way to the West: Essays on the Central Plains* (Albuquerque: University of New Mexico Press, 1995), 139. West argues that the West as a land without history—free to be reshaped in the image of other places, to have history brought to it, or else to be left as "wilderness"—has been an enduring theme in how nonnatives have thought about the region. In a brilliant essay, "Stories," West contrasts his view of the west as "placeless" with that of Native Americans and descendants of pioneers.

8. On the process of Anglos recognizing Mexican land grants to maintain their own large landholdings, see Carey McWilliams, *Factories in the Field* (Boston: Little, Brown, 1939), and Leonard Pitt, *The Decline of the Californios: A Social History of Spanish-Speaking Californians, 1846–1890* (Berkeley: University of California Press, 1966), 83–103.

9. "Sons of New England," *Californian*, November 24, 1847; "City Items," San Francisco *Alta California*, October 20, 1850; "Thanksgiving Dinner Given by Sons of New England," *Sacramento Transcript*, December 2, 1850, 2; "New England

Festival," *Alta California*, December 23, 1851, 2. On the continued celebration of Forefathers Day by the New England Society of San Francisco, see "Forefathers Day," *Alta California*, November 27, 1877, 1.

10. Society of California Pioneers, *Constitution and Bylaws* (San Francisco, 1912); quote from 1863 constitution reprinted in 1912 volume, page 4. Pioneer societies were common also in the Midwest and the Plains in this period. While much history was published under their auspices, little has been written about them—who they were, how they functioned, what they stood for. Among the few such accounts is John Mack Faragher's fascinating portrait of the Sangamon County (Illinois) Old Settlers Society, founded in 1859, in which he notes that the membership was disproportionately the urban merchant and professional children of pioneers rather than the pioneers themselves. Faragher, *Sugar Creek: Life on the Illinois Prairie* (New Haven: Yale University Press, 1986), 216–33. This profile may have held true for the California pioneer societies as well, though the children formed their own organizations in the 1870s and 1880s rather than joining the ranks of their parents.

11. *Constitution and Bylaws of Sacramento Society of California Pioneers* (Sacramento: Jefferis, 1872). In 1905, the Society of California Pioneers spent over $11,000, more than one-third of its annual income, on the relief of its members.

12. Explicit mention of caring for pioneer cemetery plots appears in *Constitution and Bylaws of Sons and Daughters of Sacramento Society of California Pioneers* (Sacramento: D. Johnston, 1891). This organization, unlike the Pioneers, was largely a women's organization. Based on the membership list in the above volume, approximately two-thirds of the members were women, and they comprised three of five officers and four of nine directors.

13. Josiah Royce, "Provincialism: Based upon a Study of Early Conditions in California," *Putnam's Magazine* 7 (November 1909): 232–40.

14. A more complete study would analyze the intersection at the local level among memories of the Gold Rush experience, the efforts of later settlers to disassociate themselves from the immorality of the era, and the national myth of the Gold Rush as a picturesque adventure. The historian Susan Lee Johnson does this for the southern region of the Mother Lode in "Telling Tales," the epilogue to her book *Roaring Camp: The Social World of the California Gold Rush* (New York: Norton, 2000), 315–44.

15. "The Calaveras Reunion," *Alta California*, June 14, 1874, 1. On the Tuolumne Pioneer Association, see "Novel Pioneer Organization," *Alta*, June 19, 1869, 1; "Oakland Observations," *Alta*, June 18, 1875, 1; "Auld Lang Syne: Tuolumne Reunion Met Today," *Alta*, June 16, 1877, 2; "Tuolumneites," *Alta*, June 17, 1877, 1. On the Pioneers of El Dorado County, see "El Dorado Pioneers," *Alta*, November 15, 1870, 1; "El Dorado Pioneers Third Annual Reunion," *Alta*, May 11, 1877, 1. On the Placer County Pioneers, see "1851–74: Reunion of Placer County Pioneers," *Alta*, May 17, 1874, 1; "Festive Pioneers," *Alta*, May 16, 1875, 1. On the

Old Calaveras Association, see "The Calaveras Reunion," *Alta*, June 14, 1874, 1. On Nevada County, see "Old Nevada," *Alta*, June 10, 1877, 1.

16. Kevin Starr notes that early historians of California such as Bancroft were influenced by Harte's fictional portraits of the mining era. Starr, *Americans and the California Dream, 1850–1915* (New York: Oxford, 1973), 120. Starr emphasizes the importance of Bancroft and other written California histories of the 1860s–90s but does not place them in the context of the variety of other historical activities and population movements of the period. On Bancroft's collecting of pioneer stories, see Willa Krug Baum, "Oral History: A Revived Tradition at the Bancroft Library," *Pacific Northwest Quarterly* 58 (April 1967): 57–64.

17. Nicholas Ball, *The Pioneers of '49: A History of the Excursion of the Society of California Pioneers of New England from Boston to the Leading Cities of the Golden State, April 10–May 17, 1890* (Boston: Lee and Shepard, 1891).

18. Ball, *The Pioneers of '49*, 93, 97, 188. The historian Malcom J. Rohrbough interprets the New England Pioneers' return to northern California as more triumphant than disorienting. Rohrbough, *Days Of Gold: The California Gold Rush and the American Nation* (Berkeley: University of California Press, 1997), 290–93.

19. *Native Daughters of the Golden West, 1886–1986* (Fresno: Pioneer Publishing Company, 1986). Membership figures come from annual proceedings for the years concerned, in bound annual reports in Native Daughters of the Golden West Home Office, San Francisco.

20. Eliza D. Keith, *Report of the Historical Landmarks Committee, Native Daughters of the Golden West* (San Francisco: Walter N. Brunt, 1902), 7.

21. Ibid., 9. On the congruence between women's historical organizations and village improvement societies in other parts of the United States see the essays in Alan Axelrad, ed., *The Colonial Revival in America* (New York: Norton, 1985); James Lindgren, *Preserving the Old Dominion: Historic Preservation and Virginia Traditionalism* (Charlottesville: University of Virginia Press, 1993); and Lindgren, *Preserving Historic New England: Preservation, Progressivism, and the Remaking of Memory* (New York: Oxford University Press, 1995).

22. Mrs. William Fairchild, "Neglected Landmarks of California," *Grizzly Bear* 5 (June 1909): 1, 31. This parallels the concern of Yankee preservationists that the Paul Revere house would become lost in its Italian neighborhood in the North End of Boston.

23. Keith wrote: "No organization composed entirely of women has the same opportunity of raising funds as have those whose membership embraces independent businessmen and capitalists and state legislators." Keith, *Report of the Historical Landmarks Committee*, 28.

24. According to family lore, Knowland's father first met Hannah Russell's sister, who persuaded the thirty-year-old Hannah to come west and marry him.

25. The "Maiden's Grave" story is courtesy of Professor Kenneth N. Owens of

California State University, Sacramento, personal correspondence, April 25, 2000. It is difficult to determine what markers might have been erected when. Despite Knowland's insistence that local NSGW chapters submit all wording of inscriptions to the Historical Landmarks Committee, the marking process in these years was highly decentralized. Central listings, such as the one Knowland published in the appendix of his book *California: A Landmark History* (Oakland: Tribune Press, 1941), or the one the state compiled in the 1930s in an effort to "register" all historical landmarks, are incomplete. As nearly as I can determine, the earliest marked historical site in California was a monument erected by the Masons of Susanville, Lassen County, in 1862 "in memory of Peter Lassen, the pioneer, who was killed by the Indians April 26, 1859 at age 66 years." Though when three members of the Mormon Battalion were killed by Native Americans on their way back to Utah in 1848, an account of the "Tragedy Springs Massacre" and the names of the three men were carved in a nearby tree, which is now preserved in a museum at Sutter's Fort in Sacramento. Douglas E. Kyle, *Historic Spots in California*, 4th ed. (Stanford, Calif.: Stanford University Press, 1990), 27. My information about these and the other early monuments mentioned in the text comes from the four-volume notebooks of Erastus Holden in the California Room, California State Library, Sacramento, as confirmed by Douglas Kyle, *Historic Spots in California*, 4th ed. (Stanford, Calif.: Stanford University Press, 1990). Holden was a retired railroad worker who in the 1930s compiled information about every historic site he could find; *Historic Spots* originated as a project of the state chapter of the DAR in the 1930s. In addition I have relied on centralized lists compiled by Knowland for his *California: A Landmark History*, and by the State Office of Historic Preservation, Sacramento; on the records of the Native Sons of the Golden West Historical Landmarks Committee in the Joseph R. Knowland Papers, Bancroft Library, University of California, Berkeley; and on a ten-volume photographic survey of marked sites which the Native Daughters compiled in the 1950s, in the Pioneer Library, Native Daughters of the Golden West Home Office, San Francisco. This latter source is especially valuable because it shows sites that lost their markers or markers that lost their sites (for example, because a marker was moved when the site was flooded by a water project or engulfed by a freeway) since their dedication.

26. Daughters of the American Revolution, *California's Seventy-five Years: The DAR 1891–1960*, ed. Eunice Moore Anderson (California State DAR, 1966).

27. "Indian Monument Is Presented to Alameda," *Alameda Times-Star,* June 18, 1914, 1, 7. Ishi had been living in the foothills south of Mount Lassen. Upon his "discovery" in 1911, he went to live at the University of California, Berkeley, under the auspices of the anthropologist Alfred Kroeber, where he died in 1916. See Theodora Kroeber, *Ishi in Two Worlds: A Biography of the Last Wild Indian in North America* (Berkeley: University of California Press, 1971). Recent research suggests that though Ishi spoke a Yahi dialect, he was likely descended from other tribes as

well. Charles Petit, "Ishi May Not Have Been All Yahi," *San Francisco Chronicle*, February 6, 1996, A3.

Of course, in Alameda the mound site that generations of Native Americans may have known as a landmark was destroyed; the marker was in a public park 1,000 feet away. Two other examples of marked Native American graves were the cross and monument dedicated October 1915 in the Indian cemetery of Mission San Jose, and a tall, snow-white cross memorial 9 feet high and 6 feet across dedicated in 1923 on J. D. Gallagher's ranch in Bodega to the Christianized Indians buried in the former Bodega Rancheria's graveyard. The author of this account mentioned that in Bodega, as in Alameda, the actual burial grounds had long been leveled. Honoria Toumey, "Bodega Cross Erected in Memory of Indians Who Inhabited Country," *Santa Rosa Republican*, January 18, 1923, 4. On Mission San Jose, see *San Francisco Examiner*, October 21, 1915, 19.

28. On Lummis, see Starr, *Americans and the California Dream*, 397–401. The California Federated Women's Clubs played an important role in various communities, though they were not represented in the California Historical Landmarks League. In 1907, paralleling Keith's call of five years earlier, the History and Landmarks Section of the California Federated Women's Clubs issued a call to local chapters to contribute to a book titled *Historic Facts and Fancies* (California Federated Womens Clubs, 1907). The book consisted of short stories divided into three sections: "Landmarks," "Pioneers," and "Indians."

29. On the romanticization of Native American and Spanish history behind the movement for mission preservation, see Nathan Gerald Weinberg, "Historic Preservation and Tradition in California: The Restoration of the Missions and the Spanish-Colonial Revival" (Ph.D. diss., University of California at Davis, 1974); James J. Rawls, "The California Mission as Symbol and Myth," *California History* 71 (Fall 1992): 343–60; Michele Moylan, "Reading the Indians: The Ramona Myth in American Culture," *Prospects* 18 (1993): 153–86.

30. Hearst launched a fund-raising drive to purchase the buildings in Monterey and Sonoma. He sought to preserve structures with evidence of both Mexican and Anglo presence, such as the "cottage where General Sherman wooed beautiful Senorita Bonafacio and where a historic rose bush was planted." "California's Ancient and Picturesque Landmarks Must Not Be Destroyed," *Examiner*, April 26, 1903, magazine section, 6–7.

31. Laura Bride Powers, "Saving Mission Santa Inez," *Grizzly Bear* 36 (April 1925): 2.

32. Joseph Knowland, *California Historical Landmarks League: What It Has Accomplished in Three Years, What It Hopes to Accomplish* (San Francisco: 1905), 5. Lisbeth Haas shows how the mission movement had the effect of revitalizing Californio identity in southern California. Haas, *Conquests and Historical Identities in California, 1769–1936* (Berkeley: University of California Press, 1995).

33. "The Tile Roof: A Relic of Old Days That Has Almost Wholly Disappeared," *San Francisco Call*, October 9, 1897, 3. Throughout the twentieth century, Anglos invariably described California as having a "Spanish" heritage, which they associated with pure-blooded European nobility, rather than a "Mexican" one, which they associated with mixed-race peasants south of the border—though, as evident in San Francisco's Portolá Festival of 1909, and Los Angeles's creation of a festival marketplace on Olvera Street in 1930, sometimes this carefree peasant Mexican image was useful for Anglos looking to shed their inhibitions. See Phoebe Kopp, "A Mexican Street of Yesterday in a City of Today: Historical Memory and Cultural Power on Olvera Street, Los Angeles, 1926–1939," Pacific Coast Branch of the American Historical Association Annual Meeting, August 1996.

34. John C. Merriam, *A Living Link with History* (1934; reprint, San Francisco: Save the Redwoods League, 1978); Madison Grant, "Saving the Redwoods," *National Geographic* 37 (June 1920): 529. The quote from Enos A. Mills appears in a solicitation Joseph Knowland received from "California Restoration Society," folder "Historic Landmarks-32," carton 4. J. R. Knowland Papers, Bancroft Library, University of California, Berkeley. Among Mills's publications was *The Story of a Thousand Year Pine* (Boston: Houghton Mifflin, 1914). In it, Mills tells the "biography" of a tree in southwest Colorado and the events it witnessed. For more on the Save the Redwoods League, see Susan R. Schrepfer, *The Fight to Save the Redwoods: A History of Environmental Reform, 1917–1978* (Madison: University of Wisconsin Press, 1983). Besides his activities on behalf of the Save the Redwoods League, Grant was also the founder and chair of the New York Zoological Society and, as a charter member of the Society of Colonial Wars, active in genealogy. For more on Grant, see John Higham, *Strangers in the Land: Patterns of American Nativism, 1860–1925* (1955; reprint, New York: Atheneum, 1970), 155–57.

35. See, for example, the big tree diagram used as a frontispiece to Daughters of the American Revolution, *California's Seventy-five Years*.

36. A list of memorial groves in northern California appears in Save the Redwoods League, *Brief Guide to the Northern Redwoods* (Berkeley: University of California Press, n.d.). The guide was enclosed with a "Memorandum on Memorial Redwood Groves, July 11, 1936" from Newton B. Drury to Joseph Knowland, in Joseph Knowland Papers, University of California, Berkeley. For urban memorial groves, see the Erastus Holden notebooks, California State Library, Sacramento.

37. Thomas Dykes Beasley, *A Tramp Through the Bret Harte Country* (San Francisco: Paul Elder & Co., 1914), 40. For the quotation in the epigraph, see pp. 60–61.

38. See, for example, Chauncey L. Canfield, "In Bret Harte Land," *Sunset* 19 (May 1907): 76–91, and R. A. Doub, "A Trip through Bret Harte Country," *Overland* 60 (September 1912): 234–36.

39. Leolin T. Sinnott, "The Mother Lode Pilgrimage," *Grizzly Bear* 31 (July 1922): 1–2, 21.

40. The complete list is in "Landmarks and Monuments," Vertical File, California State Library, Sacramento.

41. Harry C. Peterson, "Ghost Towns on '49 Tour: Historic Spots to Live Again in Story," *Call*, May 15, 1922, 2. The *Call* published a series of five dispatches from Peterson describing the pilgrimage between May 12 and 17, 1922.

42. Peterson reported that when the group reached San Andreas, "The lone Chinaman of San Andreas, Ah Noo, is expected to be out with his quaint little smile of greeting. He is one of the real old timers." Peterson, "Ghost Towns on '49 Tour: Historic Spots to Live Again in Story," 15.

43. Among the guidebooks that used the NSGW temporary numbers was Fremont Rider, *Rider's California: A Manual for Travelers* (New York: Macmillan, 1925).

44. Arthur Dunn, *Tuolumne County California* (published for Tuolumne County Board of Supervisors by Sunset Magazine Homeseekers Bureau, n.d., and Katherine Lee Chambers, *Up the Trail to Tuolumne* (Sonora, 1915) both in Vertical File, Tuolumne County: Pamphlets, California State Library.

45. Tuolumne County Board of Supervisors, *Tuolumne County* (Sonora, 1930), brochure in Vertical File, Tuolumne County: Pamphlets, California State Library.

46. "History of Twain Harte," Brochure, Twain-Harte Chamber of Commerce, 1996.

47. Cyril Clemens, "A Visit to Mark Twain's Country," *Overland Monthly* 7 (April 1929): 116–17, 127; (May 1929): 145–46, 158.

48. Leo Richards, the grandson of Nevada County miners, recalls seeing a picture of Bill Haywood on the wall of the Miners Hospital in Grass Valley as late as the 1950s. Author conversation with Leo Richards, 1998.

49. See Lois Rather, *Men Will Be Boys: The Story of E Clampus Vitus* (Oakland, Calif.: Rather Press, 1980). A list of ECV marked sites appears in Kenneth M. Castro, *Clamplaques: Report #9 to the Clamproctors of the Grand Council of the Ancient and Honorable Order of E Clampus Vitus* (Murphy's, Calif., 1978) in California State Library, Sacramento.

50. Focusing squarely on their ancestors, the Native Sons and Daughters' view of the Gold Rush was never what could be termed "multicultural," but I suspect that it might have become even less so in the 1920s. Mike Davis describes the exclusion of the old Jewish families from Los Angeles' downtown institutions in the decade; was this paralleled by an effort to purge Jews from the Pioneer rosters? Davis, *City of Quartz* (New York, 1990), 110–16.

51. Clarence M. Hunt, "Grizzly Growls," *Grizzly Bear* 36 (April 1925): 1–2; Fletcher A. Cutler, "The Order of the NSGW," *Grizzly Bear* 38 (November 1925): 50. Note that the "white race" was not part of the credo in 1923 (but "complete Americanism" was featured).

52. A number of states established such programs in response to recreational automobile travel in the 1920s. Virginia's began in 1927; Massachusetts launched

one in 1930 in conjunction with the tercentenary celebration of the Common-wealth. See Raymond Pisney, *Historical Markers: A Bibliography* (Verona, Va.: Mc-Clure Press, 1977).

53. On the emergence of state societies, see Carey McWilliams, *Southern California: An Island on the Land* [1946] (Salt Lake City: Peregrine Smith Books, 1973), and Joseph Boskin, "Associations and Picnics as Stabilizing Forces in Southern California," *California Historical Society Quarterly* 44 (March 1965): 17–26.

54. On the new involvement of state government in historical activities in California, see Kenneth N. Owens, "Historic Resources Management in a Growth State: California," in *Cultural Resources Management*, ed. Ronald W. Johnson and Michael Schene (Malabar, Fla.: Krieger, 1987), 173–85. Among the organizations campaigning for the creation of a comprehensive state park system in California were the Save the Redwoods League, the Sierra Club, the California State Automobile Association, and the California State Chamber of Commerce, as well as the Native Sons and Native Daughters of the Golden West. On the origins of the state park system and the Olmsted survey, see Joseph H. Engbeck, Jr., *State Parks of California from 1864 to the Present* (Portland, Ore.: Charles H. Belding, 1980), 47–55.

55. Information on Drury's family came from the Aubrey Drury Papers, Bancroft Library, University of California, Berkeley, and from the Church of Jesus Christ Latter Day Saints Family Search Internet Genealogical Service, Family History Catalogue, Film no. 1761042. On Drury's early career as a publicist and writer of tourist guidebooks, see Wells Drury and Aubrey Drury, *California Tourist Guide and Handbook* (Berkeley: Western Publishing, 1913), and "List of Drury Company Accounts, 1924–26," Aubrey Drury Papers, 81/52 carton 1.

56. Aubrey Drury, "Historic Sites in California" (1928), typescript in Aubrey Drury Papers, 73/3 carton 3.

57. The registration procedures are described in Minutes, California State Parks Commission, October 12, 1931, in the California State Archives, Sacramento. The Approval Committee appointed in 1931 consisted of (from northern California) Aubrey Drury, San Francisco lawyer Francis Farquhar, San Francisco lawyer Carl Wheat (a founder of E Clampus Vitus), and University of California, Berkeley, professor Herbert Bolton; (from southern California) Orra Monette (vice president of the Bank of America) from Los Angeles, Dewitt Hutchings from Riverside, Lawrence Hill from Los Angeles, Leroy Wright from San Diego, and Harry Conn of the Los Angeles *Times*. The same group met virtually unchanged for twenty years; Bolton was replaced by Knowland in 1941, and John Caughey of UCLA joined the board in 1944. Historic Landmarks Committee minutes, October 5, 1944, in Director's Correspondence, California State Parks Commission, California State Archives. These materials constitute a rich historical source, and include summary descriptions not only of the 474 sites approved for registration, through 1946, but also of the 107 that were rejected. "Reports Showing Applications for Registration as

Historic Points of Interest Held in Abeyance by the Official Approval Committee," accompanying correspondence from Frank McKee, California Chamber of Commerce, to J. H. Covington, State Park Commission, April 24, 1936, in Chief's Correspondence 1929–40, Division of Natural Resources, F3735:213, California State Archives; also "Rejected Applications for Registration of Historic Landmarks," June 15, 1946, in Directors Subject File–Historical Landmarks, 1943–49, Department of Natural Resources, F3735:256, California State Archives, Sacramento.

The state continued to rely on the chamber of commerce in the registration process until 1951. Critics complained that this resulted in great unevenness—eight of fifty-eight California counties had no historic sites, while others had too many. In the words of one critic in 1948, "the omissions are as glaring as some of the inclusions are preposterous." Phil Townsend Hanna of the Automobile Club of Southern California to Warren Hannum, director of California Department of Natural Resources, December 26, 1948; copy, with reply by J. E. Carpenter of State Chamber of Commerce, January 6, 1949. On this later period, see Nadine Ishitani Hata, *The Historic Preservation Movement in California, 1940–1976* (Sacramento: California Department of Parks/Office of Historic Preservation, 1992), and Owens, "Historic Resources Management in a Growth State."

58. Historic Landmarks Files, 1936–40, Department of Natural Resources, California State Archives, Sacramento.

59. James Gregory notes that the popularity of Pioneer heritage among both white native and white migrant Californians in the 1930s further consolidated racial lines. Gregory, *American Exodus: The Dust Bowl Migration and Okie Culture in California* (New York: Oxford University Press, 1989), 237.

60. J. E. Carpenter, "Historic Landmarks," California State Chamber of Commerce, October 17, 1944, in Directors Files, California State Archives. On preservation activities associated with the centennial, see Hata, *The Historic Preservation Movement in California*, 31–39. Knowland's role in the California Centennial Commission is documented in the Joseph Russell Knowland Papers, California Historical Society, San Francisco.

61. A prominent example of this is Dolores Hayden's efforts in the 1980s to develop a network of new historic sites for the city of Los Angeles, described in Hayden, *The Power of Place: Urban Landscapes as Public History* (Cambridge: MIT Press, 1995). See the map/walking tour of Los Angeles by Dolores Hayden, Gail Dubrow, and Carolyn Flynn, *The Power of Place: Los Angeles* (Los Angeles, 1985). In many ways, activist historians have been seeking material embodiment for the critique of California history as Pioneer boosterism that emerged in the interwar years in work of Carey McWilliams. See Robert Dorman, *The Revolt of the Provinces: The Regionalist Movement in America 1920–1945* (Chapel Hill: University of North Carolina Press, 1993).

62. The Manzanar plaque was installed at the instigation of the Japanese American Citizens League in 1973; Colonel Allensworth State Park in Tulare County was

established in 1974. In 1978, the State Office of Historic Preservation Department of Parks completed an Ethnic Minorities Survey of black, Spanish-surnamed, Japanese, Chinese, and Native American sites. On the controversy over the Manzanar plaque and changes in the state program, see Hata, *The Historic Preservation Movement in California.*

63. For the quotation in the epigraph, see Joan Didion, "Notes From a Native Daughter," in *Slouching towards Bethlehem* (New York: Noonday Press, 1990), 176. Her essay originally appeared in *Holiday Magazine* in 1968.

64. Conversation with Mary Fuhrer, Framingham, Mass., May 6, 1997. Fuhrer also told the story of discovering a barn where part of the foundation of a section added in the 1950s consisted of broken-up gravestones. When she asked a member of the local historical society how this had happened, he replied, "If you had lived here then, you would know."

65. Of course, since the 1970s many Californians, especially inhabitants of urban industrial areas, have been relatively immobile geographically and, like the residents of old New England textile towns, can remember their places as more vital than they are now.

66. Carey McWilliams, *California: The Great Exception* (1949; Berkeley: University of California Press, 1999).

67. On the Sons and Daughters of Vermont gatherings in Worcester in the 1870s and 1880s, see Timothy J. Meagher, "The Lord Is Not Dead: Cultural and Social Change among the Irish in Worcester, Mass., 1880–1920" (Ph.D. diss., Brown University, 1982); Meagher's evidence comes from the Clipping and Pamphlet files, Worcester Historical Museum.

68. Examples of ex-historic places abound. The ten-volume photographic survey of marked sites that the Native Daughters compiled in the 1950s reveals several sites that lost their markers or markers that lost their sites since their dedication (for example, because a marker was moved when the site was flooded by a water project or engulfed by a freeway). The same is also evident from the Holden notebooks.

## Conclusion

1. Nora argues that the emergence of the modern nation-state in the eighteenth century created discontinuity with previous regimes, and the geographical mobility imposed by modern capitalism undermined rooted knowledge of particular locales, obliterating local oral traditions and memories. Pierre Nora, "Between Memory and History: Les Lieux de Mémoire," *Representations* 26 (Spring 1989): 7–25.

2. John Gillis and Charles Maier speculate that in the late twentieth century we entered a postnationalist era in which an explosion of interest in local and family history has been fueled by disillusion with the modern nation-state. John Gillis, "Introduction," in *Commemorations: The Politics of National Identity* (Princeton, N.J.: Princeton University Press, 1994), 3–24; Charles Maier, "A Surfeit of Memory?

Reflections on History, Melancholy, and Denial," *History and Memory* 5 (Fall–Winter 1993): 136–52. On the persistence of nationalism evident in the defense of venerated relics, see Edward T. Linenthal, *Sacred Ground: Americans and Their Battlefields* (Urbana: University of Illinois Press, 1991).

3. The historian David Thelen correctly distinguishes between the "intimate past" as content (personal and family history) and the intimate uses of the past, how we discuss past national and global events, such as World War II, in the context of our family and friends. Roy Rosenzwieg and David Thelen, *The Presence of the Past: Popular Uses of History in American Life* (New York: Colombia University Press, 1998), 195. In many ways, my findings about how Americans understand and use the past mirror those in Thelen and Rosenzwieg's book, which is based on their national telephone survey of March 1994. I think our principal difference lies in the greater importance I assign to the experience of place and attachments to locale, something that would be difficult to discern in a national survey.

4. Genealogists are expecting an enormous boom as the generation born in the two decades after World War II turns fifty. "Climbing the Family Tree," *American Demographics*, December 1995, 42–50. Already, there has been a takeoff in the sale of genealogical software and courses, from those imparting the traditional skills in hunting down ancestors to the more psychodynamic, New Age "Reclaiming Your Roots: Honoring the Legacy of Your Family History," a course offered at the Kripalu Institute in Lenox, Massachusetts, May 10–15, 1998. *Kripalu*, January–June 1998, 31.

5. Peter Novick, *That Noble Dream: The Objectivity Question and the American Historical Profession* (New York: Cambridge University Press, 1988), 181, 367.

6. The regional identifications of Webb and Morison are well known. On Robert Kelley, see John Higham, "Robert Kelley: Historian of Political Culture," *Public Historian* 17 (Summer 1995): 61–75. One could add to this list William Cronon in Wisconsin and Donald Worster in Kansas, who were fortunate enough to be able to return to their native state universities with endowed chairs.

7. Few works by academic historians combine personal and professional approaches to the past. Timothy Breen's *Imagining the Past: East Hampton Histories* (Reading, Mass.: Addison-Wesley, 1989), a first-person account of his year as a scholar in residence in one Long Island community, contains many insights about how local residents understand and use the past, but not much about how Breen does. Richard White's *Remembering Ahanagran: Storytelling in a Family's Past* (New York: Hill & Wang, 1998) contrasts a "professional" account of his mother's life in Ireland and America with her own stories about it, but White limits his narrative to the time before his own memories of events.

# INDEX

DAVID GLASSBERG grew up in Springfield, Pennsylvania, a suburb of Philadelphia. He now lives in Amherst, Massachusetts, where he teaches history and directs the Public History Program at the University of Massachusetts. He is the author of *American Historical Pagentry: The Uses of Tradition in the Early Twentieth Century.*